In the Irish Brigade

G. A. Henty

Contents

Preface. 7
Chapter 1: Fresh from Ireland. 9
Chapter 2: A Valiant Band. 25
Chapter 3: A Strange Adventure. 40
Chapter 4: At Versailles. 56
Chapter 5: A New Friend. 73
Chapter 6: An Ambuscade. 88
Chapter 7: In Paris Again. 103
Chapter 8: To Scotland. 117
Chapter 9: An Escape From Newgate. 132
Chapter 10: Kidnapping A Minister. 147
Chapter 11: On the Frontier. 159
Chapter 12: Oudenarde. 174
Chapter 13: Convalescent. 191
Chapter 14: A Mission. 203
Chapter 15: Treachery. 219
Chapter 16: Captured. 234
Chapter 17: An Old Friend. 250
Chapter 18: War. 265
Chapter 19: In Search of a Family. 278
Chapter 20: Gerald O'Carroll. 292

IN THE IRISH BRIGADE

BY

G. A. Henty

Preface.

The evils arising from religious persecution, sectarian hatred, ill government, and oppression were never more strongly illustrated than by the fact that, for a century, Ireland, which has since that time furnished us with a large proportion of our best soldiers, should have been among our bitterest and most formidable foes, and her sons fought in the ranks of our greatest continental enemy. It was not because they were adherents of the house of Stuart that Irishmen left their native country to take service abroad, but because life in Ireland was rendered well-nigh intolerable for Catholics, on account of the nature and severity of the laws against them, and the bitterness with which those laws were carried into effect.

An Irish Catholic had no prospects of employment or advancement at home. He could hold no civil appointment of any kind. He could not serve as an officer, nor even enlist as a private, in the army. He could not hold land. He was subject to imprisonment, and even death, on the most trifling and frivolous accusations brought against him by the satellites of the Irish Government. Not only could he not sit in the parliament of Dublin, but he could not even vote at elections. It was because they believed that the return of the Stuarts would mean relief, from at least some of their disabilities, and liberty to carry out the offices of their religion openly, and to dwell in peace, free from denunciation and persecution, that the Irish remained so long faithful to the Jacobite cause.

It was not, indeed, until 1774 that the Catholics in Ireland were admitted to qualify themselves as subjects of the crown, and not until the following year that they were permitted to enlist in the army. Irish regiments had enlisted in France, previous to the Convention of Limerick; but it was the Irish army that defended that town, and, having been defeated, passed over to France, that raised the Irish

Brigade to the position of an important factor in the French army, which it held for nearly a hundred years, bearing a prominent part in every siege and battle in Flanders, Germany, Italy, and Spain. A long succession of French marshals and generals have testified to the extraordinary bravery of these troops, and to their good conduct under all circumstances. Not only in France did Irishmen play a prominent part in military matters, but they were conspicuous in every continental army, and their descendants are still to be found bearing honoured names throughout Europe.

Happily, those days are past, and for over a hundred years the courage and military capacity of Irishmen have been employed in the service of Great Britain. For records of the doings of some of the regiments of the Irish Brigade, during the years 1706-1710, I am indebted to the painstaking account of the Irish Brigade in the service of France, by J. C. O'Callaghan; while the accounts of the war in Spain are drawn from the official report, given in Boyer's Annals of the Reign of Queen Anne, which contains a mine of information of the military and civil events of the time.

G. A. Henty.

Chapter 1: Fresh from Ireland.

A number of officers of O'Brien's regiment of foot, forming a part of the Irish Brigade in the service of France, were gathered in a handsome apartment in the Rue des Fosses, on the 20th of June, 1701, when the door opened, and their colonel entered with a young officer in the uniform of the regiment.

"I have asked you here, gentlemen all," he said, "to present to you a new comrade, Desmond Kennedy, who, through the good offices of the Marshal de Noailles, has been appointed, by His Gracious Majesty, to a cornetcy in our regiment.

"Now, gentlemen, I have known, and doubtless you can all of you recall, instances where the harmony of a regiment has been grievously disturbed, and bad blood caused, owing to the want of a clear understanding upon matters connected with a family; which might have been avoided, had proper explanations been given at the commencement. I have spoken frankly to Mr. Kennedy, and he has stated to me certain particulars, and has not only authorized me, but requested me to repeat them to you, feeling that you had a right to know who it was that had come among you, and so to avoid questioning on matters that are, of all others, prone to lead to trouble among gentlemen.

"Beyond the fact that he is a Kennedy, and that his father had to fly from Ireland, two years after the siege of Limerick, owing to a participation in some plot to bring about a fresh rising in favour of King James, he is unacquainted with his family history. He has never heard from his father, and only knows that he made for France after throwing the usurper's spies off his track, and there can be little doubt that it was his intention to take service in this brigade. There have been several Kennedys in the service, and I have little doubt that this young gentleman's father was the Murroch Kennedy who joined the third regiment, about that time, and was killed a few months afterwards at the battle of Breda. His death would account for the fact that his son never received a letter from him. At the time when he left Ireland, the child was some two years old, and, as communication was difficult, and the boy so young, Murroch might very well have put off writing until the boy grew older, not thinking that death might intervene, as it did, to prevent his doing so.

"This is all simple and straightforward enough, and you will, I am sure, have no hesitation in extending the hand of friendship to the son of a gallant Irishman, who died fighting in the ranks of the Irish Brigade, exiled, like the rest of us, for loyalty to our king.

"Still, gentlemen, you might, perhaps, wonder how it is that he knows no more of his family, and it was that this question might be disposed of, once for all, that I am making this statement to you on his behalf. He was not brought up, as you might expect, with some of his father's connections. Whether the family were so scattered that there was no one to whom he could safely entrust the child, I know not, but, in point of fact, he sent him to one of the last houses where a loyal gentleman would wish his son to be brought up. We all know by name and reputation--I and your majors knew him personally--the gallant James O'Carroll, who died, fighting bravely, at the siege of Limerick. He was succeeded in his estate by his brother John, one of the few Irishmen of good family who turned traitor to his king, and who secured the succession to his brother's possessions by becoming an ardent supporter of the usurper, and by changing his religion.

"Why Murroch Kennedy should have chosen such a man as the guardian of his son is a mystery. Whether they had been great friends in earlier times, when John O'Carroll professed as warm an attachment to the Stuart cause as did his brother James, or whether Kennedy possessed such knowledge of O'Carroll's traitorous dealings with the Dutchman as would, if generally known, have rendered him so hateful to all loyal men that he could no longer have remained in the country, and so had a hold over him, Mr. Kennedy can tell us nothing. He was brought by his nurse to Castle Kilkargan, and was left with John O'Carroll. It is clear that the latter accepted the charge unwillingly, for he sent the child to a farm, where he remained until he was eight years old, and then placed him with the parish priest, who educated him. The lad visited at the houses of the neighbouring gentry, shot and rowed and fished with their sons. O'Carroll, however, beyond paying for his maintenance, all but ignored his existence, showing no interest whatever in him, up to the time when he furnished him with a letter of introduction to de Noailles, except that he made him a present of a gun, as soon as he became of an age to use one. He never attempted to tamper with his loyalty to King James, and in fact, until he sent for him to ask what profession he would choose, he never exchanged ten words with him, from the time that he was brought to the castle.

"We can each form our own theory as to the cause of such strange conduct. He may have given a pledge, to Murroch, that the boy should be brought up a loyalist, and a true son of the church. It may have been that the loyalty of the boy's father formed so unpleasant a contrast to his own disloyalty, and apostasy, that he disliked the sight of him. However, these theories can make no difference in our reception of Desmond Kennedy, as a gentleman of a good family, and as the son of a loyal adherent of the king; and as such, I think that I can, from what I have already seen of him, assert that he is one who will be a good comrade, a pleasant companion, and a credit to the regiment."

The subject of these remarks was a tall and handsome young fellow, some sixteen years of age. He was already broad at the shoulders, and promised to become an exceedingly powerful man. He had stood somewhat behind the colonel, watching calmly the effect of his words on those whose comrade he was to be, for he knew how punctilious were his countrymen, on the subject of family, placing as much or even more value than did the Scots, on points of genealogy, and of descent from the old families. His frank open face, his bearing and manner, did as much to smooth his way as did the speech of his colonel, who, when he had been introduced to him, two days before, had questioned him very closely on the subject of his family. It had almost been a matter of satisfaction to Desmond when he heard, from the colonel, that the officer who had fallen at Breda was probably the father of whom he had no remembrance; for, from the time he attained the age of boyhood, it had been a grief and pain that he should never have heard from his father, who, it now appeared, had been prevented by death from ever communicating with him.

The officers received him cordially. They had little doubt that he was the son of the Murroch Kennedy, of Dillon's regiment, although, after they separated, some wonder was expressed as to the reason why the latter had committed his son to the care of so notorious a traitor as John O'Carroll.

Desmond had been specially introduced to two of the young lieutenants, Patrick O'Neil and Phelim O'Sullivan, and these took him off with them to their quarters.

"And what is the last news from Ireland? I suppose that the confiscations have ceased, for the excellent reason that they have seized the estates of every loyal gentleman in the country?"

"That was done long ago, in the neighbourhood of Kilkargan, and, so far as I know, everywhere the feeling is as bitter as ever, among those who have been dispossessed, and also among the tenants and peasantry, who have found themselves handed over to the mercies of Dutchmen, or other followers of William. At Kilkargan there was not that grievance; but, although they had still one of the old family as their master, they could not forgive him for deserting to the side of the usurper, nor for changing his religion in order to do pleasure to William. Certainly, he can have derived but little satisfaction from the estates. He seldom showed himself out of doors, never without two or three armed servants, all of whom were strangers from the north, and he was often away, for months together, at Dublin."

"And what did you do with yourself?"

"I fished, shot, and rode. I had many friends among the gentry of the neighbourhood, who would, doubtless, have shown less kindness than they did, had it not been for the neglect with which O'Carroll treated me. His unpopularity was all in my favour.

"However, I have one good reason for being obliged to him, since it was through him that I obtained my commission. He told me that, in his young days, he had been at a French college with the duke. They had been great friends there, and he thought that, in memory of this, de Noailles would procure me a commission."

"I suppose the real fact was, Kennedy, that he was glad to get rid of you altogether?"

"I think that is likely enough. He certainly raised no objection, whatever, to my going abroad, and seemed to think it natural that I should choose the Irish Brigade, here, in preference to the British service. He said something unpleasant about its not being singular that I should be a rebel, when I always associated with rebels, to which I replied that it seemed to me that I could hardly be blamed for that, seeing that my father had been what he called a rebel, and that I had little choice in the matter of my associates; and that if I had been educated at a school in England, instead of by good Father O'Leary, I might have had other sentiments. He replied that my sentiments were nothing to him, one way or the other. He was glad to wash his hands of me altogether; and, at any rate, if I went to France, I could drink the health of King James every day without his being involved in my treason."

"It almost looked as if he wished you to grow up a rebel, Kennedy, or he would hardly have placed you in the charge of a priest. He may have reckoned that if there was another rising, you might join it, and so be taken off his hands, altogether."

"Whatever the reason was, I have certainly cause for satisfaction that he removed me from the care of the farmer's wife, with whom he at first placed me, and arranged with the priest to take charge of me altogether. O'Leary himself had been educated at Saint Omer, and was a splendid fellow. He was very popular on the countryside, and it was owing to my being with him that I was admitted to the houses of the gentry around, whereas, had I remained in the farmhouse in which O'Carroll first placed me, I should only have associated with the sons of other tenants."

"It looked, at any rate, as if he wished to make a gentleman of you, Kennedy."

"Yes, I suppose my father had asked him to do so. At any rate, I was infinitely better off than I should have been if he had taken me in at Kilkargan, for in that case I should have had no associates, whatever. As it was, I scarcely ever exchanged a word with him, until that last meeting. He sent down, by one of his servants, the letter to the Duc de Noailles, and a bag containing money for my outfit here, and for the purchase of a horse, together with a line saying that he had done his duty by me, and had no desire to hear from me in the future. I was inclined to send the money back to him, but Father O'Leary persuaded me not to do so, saying that I must be in a position to buy these things, if I obtained a commission; and that, no doubt, the money had been given me, not for my own sake, but because he felt that he owed it to me, for some service rendered to him by my father."

"It was an ungracious way of doing it," O'Sullivan said, "but, in your circumstances, I should have taken the money had it come from the old one himself. It is, perhaps, as well that it should have been done in such a manner that you may well feel you owe no great gratitude towards such a man."

"And how did you get over here?"

"There was no great difficulty about that. In spite of the activity of the English cruisers, constant communication is kept up between Ireland and France, and fortunately I had, a short time before, made the acquaintance of one of your officers, who was over there, in disguise, gathering recruits for the Brigade."

"Yes, there are a good many agents in Ireland engaged in that work. There is no difficulty in obtaining recruits, for there is scarcely a young Irishman who does not long to be with his countrymen, who have won such credit out here, and many abstain from joining only because they do not know how to set about it. The work of the agents, then, is principally to arrange means for their crossing the channel. It is well that the supply is steadily kept up, for, I can assure you, every battle fought makes very heavy gaps in our ranks; but in spite of that, three fresh regiments have been raised, in the last year, partly by fresh comers from Ireland, and partly by Irish deserters from Marlborough's regiments.

"But I am interrupting your story."

"Well, after leaving Mr. O'Carroll, and making my preparations, I paid a visit to the cottage where the officer was staying, in disguise, and told him that I wanted to cross. He gave instructions as to how to proceed. I was to go to a certain street in Cork, and knock at a certain door. When it was opened, I was to say, 'The sea is calm and the sky is bright'.

"'Then', he said, 'you will be taken in hand, and put on board one of the craft engaged in the work of carrying our recruits across the water. You will be landed at Saint Malo, where there is an agent of the Brigade, who gives instructions to the recruits as to how they are to proceed, supplies them with money enough for the journey, and a man to accompany each party, and act as interpreter on the way.

"I carried out his instructions, crossed the channel in a lugger with thirty young peasants, bound also for Paris, and, on landing at Saint Malo, took my place in the diligence for Paris; having, fortunately, no need for an interpreter. On my presenting my letter to the Marquis de Noailles, he received me with great kindness, and treated me as a guest, until he had obtained me a commission in your regiment."

"Now, when are we likely to go on active service?"

"Soon, I expect," O'Neil said; "but whether we shall be sent to the Peninsula, or to Flanders, no one knows. In fact, it is likely enough that we shall, for the present, remain here; until it is seen how matters go, and where reinforcements will be most required. It is but ten months since we came into garrison, in Paris, and we may therefore expect to be one of the last regiments ordered off.

"For my part, I am in no particular hurry to exchange comfortable quarters, and good living, and such adventures as may fall to the lot of a humble subaltern, for roughing it in the field; where, as has been the case ever since the Brigade was formed, we get a good deal more than our fair share of hard work and fighting."

"I should have thought that you would all have liked that," Desmond said, in some surprise.

"Enough is as good as a feast," the other said; "and when you have done a few weeks' work in trenches, before a town you are besieging; stood knee deep for hours in mud, soaked to the skin with rain, and with the enemy's shot coming through the parapet every half minute or so; you will see that it is not all fun and glory.

"Then, too, you see, we have no particular interest in the quarrels between France and Germany. When we fight, we fight rather for the honour of the Irish Brigade, than for the glory of France. We have a grudge against the Dutch, and fight them as interested parties, seeing that it was by his Dutch troops that William conquered Ireland. As to the English troops, we have no particular enmity against them. Cromwell's business is an old story, and I don't suppose that the English soldier feels any particular love for Queen Anne, or any animosity against us. And after all, we are nearer in blood to them than we are to the Germans, Austrians, or Spaniards, for there are few, even of our oldest families, who have not, many times since the days of Strongbow, intermarried with the English settlers. At any rate, there are still plenty of adherents of King James in England and Scotland. We speak the same language, and form part of the same nation, and I own that I would rather fight against any foreign foe than against them."

"So would I," Desmond said heartily. "Our only point of difference is that we don't agree as to who should be king. We want a Catholic king, and the majority of the English want a Protestant king. We have fought on the subject, and been beaten. Next time, we hope that we may succeed. If the king were to land in England again, I would fight heart and soul in his cause; but whether the French beat the English, in the present war, or the English beat the French, will not, as far as I can see, make much difference to King James; who, Father O'Leary tells me, is, in his opinion, supported here by the French king from no great love for himself, but because, so long as James has adherents in Ireland, Scotland, and England, he is able to play him off against the English Government."

The other young men laughed.

"For heaven's sake, Kennedy, keep such sentiments as these to yourself. It is a matter of faith, in our brigade, that we are fighting in the cause of King James, as against the English usurper. Now that William is dead, and James's daughter on the throne, matters are complicated somewhat; and if the Parliament had settled the succession, after Anne, on her brother, there might have been an end of the quarrel altogether. But now that they have settled it on Sophia of Hanover, granddaughter of James the 1st, and her descendants, subject to the restriction that they shall be Protestants, the quarrel does not seem likely to be healed."

"This priest of yours must be a dangerous man," O'Sullivan said.

"Not at all. I can assure you, he is devoted to the king; but, as he told me, there is no use in Irishmen always closing their eyes to the true state of things. He says that we must rely upon ourselves, and our loyal friends in Scotland and England, but that he is sure the king will never be placed on his throne by French bayonets. A small auxiliary force may be sent over, but, in all these years, Louis has made no real effort to assist him; and even if, for his own purposes, he sent a great army to England, and placed him on the throne, he would not be able to maintain himself there for a month after the French had withdrawn, for even a rightful king would be hated by the people upon whom he had been forced, by a foreign power, especially a power that had, for centuries, been regarded as their chief enemy. If he had been in earnest, Louis would have sent over a great army, instead of a few thousand men, to Ireland, when such a diversion would have turned the scale in our favour. As he did not do so then, he is not likely to do so in the future. The king is useful to him, here, by keeping up an agitation that must, to some extent, cripple the strength of England; but, were a Stuart on the throne, he would have to listen to the wishes of the majority of his people, and France would gain nothing by placing him there. Moreover, she would lose the services of twenty thousand of her best soldiers, for naturally the exiles would all return home, and what is now the most valuable force in the French service, might then become an equally important one in the service of Britain."

"I am glad that this priest of yours remains quietly in Kilkargan, for, if he were to come here, and expound his views among our regiments, he might cause quite a defection among them. At any rate, Kennedy, I should advise you not to take to propagating his views in the regiment. It would not add to your comfort, or ours, and there are a good many hot-headed men who would take up the idea that you had been infected by O'Carroll's principles."

"It would not be well for anyone to say as much to my face," Desmond said. "Father O'Leary is loyal to the backbone, although he has his own ideas as to the hopelessness of our obtaining any efficient help from Louis. He thinks that it will be far better to trust to our friends at home, and that, even did Louis carry out his promises, it would in the long run harm rather than benefit King James."

"I am not saying that his view may not be correct, Kennedy. I am only saying that the view would be a very unpopular one, among the Brigade. We are fighting for France because we believe that France, in turn, will aid in placing our rightful king on the throne, and if we once entertained the notion that Louis was deceiving us, that he had no intention of helping us, and that, if he did place James on the throne, he would alienate all his sympathizers at home, we should ask ourselves of what use was it, spending our blood in fighting the battles of France."

"At any rate, I will take your advice, O'Sullivan, and will keep my lips sealed, as to Father O'Leary's views. As you see, by my presence here, he has not convinced me, and as long as there is a hope that, by the aid of a French army, we may yet see our king come to his own again, I shall do my best to prove myself a faithful soldier of France. I have chosen my career with my eyes open. A loyal Irishman cannot obtain employment, still less military employment, in his own country, and accordingly, we are to be found fighting as soldiers of fortune in every country in Europe. At least there is some chance that we may be benefiting the royal cause by fighting for the country that gave King James shelter, and rendered him armed assistance in his struggle with the usurper, and will probably give aid, more or less efficient, when the next attempt is made. In other countries we are but soldiers of fortune. In France we may regard ourselves as serving our own king by serving King Louis."

"Do you speak French well, Kennedy?" O'Neil said, changing the conversation abruptly.

"Yes. Father O'Leary took care of that, for I always said that I should take service abroad, as there was clearly nothing else to do for a living, and, consequently, he generally talked to me in that language, and I speak it as well as I do English or Irish."

"You have not had much practice with the sword, I suppose?"

"Not so much as I could wish, though I never lost an opportunity of practising. There were several of the tenants who served in the regiment James O'Carroll raised. I used to practise with them, but I shall lose no time in getting the best instruction I can, here."

"You may want it, Kennedy. We are not particularly liked by the French officers, because we are generally chosen to lead an assault, or for other desperate service. Duelling is, of course, forbidden, but that in no way prevents duels from being frequent. As for fighting in action, as far as I have seen or heard, swordsmanship does not go for a great deal. If you press on hard enough, and there are men following you, the enemy give way, generally, before it comes to hand-to-hand fighting. If, on the other hand, they are the more numerous, and hold their position in the breach, it is the musketry that settles it. It is only when two officers happen to meet, in a fierce fight, that swordsmanship becomes of importance.

"We have a good school in the regiment, and there are several famous masters of fence in the town, so I should advise you to give a couple of hours a day, for a time, to making yourself a first-rate swordsman. I have just left off. Our maitre d'armes tells me I am too hotheaded ever to make a fine blade; but I should fancy, from the way you have been arguing, that you are likely to be cooler than most of us in a fencing bout. It is the fault with us all that we are apt to lose our tempers, and indeed Maitre Maupert, who is the best teacher here, declines absolutely to take any of us as pupils, saying that, while we may do excellently well in battle, he can never hope to make first-class fencers of men who cannot be relied upon to keep their heads cool, and to fight with pointed weapons as calmly as they might fence with a friend in a saloon."

"Well, I shall work hard to become a fair swordsman," Desmond said, with a laugh. "I suppose there is plenty of time to spare."

"Plenty. We have a couple of hours' drill in the morning, and after that, except when you are officer of the day, you can spend your time as you like. The colonel and two of his officers attend at the king's levees, when he is in Paris, but, as he spends the greater portion of his time at Versailles, we are seldom called upon for that duty."

A few days after Desmond's arrival, the colonel took him with him to Saint Germain, where James the 3rd, as his supporters called him, held a miniature court. The colonel presented Desmond as a loyal subject of His Majesty, and a newly-joined cornet in his regiment.

The young prince was a lad of eighteen. He was surrounded by a group of courtiers, who had accompanied or followed his father into exile, and whose insistence upon treating him with the respect due to a monarch was in no slight degree galling to him, for, as he often declared to the few friends he had about his own age, he had all the disadvantages of being a king, without any of the advantages.

He was at once taken with the appearance of Desmond Kennedy.

"Ah, Monsieur Kennedy," he said, after the ceremony of presentation had been completed; "I wish that I had all my faithful subjects, of the Irish Brigade, across the water with me; and that I could put on a uniform like yours, and fight at their head for my rights."

"I would that you had, Sire. It would be a good day for us all; and believe me, that either in Ireland or Scotland you would soon find yourself at the head of an army, many times more numerous than our brigade."

"They all tell me that I must wait," the young prince said, with a sigh, "but I have been waiting a long time now, and it seems no nearer than when I was a child. However, the King of France has promised me that it cannot be much longer; and that, when Marlborough is defeated, and his army driven back across the sea, he will send a fleet and an army to place me on my throne."

"We shall all rejoice, indeed, when that time comes, Sire; and I am sure there is not a man in the Irish Brigade who will not follow you to the death, and serve you as faithfully as many of them did your royal father."

"I hope you will come here often, Monsieur Kennedy. I am sure that I shall like you very much, and I think that you would always say what you thought, and tell me the real truth about things."

"Sire!" one of the older men exclaimed, reproachfully.

"I mean no reflection on anyone, Dillon. You all say what I am sure you feel, but you have grown accustomed to waiting, and all think of what is politic, and complain that I speak too frankly. Monsieur Kennedy comes straight from Ireland,

and he is not old enough, yet, to have learned to measure his words, and will not be always afraid that anything he may say will be carried to the king.

"How I wish that the king would send me with Marshal Tallard!"

"That would never do, Sire. The English are your subjects, and they would never forgive you, if you were to appear in the field with a French army, fighting against them."

"But the Irish Brigade fight, Dillon?"

"Yes, Your Majesty, but they are in the service of France, and, by the terms of the treaty of Limerick, were allowed to expatriate themselves, and to enter the French service. We have, in fact, renounced our nationality, with the consent of the English, and, if taken prisoners, could only be treated as captured foes, and not as traitors. Of course, when Your Majesty ascends the throne, we shall again become British subjects."

"I trust that that may come soon, Dillon, and for your sake, rather than my own. When the time comes, you will not find me backward, but this weary waiting tries me sorely, and, were it not for those who have remained faithful to our cause, I would gladly resign such chances as I have of succeeding to the throne of England, and take a commission in the Irish Brigade."

Dillon and some of the elder men shook their heads.

"Can you wonder?" the young prince said, passionately. "Here is Master Kennedy, who is younger than myself, though a free life and exercise have made him a man, in comparison to me. He has his life before him. He will bear his part in many a pitched battle, and, doubtless, in many a private adventure. He is his own master, and, as long as he does his duty, there are none to say, 'you must not do that; you must not say that; you must preserve your dignity; you must speak softly and discreetly; you must wait patiently.'

"I envy you, Master Kennedy. I envy you, from the bottom of my heart! Come often to see me. You will always be welcome;" and, turning abruptly away, he left the chamber hurriedly, to conceal the tears which filled his eyes.

His counsellors shook their heads solemnly, but Colonel O'Brien said, warmly:

"What the king says is natural, for a man of his age; and, for my part, it has increased my respect for him. I say it without offence, but what could be duller than the life this lad leads here? He has been brought up, literally, without a pleasure. His late Majesty, heaven rest his soul! was absorbed in his religious exercises, and nothing could have been more trying, to a boy, than a court in which the priests and confessors were practically supreme. Since his father's death, things have been but little better, and now I see that, at heart, the young king has plenty of spirit and energy, I can feel that his life has been that of a caged hawk, and I am not surprised that he occasionally breaks out into revolt against it. It would, methinks, do him a world of good, had he a few companions about his own age, like Ensign Kennedy. I would even say that, although I can quite understand that, as King of England, he could not well take a commission in one of our regiments, he might at least be placed with one of our most experienced and honoured colonels, in order to learn military exercises, and to mix with the officers as any other nobleman might do, when attached to the regiment."

Murmurs of dissent arose among the counsellors.

"Well, gentlemen," the colonel went on, "I have no desire to interfere with your functions, but, in my opinion, it is good that a king should also be a general. Did anyone think any the worse of Dutch William, that he was able to command his army, personally? None of us can believe that King James will ever succeed to the inheritance of his fathers, without fighting; and it would be well, indeed, that he should not appear as a puppet, but as one qualified to command. It was the fault, or rather the misfortune, of his father, that he was unfit to lead his troops in the field. Had he been able to do so, he would, in all probability, have died King of England, instead of as a fugitive and a pensioner of King Louis. In one way, it grieves me to see that the young king feels his position acutely; but, on the other hand, I am rejoiced to see that he is in no way lacking in spirit, and that he longs to be out of his cage, and to try his wings for himself.

"Well, gentlemen, having had my say, I will take my leave of you, as duty calls me back to my regiment. I trust that the frankness with which I have spoken will not be misunderstood."

So saying, with a bow to the courtiers he left the room, followed by Kennedy.

"They mean well," he said, after they had mounted, and ridden off at a gallop; "but it is a pity that these gentlemen, all loyal and honourable men as they are, should surround the young king. They suited, well enough, to the mood of his father, who was always wanting in spirit, and was broken down, not only by the loss of his kingdom, but by the conduct of his daughters; and, what with that, and his devotion to religion, he was rather a monk than a monarch. He believed--but most mistakenly--that he had a genius for politics, and was constantly intriguing with his adherents at home, notably Marlborough and other lords, from whom he obtained fair words and promises of support, but nothing else. But though he could plan, he did not possess a spark of energy, and was one of the most undecided of men, though, like most undecided men, he could be extremely obstinate; and, unfortunately, the more wrong he was, the more obstinately he held to his course.

"However, all this can make no difference in our devotion to the Stuart cause. But I hail, with satisfaction, the prospect that, in his son, we may have one to whom we may feel personally loyal; for there can be no doubt that men will fight with more vigour, for a person to whom they are attached, than for an abstract idea."

"I have heard Father O'Leary say the same, sir. His opinion was that, had the late king possessed the qualities that commanded the personal admiration and fidelity of his followers, and excited something like enthusiasm among the people at large, he would never have lost his throne; nor, could he have led his armies, as did Gustavus or Charles the 12th of Sweden, would William of Orange ever have ventured to cross to England."

"It was a bad business, altogether, lad. His cause was practically lost, from the day that William set foot upon English soil. He had, in reality, no personal friends; and those who would have remained faithful to the cause, were paralysed by his indecision and feebleness. Charles the Martyr made many mistakes, but he had the passionate adherence of his followers. His personality, and his noble appearance, did as much for him as the goodness of his cause; while his son, James, repelled rather than attracted personal devotion. I trust that his grandson will inherit some of his qualities. His outburst, today, gave me hope that he will do so; but one must not build too much on that. It may have been only the pettishness of a young man, sick of the constant tutelage to which he is subjected, and the ennui of the life he leads, rather than the earnestness of a noble spirit.

"Of course, Kennedy, I need not tell you that it would be well to make no mention, to anyone, of the scene that you have witnessed."

"I shall certainly make no mention of it to anyone, sir. I am sorry, indeed, for the young king. His life must be a dreadful one, conscious of the impossibility of breaking the bonds in which he is held, and knowing that his every word and action will be reported, by spies, to the King of France."

For three months, Desmond Kennedy worked hard at drill and sword exercise. He became a general favourite in the regiment, owing to his good temper, high spirits, and readiness to join in everything that was going on.

He went over, several times, to Saint Germain. At first, the king's counsellors looked but coldly upon him, and he would have ceased to come there, had it not been for the unaffected pleasure shown by the king at his visits. In time, however, two of the principal men at the little court requested him to have a conversation with them, before going into the king's chamber.

"You will understand, Mr. Kennedy," one of them said, when they had seated themselves in a quiet spot in the garden; "that we, standing in the position of His Majesty's counsellors, are in a position of great responsibility. His Majesty, as we admit is but natural, chafes over the inaction to which he is condemned by circumstances; and is apt, at times, to express his desire for action in terms which, if they came to the ears of King Louis, as we have every reason to believe is sometimes the case, would do him and the cause serious injury. Naturally, we should be glad for him to have companions of his own age, but it behoves us to be most careful that such companionship should not add to our difficulties in this direction; and we should view with satisfaction a friendship between the young king and one who, like yourself, is nearly of his own age and, as we can see, full of spirit and energy. In these matters the king is deficient; but it would be better that he should, for the present, remain as he is, rather than that he should, in acquiring more manly habits, grow still more impatient and discontented with his position.

"We have naturally taken some little trouble in finding out how you stand in your regiment, and we hear nothing but good of you. You are much liked by your comrades, pay the greatest attention to your military exercises, and are regarded as one who will, some day, do much credit to the regiment; and we feel that, in most respects, your influence could not but be advantageous to the young king; but the good that this might do him would be more than balanced, were you to render him still more impatient than he is for action. You may well suppose that we, exiles as we have been for so many years from our country, are not less impatient than he for the day of action; but we know that such action must depend upon the King of France, and not upon ourselves. We would gladly risk all, in an effort to place him on the throne of England, to repair past injustices and cruel wrongs; but, were we to move without the assistance of Louis, instead of achieving that object we might only bring fresh ruin, confiscations, and death upon the royalists of England, Scotland, and Ireland. Are you of our opinion?"

"Completely so, sir. Of course, I know but little of what is passing, save in the neighbourhood where I have been brought up; but I know that there, even among the king's most devoted adherents, there is a feeling that nothing can possibly be done until France lends her aid, in earnest. The English army is far stronger than it was when we were last in arms, and when William had to rely, almost entirely, upon his Dutch troops and Dutch generals; while the friends of the Stuarts are almost without arms, without leaders, and without organization."

"That is good, Mr. Kennedy; and, if we were to sanction King James's forming an intimacy with you, can I understand that we could rely upon your not using your influence to add to his impatience for action, and discontent with his present position?"

"Certainly, sir. Being so recently from Ireland, I could assure him that even his most devoted adherents, there, are of opinion that no rising could be attended with success, unless backed by French arms, and especially by the aid of the Irish Brigade, which has already won such renown for itself, and whose appearance would excite the greatest enthusiasm among all Irishmen."

"In that case, Mr. Kennedy, so far from throwing any difficulties in the way of His Majesty seeking your companionship, we shall encourage him, and shall be glad to see you here, as often as your military duties will permit."

Chapter 2: A Valiant Band.

The permission was not attended with the result that the young prince's counsellors had hoped. For a time, James showed a lively pleasure when Desmond rode over to Saint Germain, walked with him in the gardens, and talked to him alone in his private apartments, and professed a warm friendship for him; but Desmond was not long in discovering that his first estimate of the prince's character had been wholly erroneous, and that his outburst at their first meeting had been the result of pique and irritation, rather than any real desire to lead a more active life. Upon the contrary, he was constitutionally indolent and lethargic. There were horses at his command, but it was seldom, indeed, that he would take the trouble to cross the saddle, although walking was distasteful to him. Even when speaking of his hopes of ascending the throne of England, he spoke without enthusiasm, and said one day:

"It is a pity that it cannot be managed without fuss and trouble. I hate trouble."

"Nothing can be done worth doing, without trouble, Your Majesty," Desmond said sturdily. "It almost seems to me that, if everything could be had without trouble, it would not be worth having."

"How do you mean, Mr. Kennedy?"

"I may illustrate it by saying, Sire, that no true fisherman would care about angling in a pond, close to his house, and so full of fish, that he had but to drop a baited hook into the water to bring up one immediately. The pleasure of fishing consists largely in the hard work that it demands. It is, perhaps, miles to a stream across the hills, and a long day's work may produce but a half dozen fish; but these the angler prizes in proportion to the trouble he has had to get them. I think that, were I born heir to a throne, I would rather that it should cost me hardship, toil, and danger to obtain it, than walk into a cathedral, a few days after my father's death, and there be crowned."

"I do not agree with you, at all," James said, shortly. "If anything could not be had without toil, hardship, and danger, as you say, I would willingly go without it."

"Then, Sire, I can only hope that the toil and danger may be borne by your devoted followers, and that you may be spared them, personally."

James looked sharply up at his companion, to gather whether the words were spoken sarcastically, but Desmond's face, though flushed, was calm and serious. Nevertheless, indolent as he was, James felt that the words were a reproof; that, although he had at first liked him, there was in reality little in common between him and this energetic young fellow; and the next time he came, he received him with much less cordiality than before; while Desmond, who was beginning to tire of the companionship of one who lacked, alike, the fun and humour, and the restless activity of his comrades, Patrick and Phelim; and who saw that the professions of James's friendship were but short lived, came over to Saint Germain less frequently, until, at last, he only rode over with his colonel, or when some duty called him there.

"So you have been a failure, Master Kennedy," the counsellor who had first spoken to him said, one day, when the change in the king's manner became evident to them all.

"I am afraid so, sir," Desmond replied with a smile. "I have no doubt that it was my fault. Perhaps I was not patient enough with him; but, indeed, my efforts to rouse him to take exercise, to practise in arms, and so on, were so ill received, that I felt I was doing more harm than good."

"I was afraid that it would be so," the other said, regretfully. "You see, during his later years, his father gave up his time almost entirely to religious observances; and, consequently, the lad's life was very dull and monotonous. Constitutionally, he undoubtedly takes after his father, who, with all his virtues, was at once indolent and undecided. We have observed, with regret, his disinclination to bestir himself in any way. Seeing that we, who were his father's companions, are too old, or too much disheartened, to be lively companions for him, we had hoped that the talk of one of spirit, and of his own age, might have roused him to make some exertions to overcome his disinclination for anything like active exercise. I think now, however, that we were wrong; that the tonic was too strong; that he could not but feel that your abundance of spirits, and life, were too much for him; and that the companion he needs is one who could, to some extent, sympathize with him, and who could, perhaps, make more allowance for the manner in which he has been brought up.

"We do not blame you at all. I am sure that you have done your best. But it is evident that the contrast between you and himself has been too strong a one; and that, feeling he cannot hope to emulate your soldierly activity, he has come to resent it, as a sort of reflection upon himself."

Desmond was, by no means, sorry at being relieved of the necessity of paying frequent visits to Saint Germain. In the first place, he begrudged the time that was taken from his fencing lessons, at which he had worked enthusiastically; and in the next, he had felt, after two or three visits, that between himself and the young king there was really nothing in common. Full of life and spirits himself, it seemed to him nothing short of disgraceful that one, who aspired to rule, should take no pains whatever to fit himself for a throne, or to cultivate qualities that would render himself popular among a high-spirited people. And, as he came to understand James more thoroughly, he had found his visits increasingly irksome, all the more so, as he felt their inutility.

"Thank goodness," he said, to his two friends, when he went home that day, "I have done with Saint Germain. I am as warm an adherent as ever of the cause of the Stuarts, and should be perfectly ready, when the time comes, to fight my hardest for them; but I would vastly rather fight for the king, than converse with him."

"I suppose, by what I have seen of him, that he must be somewhat wearisome," Phelim O'Sullivan said, with a laugh. "Fortunately, wit and gaiety are not essential qualities on the part of a monarch; but I must own that, treasonable as it may sound, I fear His Majesty is lacking in other qualities, far more essential in a monarch. I should say that he is kindly and well disposed, he wishes to be fair and just, and may turn out a wise ruler; but he is altogether deficient in energy. I suppose there is no occasion for a king, safely seated upon a throne, to be energetic; but a prince in exile should possess the qualities that excite enthusiasm, and bind men to him. Possibly, the qualities King James possesses would be highly valued by the Scotch, but they would certainly fail to inspire our people."

"Yes," Patrick O'Neil agreed. "His father did more to ruin his cause, in Ireland, than all William's Dutch generals and troops, together. It was disheartening to be risking life and possessions for a man who would do nothing for himself, whose indecision paralysed our leaders, and who, the moment a reverse came, sought safety in flight, instead of taking his place among the men who were devoted to his cause. I can understand that, in England, where the majority of those who professed to be devoted to him were betraying him, and were in secret communication with William, he should be by turns obstinate and vacillating; but in Ireland, where every man who surrounded him was risking his life in his cause, he should have shown absolute confidence in them, listened to their advice, set an example of personal gallantry and courage, and, at least, remained among them until all was definitely lost. It was the desertion of James, rather than the loss of the battle of the Boyne, that ruined his cause.

"Well, I am glad you are out of it, for it was a pity that you should be going without your work at the salle d'armes, when you were making such progress that, the master reported, in a few months you would become one of the best swordsmen in the regiment."

There were, in Paris, many Irish officers besides those belonging to Colonel O'Brien's regiment. These were, for the most part, men who had been severely wounded in the preceding campaign, and who now remained in the capital with the depots of their regiments. These were constantly recruited by fresh arrivals from Ireland, by which means the Irish Brigade was not only kept up to their original strength, in spite of the heavy losses they suffered, in the engagements in which they had taken part, but largely increased its force, new regiments being constantly formed. Naturally, O'Brien's corps, being the only complete regiment in Paris, at the time, was regarded as the headquarters and general meeting place of all the Irish officers there; and, as some of these had campaigned in Flanders, in Italy, and in Spain, Desmond learned, from their talk and anecdotes, far more of the doings of the Brigade than he had hitherto known. From the first they had, by their reckless bravery, in almost every engagement that had taken place, so distinguished themselves that they received the highest commendation from the French generals, and were almost invariably selected for specially dangerous service.

"I think the hottest affair I was ever engaged in," a major, who had served in

Burke's regiment, said one evening, when some ten or twelve of his companions had gathered, at the room which was the general meeting place of the officers of the corps, "was at the attack on Cremona by Eugene. You have all heard how our regiment, and that of Dillon, distinguished themselves there, but you may not have heard particulars. The place was a strong one, and it was garrisoned by some 4000 men--all French, with the exception of our two regiments. Marshal Villeroy was himself in command; an excellent officer, but, as is often the case in the French army, very badly served by his subordinates.

"Here, as you know, almost everything goes by influence; and the generals are surrounded by men who have been forced upon them by powerful persons, whom they cannot afford to disoblige. The consequence was that, relying upon the strength of the place, no proper watch was set. There were guards, indeed, at the gates, but with no communication with each other; no soldiers on the ramparts; no patrols were sent out beyond the town, or maintained in the streets.

"No harm might have come of this, had it not been that treachery was at work. There was a scoundrel, who was brother of the priest of one of the parishes near the wall, and both were in favour of the enemy. The priest's residence was near a sewer, which communicated with the moat outside the walls. The entrance was closed by an iron grating. Were this removed, troops could enter, by the sewer, into the priest's wine cellar.

"The priest, being promised a large sum of money, set to work. First, he laid a complaint before the governor that the sewer was choked with filth, which might be a source of disease to the town unless removed; and to do this, it was necessary that the grating should be taken down. Being altogether unsuspicious of evil, the governor granted his request.

"As soon as the grating was removed, Eugene despatched eight miners, who crossed the moat at night, made their way up the sewer, and opened a communication between it and the priest's house. When all was ready, four or five hundred picked grenadiers entered, and were concealed in the house of the priest, and other adherents of the emperor.

"Eugene set two strong bodies of picked troops in motion. The one was to enter by the Saint Margaret gate, which would be seized by the force already in the city. This column consisted of five thousand men. The second force, of two thousand infantry and three thousand cavalry, under the Prince de Vaudemont, was to cross the river by a bridge of boats.

"We slept like stupid dogs. Such watchmen as there were on the walls gave no alarm. The gate of All Saints was seized, its guard being instantly overpowered, and a party of engineers broke down the gate of Saint Margaret, which had been walled up; and at daylight Eugene rode into the town, followed by his troops and one thousand cavalry; while another mounted force watched the gate, and the country round, to prevent the escape of fugitives.

"Before any alarm was given, Eugene had established himself at the Hotel de Ville, was master of the great street that separated half the garrison from the other half, had taken possession of the cathedral; and, in fact, the place was captured without a shot being fired.

"Then the uproar began. Parties of troops, led by natives of the town, seized a large number of officers at their lodgings; and as the alarm spread, the troops seized their muskets and rushed out, only to be sabred and trodden down by the enemy's cavalry. I was asleep, and dreaming, when my servant rushed into my room, and said:

"'The Germans are in possession of the town, Captain.'

"'You are a blathering idiot,' I said.

"'It's true, your honour. Get up and listen.'

"Very unwillingly, I got out of bed and opened the window, and, by the holy poker, I found that Pat was right. There was a sound of firing, shouting, and screaming, and I heard the gallop of a heavy body of horsemen, and, directly afterwards, a squadron of German cuirassiers came galloping down the street.

"'It is time for us to be out of this, Pat,' I said, and jumped into my clothes, quicker than I had ever done before.

"We went downstairs, and I borrowed two overcoats that we found hanging there, and put them on over our uniforms. Then we went out, by the back door, and ran as hard as we could, keeping through narrow lanes, to the barracks.

"On my way, I had to pass a barrier near a toll gate. Here there were thirty-six of our men under a sergeant. Not knowing where the enemy were, or whether they were between me and the barracks, I thought it best to stay there, and of course took the command. Just as I had done so, I heard the tramping of cavalry, and had the gate shut. We were just in time, for two hundred and fifty cuirassiers came galloping along.

"Their leader, Baron de Mercy, as soon as the troops began to enter Saint Margaret's gate, was ordered to dash round and capture the Po gate, through which Vaudemont's corps would, after crossing the bridge, enter the town. He shouted to me to surrender, promising us our lives. I told him that if he wanted the place, he would have to come and take it. He used language which I need not repeat, but he did not attack us, waiting for the arrival of four hundred infantry, who had been ordered to follow him. They were some time in coming up, having lost their way, owing to the rascally native who was their guide being killed by a shot from a window.

"I was not sorry for the delay, for it gave us time to look at matters quietly, and prepare for defence. Another six hundred cavalry now came up, and Mercy placed them so as to cut off, altogether, the French cavalry, who were quartered away to the right; then he ordered the infantry to attack us.

"Our position was a good one. The barricade was formed of square piles, driven into the ground with small narrow openings between them. I ordered the men to keep behind the timbers until the enemy came up. The Germans opened a murdering fire as they approached, but, though the bullets pattered like rain against the palisades, and whistled in between them, not a man was touched. I waited till they were within two paces, and then gave the word, and you may well guess that there was not a bullet thrown away, and the Germans, mightily astonished, drew back, leaving nigh forty of their men behind them. Then, falling back a bit, they opened fire upon us, but it was a game that two could play at. We could see them, but they could not see us; and while we loaded our muskets in shelter, they were exposed, and we picked them off by dozens.

"The firing had, of course, given the alarm to our two regiments, who turned out just as they were, in their nightshirts. Major O'Mahony, who was in command of Dillon's regiment, as Lally was away on leave, luckily made his way in safety from his lodgings to the barracks, got his own men in order, while Colonel Wauchop, who commanded our regiment, took the command of the two battalions. Fortunately, a portion of the regiment had been ordered to fall in early for inspection, and this gave time for the rest to get into their uniforms; and, as soon as they were ready, Wauchop led them out and fell suddenly upon a portion of Mercy's force, poured in a volley, and then charged them.

"Horse and foot fell back before the attack. Then they turned the cannon on the ramparts, and thus secured possession of the Po gate, and, pushing on, the guns helping them, drove the Austrians from the houses they occupied, and so opened communications with the French cavalry.

"A brigadier now came up, and ordered the battalions to barricade all the streets they had won, with barrels and carts. A French regiment arrived, and occupied the church of Saint Salvador, and the battery which commanded the bridge, across which Vaudemont's corps could now be seen approaching. The redoubt on the other side of the bridge was only held by fifty men, and they were now strengthened by a hundred of the French soldiers. The Austrians approached, making sure that the town had already been taken, and looking out for a signal that was to be hoisted. Their astonishment was great, when a heavy musketry fire was opened upon them by the garrison of the outpost, while the guns of the battery on the wall plunged their shot in among them.

"The column was at once halted. Eugene had regarded the struggle as over, when news was brought to him of the defeat of Mercy's corps by the Irish. Everywhere else things had gone most favourably. Marshal Villeroy had been wounded and made prisoner. His marechal de camp shared the same fate. The Chevalier D'Entregues, who advanced to meet the enemy, was defeated and killed, as was Lieutenant General de Trenan, and the Spanish Governor of the town mortally wounded.

"On receiving the news, Eugene at once sent an officer to inspect the Irish position; but his report was that they were too well placed to be driven from it. He then sent Captain MacDonnell, an officer in his service, to offer, if the Irish would leave their position, to enrol them in the Austrian service, with higher pay than they now received. You may guess the sort of answer he received, and he was at once arrested for bringing such a message to them. Eugene then endeavoured to engage Marshal Villeroy to order the Irish to lay down their arms, as further resistance would only end in their slaughter. Villeroy simply replied that, as a prisoner, he could no longer give orders.

"During this pause, the Count de Revel and the Marquis de Queslin succeeded in gathering together a considerable number of the scattered French infantry, and with these they marched to endeavour to recover the gates that had been lost, and, having occupied the church of Santa Maria, and a bastion near the gate of All Saints, ordered the Irish to leave a hundred men at the barricades, and with the rest to push forward to the gate of Mantua. So I found myself in command of a full company.

"O'Mahony was now in command of the two regiments, as Wauchop had been wounded. It was pretty hard work they had of it, and they suffered heavily in carrying the guardhouse, held by two hundred Austrians. Eugene now launched a great force against our people, and attacked them on all sides; but O'Mahony faced them each way, and received the charge of the cuirassiers with so heavy a fire that they fled in disorder. Another corps of cuirassiers came up, and these charged with such fury that their leader, Monsieur de Freiberg, pushed his way into the middle of Dillon's regiment, where he was surrounded, and, refusing quarter, was killed; and his men, disheartened by the fall of their leader, fled, carrying with them the infantry who were ranged in their rear.

"But our men were now exhausted by their exertions, and suffered heavily; and O'Mahony, seeing that he was likely to be attacked by fresh troops, and that my post guarding the approach of the Po gate would then be left altogether unsupported, returned to it. I was glad enough when I saw them coming, for it was mighty trying work being left there, and hearing the storm of battle going on all round, and knowing that at any moment we might be attacked.

"They did not stop long, for orders came from Revel, who had captured the gate of All Saints, and was preparing to attack Saint Margaret's, to march again to the gate of Mantua. It seemed a hopeless enterprise. Captain Dillon, of Dillon's regiment, marched out and, after hard fighting, drove the Austrians from house to house; but, on reaching a spot where the ground was open, he was attacked on all sides, and for a time the enemy and our men were mixed up together in a melee.

"I could hear by the sound of the firing that our men were returning, and posted my fellows so as to cover their retreat; and as they came back, hotly pressed by the enemy, we opened so warm a fire that they passed in through the gate of the barrier in safety, but only half as strong as they had gone out.

"As soon as they were in, they aided us in strengthening the position. Seeing that Vaudemont's corps was on the point of attacking the redoubt, the Marquis de

Queslin sent orders to the little garrison there to withdraw across the bridge, and destroy the boats. This they effected, in spite of the heavy fire kept up by the enemy.

"In the meantime, fighting had been going on all over the town. The gate of Mantua had been held by Captain Lynch, of Dillon's battalion, and thirty-five men. As soon as he heard the din of battle in the town, he collected a few fugitives, entrenched his position at the guardhouse, and maintained it for the whole day; not only that, but, finding that his position was commanded by a party of Austrians, who had taken post in the church of Saint Marie, close by, he sallied out, drove them from the church, and maintained possession of that as well; until, late in the afternoon, he was reinforced by two companies of our regiment, who made their way this time without opposition.

"The enemy fell back, but not unmolested, as, sallying out, we pressed hotly upon them. There now remained only the gate of Saint Margaret in the hands of the Austrians. Here a large body of troops had been stationed, and succeeded in repulsing the repeated attacks made upon them by Revel's force.

"The fight had now lasted for eleven hours, and the position of the Austrians had become critical. The desperate resistance of our men had entirely changed the position. They had repulsed every attack upon them, had given time for the scattered French to gather, and the one gate remaining in Eugene's possession was seriously threatened. Vaudemont's corps was helpless on the other side of the river, and could render no assistance, and Eugene gave the order for his troops to retire, which they did in good order.

"It had been a hot day, indeed, for us, and we were only too glad to see them go. We had lost three hundred and fifty men, out of the six hundred with which we began the fight; altogether, the garrison had lost, in killed, wounded, and in prisoners, fourteen hundred men and officers, while Eugene's loss was between fifteen and sixteen hundred.

"Personally, I have had hotter fighting, but taking the day altogether, it was the most terrible through which I have ever passed. Throughout the day we were in total ignorance of what was going on elsewhere, though we knew, by the firing in other parts of the town, that the French there had not been overpowered, and, each time the regiments left us, I was expecting every moment to be attacked by an overwhelming force. Faith, it was enough to make one's hair white! However, I have no reason to grumble. I obtained great praise for the defence of the barrier, and was given my majority; and, if it had not been for the wound I received, two years ago, which incapacitated me from active service, I might now be in command of the regiment."

"Yes, indeed," another officer said. "It was truly a gallant affair; and, although our men had fought equally as well in many another engagement, it was their conduct at Cremona that attracted the greatest attention, and showed the French the value of the Brigade. I would we had always been employed in actions on which we could look back, with the same pride and pleasure, as we can upon Cremona and a long list of battles where we bore the brunt of the fighting; and never failed to be specially mentioned with praise by the general.

"The most unpleasant work that I ever did was when under Marshal de Catinat. Eight Irish battalions were sent up, in 1694, from Pignerolle into the valley of La Perouse, to oppose the Vaudois, who had always offered a vigorous resistance to the passage of our troops through their passes. They were wild mountaineers, and Huguenots to a man, who had, I believe, generations ago been forced to fly from France and take refuge in the mountains, and maintained themselves sturdily against various expeditions sent against them.

"I own the business was not at all to my taste, and many others of our officers shared my opinions. It was too much like what we remembered so bitterly at home, when William's troopers pursued our fugitives to the hills, burning, destroying, and killing, and, above all, hunting down the priests. This was the other way, but was as cruel and barbarous. The poor people had given no offence, save that they held to their own religion. An Irishman should be the last to blame another for that, and, seeing they had successfully opposed the efforts of the French to root them out, it was much against my will that I marched with my regiment. I hope that, when it comes to fighting against regular troops, of whatever nationality, I am ready to do my work; but to carry fire and sword among a quiet people, in little mountain villages, went against the grain.

"It seemed to us that it was to be a massacre rather than fighting, but there we were mistaken. It was the hardest work that I ever went through. It was impossible in such a country to move in large bodies, and we were broken up into small parties, which advanced into the hills, each under its own commander, without any fixed plans save to destroy every habitation, to capture or kill the flocks of goats, which afforded the inhabitants their chief means of subsistence, and to give no quarter wherever they resisted.

"Even now, I shudder at the thought of the work we had to do; climbing over pathless hills, wading waist deep through mountain torrents, clambering along on the face of precipices where a false step meant death, and always exposed to a dropping fire from invisible foes, who, when we arrived at the spot from which they had fired, had vanished and taken up a fresh position, so that the whole work had to be done over again. Sometimes we were two or even more days without food, for, as you may imagine, it was impossible to transport provisions, and we had nothing save what we carried in our haversacks at starting. We had to sleep on the soaked ground, in pitiless storms. Many men were carried away and drowned in crossing the swollen torrents. Our clothes were never dry. And the worst of it was, after six weeks of such work, we felt that we were no nearer to the object for which we had been sent up than we were when we started.

"It was true that we had destroyed many of their little villages, but as these generally consisted of but a few houses, only rough buildings that could be rebuilt in a few days, the gain was not a substantial one. We had, of course, killed some of the Vaudois, but our loss had been much heavier than theirs, for, active as our men were, they were no match in speed for these mountaineers, who were as nimble as their own goats, knew everything of the country, and could appear or disappear, as it seemed to us, almost by magic. It was a wretched business, and once or twice, when our parties were caught in the narrow ravines, they were overwhelmed by rocks thrown down from above; so that, on the whole, we lost almost as many men as we should have done in a pitched battle, gaining no credit, nor having the satisfaction that we were doing good service to France.

"I hope I may never be employed in a business like that again. It was not only the Vaudois that we had to fight, for, seeing that at first we were pushing forward steadily, the Duke of Savoy, under whose protection they lived, sent six hundred regular troops to assist them, and these, who were well commanded, adopted the same tactics as the peasants, avoiding all our attempts to bring on an engagement, and never fighting except when they had us to great advantage.

"As a rule, our men were always dissatisfied when they received orders to fall back, but I think that there was not a man among us but was heartily glad, when we were recalled to rejoin Catinat at Pignerolle."

The expedition, however, although altogether unsuccessful in rooting out the Vaudois, created such terrible devastation in the mountains and valleys that the Irish name and nation will long remain odious to the Vaudois. Six generations have since passed away, but neither time nor subsequent calamities have obliterated the impression made by the waste and desolation of this military incursion.

"You were at Blenheim, were you not, Captain O'Donovan?"

"Yes. A tough fight it was, and a mismanaged one. I was in the Earl of Clare's regiment, which, with Lee and Dorrington's battalions, was stationed with the force in Oberglau in the centre of our position. It seemed to us, and to our generals, that our position was almost impregnable. It lay along a ridge, at the foot of which was a rivulet and deep swampy ground. On the right of the position was the village of Blenheim, held by twenty-seven battalions of good French infantry, twelve squadrons, and twenty-four pieces of cannon. Strong entrenchments had been thrown up round our position, but these were not altogether completed. Blenheim, moreover, had been surrounded by very heavy and strong palisades, altogether impassable by infantry, and, as the allies could not hope to get cannon across the stream and swamps, it seemed to defy any attack. From Oberglau the army of Marshal de Marcin and the Elector stretched to the village of Lutzingen. We had some five-and-twenty cannon at Oberglau.

"The weak point, as it afterwards turned out to be, was the crest between us and Blenheim. Considering that both the artillery and musketry fire from both villages swept the slope, and as in numbers we equalled the enemy, it was thought well-nigh impossible for him to cross the swamps and advance to the attack; and almost the whole of the French cavalry were massed on the crest, in order to charge them, should they succeed in crossing and try to ascend the slope.

"At first the battle went altogether favourably. We had opposite to us the English, Dutch, Hanoverians, and Danish troops under Marlborough, while facing our left were Prussians, Imperialists, and other German troops under Eugene. Marlborough's Danish and Hanoverian cavalry first crossed, but were at once charged and driven back. Then they tried again, supported by English infantry. Then Marlborough led up a still stronger force, drove back our light cavalry, and began to ascend the hill. We were attacked by ten battalions--Hanoverians, Danes, and Prussians, while the English bore against Blenheim. The fighting at both places was desperate, and I must do the Germans the justice to say that nothing could have exceeded the gallantry they showed, and that, in spite of the heavy fire we maintained, they pressed up the slope.

"We remained in our entrenchments, till it could be seen that the English were falling back from Blenheim, whose palisade, manned by twenty-seven battalions of infantry, offered an obstacle that would have defied the best troops in the world to penetrate.

"Immediately this was seen, nine battalions, headed by our three regiments, leapt from the trenches and poured down on the Germans. The enemy could not withstand our onslaught. Two of their regiments were utterly destroyed, the rest suffered terribly, and were driven back. On the left, Marcin held his ground against all the attacks of Eugene, and it seemed to us that the battle was won.

"However, it was not over yet. While the fierce fighting had been going on in front of Oberglau and Blenheim, Marlborough had passed the whole of his cavalry and the rest of his infantry across the rivulet, and, in spite of artillery and musketry fire, these moved up in grand order, the infantry inclining towards the two villages as before, the cavalry bearing straight up the slope, and, when they reached the crest, charging furiously upon our horse stationed there. They were superior in numbers, but on this head accounts differ. At any rate, they overthrew our cavalry, who fled in the greatest disorder, pursued by the allied horse.

"The infantry poured into the gap thus made, Blenheim was entirely isolated, and we were exposed to assault both in front and rear. Nevertheless, we repulsed all attacks, until Marcin sent orders for us to retire; then we sallied out, after setting fire to the village, flung ourselves upon the enemy, and succeeded in cutting our way through, our regiment forming the rear guard. The whole of Marcin's army were now in full retreat, harassed by the allied cavalry; but whenever their squadrons approached us, we faced about and gave them so warm a reception that they attacked less formidable foes. As for the garrison in Blenheim, you know they were at last surrounded by Marlborough's whole force, with artillery; and with the Danube in their rear, and no prospect of succour, they were forced to surrender.

"It was a disastrous day, and I have not yet recovered from the wound I received there. Wad five thousand infantry been posted in a redoubt, halfway between Blenheim and Oberglau, so as to give support to our cavalry, the result of the battle would have been very different. Still, I suppose that most battles are lost by some unlooked-for accident--some mistake in posting the troops. We can only say that, had the allied forces been all composed of such troops as those Eugene commanded, they would have been beaten decisively; and that had, on the contrary, Eugene commanded such troops as those under Marlborough, Marcin would never have held his ground."

"How many British troops were there in the battle, Captain O'Donovan?"

"Somewhere about twelve thousand, while the Continental troops were forty-seven or forty-eight thousand. There is no doubt that they were the backbone of the force, just as we flatter ourselves that our three regiments were the backbone of the defence of Oberglau."

Chapter 3: A Strange Adventure.

When the party broke up, O'Neil and O'Sullivan, as usual, came in for a quiet chat to Desmond's room.

"As we may be possibly ordered to Spain," Kennedy said, "I should like to know a little about what we are going to fight about; for, although I know a good deal about the war in Flanders, no news about that in Spain ever reached Kilkargan."

"Well, you know, of course," O'Neil said, "that Philip the Fifth is a grandson of Louis; and is naturally supported by France against the Archduke Charles of Austria, who is competitor for the throne, and who is, of course, supported by England. Six thousand English and Dutch troops were sent to aid the Archduke Charles in his attempt to invade Spain and dethrone Philip. The King of Portugal, who is a member of the allied confederacy, promised to have everything ready to cooperate with them. They found, however, on their arrival, that no preparations had been made, and they were accordingly distributed, for a time, among the garrisons on the frontier.

"Philip, on his part, had not been so inactive, and two armies--the one commanded by the Duke of Berwick, and the other by General Villadarias--invaded Portugal. Berwick surprised and captured two Dutch battalions, and then captured Portalagre, and compelled the garrison, including an English regiment of infantry, to surrender.

"The allies, to make a diversion, sent General Das Minas into Spain, with fifteen thousand men, who captured one or two towns and defeated a body of French and Spanish troops. The hot weather now set in, and put a stop to hostilities, and the troops on both sides went into quarters. The general--I forget his name--who commanded the English and Dutch contingent, was so disgusted with the proceedings of the Portuguese that he resigned his command, and the Earl of Galway was appointed in his place. The next year he crossed the frontier, captured several towns, without much fighting, and invested Badajos. Here, however, a stern resistance was met with. Galway's hand was carried off by a shot, and the French general (Tesse) coming up in force to the relief of the town, and the Portuguese not arriving at all, the allies were obliged to fall back upon Portugal. But Philip was threatened from a fresh quarter.

"In June, the Earl of Peterborough sailed from Portsmouth with five thousand men, and at Lisbon took on board the Archduke Charles. At Gibraltar some more troops were embarked, and Peterborough set sail for the coast of Valencia. Peterborough himself, one of the most daring of men, and possessed of extraordinary military talent, was in favour of a march upon Madrid; but, fortunately for us, he was overruled, and commenced the siege of Barcelona--a strong town garrisoned by five thousand good troops, while he himself had but a thousand more under his command. Nevertheless, by a sudden and daring attack he captured the strong castle of Montjuich, which commanded the town, which was in consequence obliged to surrender four days later, and the whole of Catalonia was then captured. Saint Matteo, ninety miles from Barcelona, which had declared for Charles and was besieged by a large force, was relieved; and so brilliant were the exploits accomplished by Peterborough, with most inadequate means, that the Spaniards came to the conclusion that he was possessed by an evil spirit.

"Large reinforcements were sent from France, and King Philip advanced upon Barcelona, and invested it by land, while a French fleet bombarded it by sea. Peterborough hurried, with a small force from Valencia, to aid the besieged, the matter being all the more important since Charles himself was in the city. Before his arrival, however, an English fleet appeared, and our fleet retired.

"Philip at once raised the siege, and retired to Madrid. His position was indeed serious. Lord Galway was advancing from the frontier, and Peterborough had gathered a force to cooperate with him. Upon the approach of Galway, Philip and the Duke of Berwick retreated to the frontier. There they received great reinforcements, and advanced against Madrid, which was evacuated by Galway, who marched away to form a junction with Lord Peterborough.

"Owing to the dilatory habits and hesitation of the Austrian prince, the junction was not effected for some time, and then, in spite of the entreaties of the two English generals, he could not be persuaded to make a movement towards Madrid. Peterborough, whose temper was extremely fiery, at last lost all patience, abused Charles openly, and then, mounting his horse, rode down to the coast, embarked upon an English ship of war, and sailed away to assist the Duke of Savoy. After his departure, the ill feeling between the English force, the Portuguese, and the leaders of the Spanish adherents of Charles increased, and they spent their time in quarrelling among themselves. They were without money, magazines, and almost without provisions. Berwick was near them with a superior force, and they took the only step open, of retreating towards Valencia, which they reached, after suffering great hardships, before Berwick could overtake them.

"French troops were poured into Spain, while no reinforcements were sent from England. Galway and the Portuguese advanced to meet the Duke of Berwick, who was marching with a large army to occupy Catalonia.

"The two forces met, on the plain of Almanza, on the 24th of April. We and the Spaniards were superior in number to the English, Dutch, and Portuguese. The battle was maintained for six hours. The Portuguese infantry did little, but the English and Dutch repulsed charge after charge, even after the Portuguese and Spanish allies on both wings were defeated. But, in the end, victory remained with us. Galway and Das Minas, the Portuguese general, were both wounded, and five thousand of their men killed, and yet the Dutch and English infantry held together.

"But on the following day, being absolutely without supplies, some effected their escape and succeeded in reaching Portugal, while the main body surrendered. Valencia, Saragossa, and other towns opened their gates to us, and, for a time, the cause of the Archduke Charles seemed lost.

"Our success was, however, balanced by the loss, in the same year, of the whole of the Spanish possessions in Italy. As yet, in spite of the disasters that had befallen him, the cause of Charles was not altogether lost, for he received fresh promises of support from England, whose interest it was to continue the war in Spain, and thus compel France to keep a considerable body of troops there, instead of employing them against Marlborough in Flanders.

"Galway and Das Minas were taken back to Portugal, in an English fleet, after their disaster, and General Stanhope, who, they say, is an officer of great military experience and talent, has been sent out to take the command; and as a portion of Catalonia is still held for Charles, there may yet be a good deal of hard fighting, before the matter can be considered finally settled."

"Thank you, O'Neil. I feel that I know something about it, now. Are there any of our regiments there?"

"Yes, three of them. There is also an Irish regiment in the Spanish service, under Colonel Crofton;" and with this, the talk ended for the night.

After three months' work Desmond was dismissed from drill, and had obtained such a proficiency with the rapier that he felt that he could now relax his work, and see something of the city, which he had been hitherto too busy to explore. He had seen the principal streets, in the company of his comrades, had admired the mansions of the nobles, the richness of the goods exposed to view in the windows, and the gaiety and magnificence of the dresses of the upper class. His friends had warned him that, if he intended to go farther, he should never do so alone, but should take with him his soldier servant, a trooper named Mike Callaghan.

Mike was some twenty-eight years old, strong and bony; his hair was red, and the natural colour of his face was obscured by a host of freckles; his eyes were blue, and his nose had an upward turn; his expression was merry and good humoured, but there was a twinkle about his eyes that seemed to show that he was by no means wanting in shrewdness.

"Even in the daytime," O'Neil said, "it is not safe for a man, if well dressed and likely to carry money in his pocket, to go into some quarters of the town. Paris has always been a turbulent city, and, while it is the abode of the richest and noblest of Frenchmen, it is also the resort of the rascaldom of all France. Some streets are such that even the city guard would not venture to search for an ill doer, unless in considerable force and prepared for battle. There are, of course, many streets, both on this and the other side of the river, where life and property are as safe as in the Rue Royal; which, by the way, is not saying much, for it was only three days ago that a man was assassinated there in broad daylight. He was a captain in the Picardy regiment, and it was supposed that his murderer was a man who had been dismissed from the regiment with ignominy. But, whoever it was, he has got clear away, for your Parisian citizen takes good care not to interfere in such matters, and no one thought of laying hands on the villain, although it is said he walked quietly off.

"It is in the streets that I am speaking of that adventures may most easily be met with. Here there are too many hotels of the nobles, with their numerous retainers, for it to be safe to commit crime, and the city guard are generally on the alert, for, were harm to come to one of the gentlemen attached to the great houses, the matter would be represented to the king, and the city authorities would come in for a sharp reproof for their failure to keep order in the city; whereas, anything that happens among the bourgeois would pass wholly without notice. However, if you keep out of the wine shops, you are not likely to become involved in trouble. Nine-tenths of the quarrels and tumults originate there. There is a dispute, perhaps, between a soldier and a citizen, or between soldiers of different regiments, and in a minute or two twenty swords are drawn, and the disturbance grows, sometimes, until it is necessary to call out troops from the nearest barracks to suppress it. However, I know that you are not likely to get into trouble that way, for you are a very model of moderation, to the corps."

"I have seen enough of the consequences of drink in Ireland," Desmond said, "to cure me of any desire for liquor, even had I a love for it. Faction fights, involving the people of the whole barony, arising from some drunken brawl, are common enough; while among the better class duels are common and, for the most part, are the result of some foolish quarrel between two men heated by wine. Besides, even putting that aside, I should have given up the habit. When I joined the regiment, I was anxious to become a good swordsman, but if one's head is overheated at night, one's hand would be unsteady and one's nerves shaken in the morning.

"Possibly," he added, with a smile, "it is this, quite as much as the hotness of their temper, that prevents the best teachers from caring to undertake the tuition of the officers of the Brigade."

"Possibly," Phelim laughed, "though I never thought of it before. There is no doubt that the French, who, whatever their faults be, are far less given to exceeding a fair allowance of wine than are our countrymen, would come to their morning lessons in the saloon in a better condition to profit by the advice of the master than many of our men."

"I don't think," Patrick O'Neil said, "that we Irishmen drink from any particular love of liquor, but from good fellowship and joviality. One can hardly imagine a party of French nobles inflaming themselves with wine, and singing, as our fellows do. Frenchmen are gay in what I may call a feeble way--there is no go in it. There is no spirit in their songs, there is no real heartiness in their joviality, and the idea of one man playing a practical joke upon another, the latter taking it in good part, could never enter their heads, for they are ready to take offence at the merest trifle.

"As you know, there are certain cabarets told off for the use of the soldiers of the Brigade. They are allowed to use no others, and no French troops are allowed to enter these wine shops. Similarly, there are certain establishments which are almost exclusively patronized by officers of the Brigade. There is, of course, no absolute rule here, and we can enter any cabaret we choose; but it is understood that it is at our own risk, and that, if we get into trouble there, we are sure to be handled over the coals pretty sharply, as it is considered that we must deliberately have gone there with the intention of picking a quarrel. The cabarets used by the men are all close to the barracks, so that, in case of a fracas, a guard is sent down to bring all concerned in it back to the barracks. Fortunately, there is no need for the places we frequent being so close to the barracks, for it is understood that anyone who takes too much liquor, outside his own quarters, brings discredit on the regiment; and it is after we adjourn to the rooms of one or other of us that liquor begins to flow freely, and we make a night of it."

"Don't you ever have quarrels among yourselves?"

"Angry words pass, sometimes, but all present interfere at once. The honour of the regiment is the first point with us all. If men want to quarrel, there are plenty of French officers who would be quite ready to oblige them, but a quarrel among ourselves would be regarded as discreditable to the corps. Consequently, a dispute is always stopped before it reaches a dangerous point, and if it goes further than usual, the parties are sent for by the colonel in the morning, both get heavily wigged, and the colonel insists upon the matter being dropped, altogether. As the blood has had time to cool, both are always ready to obey his orders, especially as they know that he would report them at once to the general, if the matter were carried further."

"Well, I shall certainly not be likely to get into a quarrel over wine," Desmond said, "nor indeed, in any other way, unless I am absolutely forced into it. As to adventures such as you speak of, I am still less likely to be concerned in them. I hope that, when we are ordered on service, I shall have a full share of adventures such as may become a soldier."

O'Neil smiled. "Time will show," he said. "Adventures come without being sought, and you may find yourself in the thick of one, before you have an idea of what you are doing. But mind, if you do get into any adventure and need assistance, you are bound to let us help you. That is the compact we made, two months ago. We agreed to stand by each other, to be good comrades, to share our last sous, and naturally to give mutual aid under all and every circumstance."

Desmond nodded.

"At any rate, O'Neil, adventures cannot be so common as you represent, since neither of you, so far, has called upon me for aid or assistance."

"Have you heard the last piece of court scandal, Kennedy?" O'Sullivan asked, as the three friends sat down to breakfast together, a few days later.

"No; what is it?"

"Well, it is said that a certain damsel--her name is, at present, a secret--has disappeared."

"There is nothing very strange about that," O'Neil laughed. "Damsels do occasionally disappear. Sometimes they have taken their fate into their own hands, and gone off with someone they like better than the man their father has chosen for them; sometimes, again, they are popped into a convent for contumacy. Well, go on, O'Sullivan, that cannot be all."

"Well, it is all that seems to be certain. You know that I went with the colonel, last night, to a ball at the Hotel de Rohan, and nothing else was talked about. Several there returned from Versailles in the afternoon, and came back full of it. All sorts of versions are current. That she is a rich heiress goes without saying. If she had not been, her disappearance would have excited no attention whatever. So we may take it that she is an heiress of noble family. Some say that her father had chosen, as her husband, a man she disliked exceedingly, and that she has probably taken refuge in a convent. Some think that she has been carried off bodily, by someone smitten both by her charms and her fortune. It is certain that the king has interested himself much in the matter, and expresses the greatest indignation. Though, as it would not seem that she is a royal ward, it is not clear why he should concern himself over it. Some whisper that the king's anger is but feigned, and that the girl has been carried off by one of his favourites."

"Why should such a thing as that be supposed?" Desmond asked, indignantly.

"Well, there is something in support of the idea. If anyone else were to steal away, with or without her consent, a young lady of the court with influential friends, he would be likely to pass the first two years of his married life in one of the royal prisons; and therefore none but a desperate man, or one so secure of the king's favour as to feel certain that no evil consequences would befall him, would venture upon such a step. You must remember that there are not a few nobles of the court who have ruined themselves, to keep up the lavish expenditure incumbent upon those who bask in the royal favour at Versailles. It would be possible that His Majesty may have endeavoured to obtain the hand of this young lady for one of his favourites, and that her father may be a noble of sufficient consequence to hold his own, and to express to His Majesty his regret that he was unable to adopt his recommendation, as he had other views for the disposal of her hand.

"The real singularity of the matter is, that no one can tell with certainty who the missing lady is. Early in the day half a dozen were named, but as I believe all of these put in an appearance at the reception in the afternoon, it is evident that, so far as they were concerned, there were no foundations for the rumour. It may be taken for certain, however, that her friends are powerful people, to have been able to impose silence upon those acquainted with the facts."

"Well, it is impossible to take very much interest in the story," Desmond said carelessly, "when we are in ignorance of the very name of the lady, and of the important point, whether she has voluntarily gone away either with a lover or to a convent, or whether she has been carried off against her will. If the latter, you were talking of adventures, O'Neil, and this would be just the sort of adventure that I should like; for us three to discover the maiden, and rescue her from her abductor."

The others both laughed loudly.

"And this is the young officer who, the other day, declared that he wished for no adventures save those that came in the course of a campaign, and now he is declaring that he would like to become a very knight errant, and go about rescuing damsels in distress!"

"I have no idea of carrying it into execution," Desmond said. "It was merely an expression of a wish. Of course, if the lady in question went willingly and to avoid persecution, I would rather help than hinder her; but if she has been carried off by some ruined courtier, nothing would please me better than to rescue her from him."

Several days had passed, and at last it was confidently believed that the missing lady was the daughter of Baron Pointdexter, a magnate of Languedoc, who had but recently come up to court, on an intimation from the king that it was a long time since he had been seen there, and that His Majesty hoped that he would be accompanied by his daughter, of whose beauty reports had reached him. It was certain that neither she nor her father had attended any of the receptions or fetes at Versailles, since the rumour first spread, although the baron had had a private interview with the king a few hours afterwards, and had left his chamber with a frowning brow, that showed that the interview had not been a pleasant one. He had not again appeared at court, whether in consequence of the royal command, or not, no one knew.

The baron was one of the richest proprietors in the south of France. He was a specimen of the best type of the French nobles, preferring to spend his time among his own wide estates to coming up to the capital, where his visits had at all times been rare.

During the daytime, Desmond went out but little. When the hours of drill and exercise were over, he spent some time in visiting the quarters of the men of his company, making their personal acquaintance, and chatting freely with them. They were glad to hear from him about their native country; and, as some of them came from his own neighbourhood, they took a lively interest in the news--the first that had reached them for years--of families with whom they were acquainted. He spent two or three hours in the afternoons in the salle d'armes of the regiment, or at the schools of one or other of the maitres d'armes most in vogue, and then paid visits, with one or other of the officers of the regiment, to great houses of which they had the entree.

Of an evening he went out, accompanied by Mike Callaghan, and wandered about the less fashionable part of the town, which pleased him better than the more crowded and busy quarters.

One evening, he had gone farther than usual, had passed through the gates, and had followed the road by the banks of the river. As an officer in uniform, he was able to re-enter the town after the gates were closed, the rules being by no means strict, as, during the reign of Louis the 14th, France, though engaged in frequent wars abroad, was free from domestic troubles.

Presently, he passed a lonely house of some size, standing back from the road and surrounded by a high wall. As he did so, he heard a scream in a female voice, followed by angry exclamations from two male voices, while loudly rose a woman's cries for help.

"There is bad work of some sort going on in there," he said to Mike. "We had better see what it is all about. Do you go round the wall by the right, and I will go round by the left, and see if there is any way by which we can climb over."

They met at the back of the house. The wall was unbroken, save by the gates in front.

"The wall is too high for us to climb, Mike," Desmond said. "Even if I stood on your head, I could not reach the top. Let us go round to the front again."

They returned, and closely scrutinized the gate. It was not so high as the wall itself, but was fully twelve feet.

"I have got a pistol with me, your honour," Mike said. "I have seen doors blown in, by firing a gun through the keyhole."

"That would do, if we were sure that there were no bars, Mike; but the chances are that it is barred, as well as locked. Besides, I am sure that we should not be justified in blowing in the door of a private house. It may be that they were the cries of a mad woman. I would rather get over as quietly as possible."

"Well, sir, I will stand against it, and if you will get on to my shoulders and put your foot on my head, you will reach the top. Then, if you lower one end of your sash to me, I can pull myself up beside you."

"Yes, I think we can manage it that way, Mike. I am convinced that there is something wrong going on here, and I don't mind taking the risk of getting into a scrape by interfering. Now do you stoop a bit, so that I can get on to your shoulder; then you can raise yourself to your full height. Take off your hat, first. I shall certainly have to put my foot on your head."

"All right, your honour. Don't you be afraid of hurting me. My skull is thick enough to stand the weight of two of you."

In a minute, Desmond had his fingers on the top of the gates, drew himself up, and, moving to the corner, where he could get his back against the end of the wall, lowered his sash to Mike.

"You are sure I shall not pull you down?"

"I am not sure, but we will try, anyhow."

This was said in a whisper, for there might, for anything he knew, be two or three men in the garden. Mike took off his boots, so as to avoid making a noise. Desmond was sitting astride of the gate, and had his end of the sash over the top of it, and under his leg, thereby greatly reducing the strain that would be thrown on it, and then leaning with all his weight on it, where it crossed the gate. Mike was an active as well as a strong man, and speedily was by his side.

"Now we will drop down," Desmond said, and, setting the example, lowered himself till he hung by his hands, and then dropped. Mike was soon beside him.

"What shall we do next?"

"We will go and knock boldly at the door; but before we do that, we will unbar the gate and shoot the bolt of the lock. We have no idea how many men there may be in the house. Maybe we shall have to beat a retreat."

The lock was shot without difficulty, but the bolts were still fast, and were not drawn without noise. They pushed back the last of these, and then opened the gates, which creaked noisily as they did so.

"They can hardly help hearing that," Desmond muttered; and indeed, as he spoke, the door of the house opened suddenly, and five men came out, two of them holding torches. A man, who seemed to be the leader of the party, uttered an exclamation of fury as the light fell upon the figures of the two men at the open gate.

"Cut the villains down!" he shouted.

"Stop!" Desmond cried, in a loud voice. "I am an officer of O'Brien's regiment of foot. I heard a scream, and a woman's cry for help, and, fearing that foul play was going on, I made my entry here."

The man, who had drawn his sword, paused.

"You have done wrong, sir. The cries you heard were those of a mad woman. You had better withdraw at once. I shall report you, tomorrow, for having forcibly made an entrance into private premises."

"That you are perfectly at liberty to do," Desmond replied quietly; "but certainly I shall not withdraw, until I see this lady, and ascertain from herself whether your story is a true one."

"Then your blood be on your own head!" the man said.

"At them, men! you know your orders--to kill anyone who attempted to interfere with us, no matter what his rank."

The five men rushed together upon the intruders.

"Hold the gate, Mike," Desmond said, "and they cannot get behind us."

They stepped back a pace or two, and drew their swords. The position was a favourable one, for the two halves of the gate opened inwards, and so protected them from any but an attack in front. The leader rushed at Desmond, but the latter guarded the sweeping blow he dealt at him, and at the first pass ran him through the body; but the other four men, enraged rather than daunted by the fall of their leader, now rushed forward together, and one of them, drawing a pistol, fired at Desmond when within three paces.

The latter threw his head on one side, as he saw the pistol levelled. The action saved his life, for it was well aimed, and the bullet would have struck him full between the eyes. As it was, he felt a sharp sudden pain, as it grazed his cheek deeply. He sprang forward, and before the man could drop the pistol and change his sword from the left hand to the right, Desmond's weapon pierced his throat. At the same moment, Mike cut down one of his assailants with his sabre, receiving, however, a severe cut on the left shoulder from the other.

Paralysed at the loss of three of their number, the remaining two of the assailants paused, for a moment. It was fatal to one of them, for Mike snatched his pistol from his pocket, and shot the man who had wounded him, dead. The other threw down his sword, and fell upon his knees, crying for mercy.

"Shall I kill him, your honour?"

"No. Fasten his hands behind him, with his own belt; and bind his ankles tightly together, with that of one of his comrades."

He paused, while Mike adroitly carried out his instructions.

"Now we will see what this is all about," Desmond said. "I don't suppose that there are any more of them in the house. Still, we may as well keep our swords in readiness."

Picking up one of the torches that had fallen from their assailants' hands, and holding it above his head with his left hand, while his right held his sword ready for action, Desmond entered the house. The sitting rooms on both sides of the hall were empty, but, upon entering the kitchen, he found an old woman crouching in a corner, in the extremity of fear.

"Stand up. I am not going to hurt you," Desmond said. "Lead us, at once, to the chamber of the lady we heard call out."

The old woman rose slowly, took down a key hanging from a peg, and, leading the way upstairs, opened a door.

"Keep a watch upon the crone," Desmond said, as he entered.

As he did so, his eye fell upon a girl of some seventeen years old. She was standing at the window, with her hands clasped. She turned round as he entered, and, as her eye fell upon his uniform, she gave a cry of delight.

"Ah, monsieur, you have rescued me! I heard the fight in the garden, and knew that the good God had sent someone to my aid. But you are wounded, sir. Your face is streaming with blood."

"'Tis but the graze of a pistol ball," he said, "and needs but a bowl of water, and a strip of plaster, to put it right. I had well-nigh forgotten it.

"I am glad, indeed, to have been able to render you this service, mademoiselle. It was most providential that I happened to come along the road, and heard your screams and cries for aid; and I determined to see if any foul business was being carried on here. What made you call out?"

"I had let myself down from the window, by knotting the bedclothes together. I was blindfolded, when they carried me in here, and did not know that the walls were so high all round, but had hoped to find some gate by which I might escape. There were only the great gates, and these were locked; and I was trying to draw the bolts when two of the men suddenly rushed out. I suppose the old woman came up here, and found the room empty. It was then that I screamed for help, but they dragged me in, in spite of my struggles, and one said I might scream as much as I liked, for there was not a house within hearing, and no one would be passing anywhere near.

"When he said that, I quite gave up hope. I had believed that I was in some lonely house, in the suburbs of the city, and I little thought that my cries could not be heard.

"But where are the men who guarded me?"

"Four of them are dead, mademoiselle, and the other securely bound. Now, if you will tell me who you are, and where your friends live, I and my soldier servant will escort you to them."

"My name is Anne de Pointdexter."

Desmond was scarcely surprised, for the care which had been taken in choosing so lonely a spot for her concealment, and the fact that an officer and four men should be placed there to guard her, showed that she must have been regarded as a prisoner of importance.

"Then I am glad, indeed, to have been the means of rescuing you. All Paris has been talking of your disappearance, for the past ten days. The question is, what would you wish done? It is too far to take you to Versailles tonight, and too late to obtain means of conveyance."

"There is a carriage in the stables behind the house, and there are some horses. I cannot say how many, but at night I have heard them stamping. I suppose the carriage was left here so that they could remove me to some other place, in case suspicion should fall upon this house. How many are there of you, monsieur?"

"Only myself, and the trooper you see at the door."

"And did you two fight with five men, and kill four of them!" she exclaimed, in surprise. "How brave of you, monsieur, and how good to run such risk, for a person of whom you knew nothing!"

"I knew that it was a woman in distress," Desmond said, "and that was quite enough to induce two Irishmen to step in, and answer to her cry for aid. However, mademoiselle, if the carriage and horses are there, this will get us out of our difficulty. The only question is, will you start at once, or wait until daylight? We may be stopped by the patrols, as we approach Versailles, but I have no doubt that my uniform will suffice to pass us into the town, where probably your father is still lodging."

"I would much rather go at once," the girl said. "There are others who come, sometimes at all hours of the night."

"Very well, then, we will see about getting the carriage ready, at once. If you will come downstairs, we will lock this old woman up in your room."

This was done at once, and the girl, who was so shaken by her captivity that she feared to remain for a moment by herself, accompanied her rescuers to the back of the house. Here, as she had said, they found a carriage and four horses, two of which stood ready saddled, while the others were evidently carriage horses. These were speedily harnessed, and put into the carriage.

"Now, Mike, you had better drive. I will mount one of these saddle horses and ride alongside. I think, mademoiselle, as the drive will be a long one, it would be as well that we should put the old woman in the carriage with you. She will be a companion, though one that you would not take from choice. Still, your father may wish to question her, and, indeed, it would be better in many respects that you should have a female with you."

"Thank you, Monsieur Kennedy,"--for she had already learned his name--she said gratefully, "it would certainly be much better."

The old woman was therefore brought down, and made to enter the carriage, and seat herself facing Mademoiselle Pointdexter. Mike took his seat on the box, and Desmond mounted one of the saddle horses, and led the other. They had already removed the bodies that lay in front of the gates.

They had to make a considerable detour round Paris, before they came down upon the Versailles road. The roads were bad and the carriage was heavy, and daylight was already breaking when they entered the town. They had twice been stopped by patrols, but Desmond's uniform had sufficed to pass them.

Baron Pointdexter had taken up his abode in a large house, standing in a walled garden in the lower part of the town. When they reached it, Desmond dismounted and rung the bell. After he had done this several times, a step was heard in the garden, and a voice asked roughly, "Who is it that rings at this hour of the morning?"

Mademoiselle Pointdexter, who had alighted as soon as the carriage stopped, called out, "It is I, Eustace."

There was an exclamation of surprise and joy, bolts were at once drawn, and the gate thrown open, and an old servitor threw himself on his knees as the girl entered, and, taking the hand she held out to him, put it to his lips.

"Ah, mademoiselle," he said, while the tears streamed down his cheeks, "what a joyful morning it is! We have all suffered, and monsieur le baron most of all. He has spoken but a few words, since you left, but walks up and down the garden as one distraught, muttering to himself, and sometimes even drawing his sword and thrusting it at an invisible enemy. He is up, mademoiselle. He has never gone to his bed since you were missing."

As he spoke, the door of the house opened, and the baron hurried out, with the question, "What is it, Eustace?"

Then, as his eye fell on his daughter, he gave a hoarse cry, and for a moment swayed, as if he would have fallen. His daughter ran up to him, and threw her arms round his neck.

"Do you return to me safe and well?" he asked, as, after a long embrace, he stepped back and gazed into her face.

"Quite safe and well, father."

"The Lord be praised!" the baron exclaimed, and, dropping into a garden seat by his side, he burst into a passion of sobbing.

As soon as he had appeared, Desmond had handed over the old woman to Eustace.

"She is a prisoner--keep a watch over her," he said. "She can tell much. We will take the carriage round to a stable, and must then return at once to Paris, where I must be on duty at seven. Please inform the baron that I shall do myself the honour of calling, tomorrow, to enquire whether Mademoiselle Pointdexter has suffered from the effects of the fatigue and excitement. Express my regret that I am obliged to leave at once, but I am sure he will have so much to hear, from his daughter, that it is best they should be alone together, for a time."

He at once remounted his horse, Mike climbed up on to his seat, and they drove off, and, knocking up the people at some large stables, left the carriage and horses there, telling the proprietors to send to the Baron Pointdexter to know his wishes regarding it. Then Mike mounted the spare horse, and they started at full speed for Paris, and arrived at the barracks in time for Desmond to take his place at the early parade.

Chapter 4: At Versailles.

The regiment was on the point of falling in, on the parade ground, when Desmond Kennedy rode up. Leaping from his horse, he threw the reins to his servant.

"Take them both round to the stables, and put them in spare stalls, Mike. I will get leave off parade for both of us, and ask the surgeon to dress your wounds properly."

Then he went up to the colonel, who was just entering the barrack yard.

"Colonel O'Brien," he said, "I must ask your leave off parade, for, as you see, I am scarcely in a condition to take my place with my company."

"So it would seem, Mr. Kennedy. You have been in trouble, I see. Nothing serious, I hope?"

"Nothing at all, sir, as far as I am concerned. It is merely a graze from a pistol ball."

"Well, I must hear about it, afterwards."

"I must also ask leave off parade for Callaghan, my servant, sir. He is hurt a good deal more than I am, though not, I hope, seriously."

The colonel nodded. "I will send the surgeon to your quarters, and he will see to you both."

As Desmond left the colonel, his two chums came up.

"Why, Kennedy, what on earth have you been doing to yourself? This is what comes of gallivanting about after dark. When we came round, yesterday evening, to go out with you as usual, you were not in. There was nothing very unusual in that, for these evening walks of yours are often prolonged; but we called again, on our return at eleven o'clock, and found you were still absent. This looked serious. We came round again at six this morning, for we were anxious about you, and learned you had not been in all night, and, on enquiring, heard that Callaghan was also absent.

"That was cheering. That you might get into some scrape or other, we could reasonably believe; but, as you had your man with you, we could hardly suppose that misfortune had fallen upon both of you."

"The wound is a mere graze. I will tell you, after parade, what I have been doing," Desmond said, "but you must nurse your curiosity till you are dismissed."

A few minutes after Desmond reached his quarters, the surgeon came in.

"I do not think that I have any need of your services, doctor. I got a piece of plaster, and stuck it on two hours ago, and I have no doubt that the wound will heal in a few days."

"However, I will, with your permission, take it off, Mr. Kennedy. It is much better that the wound should be properly washed, and some dressing applied to it. It will heal all the quicker, and you are less likely to have an ugly scar.

"It is a pretty deep graze," he said, after he had carefully removed the plaster. "An eighth of an inch farther, and it would have made your teeth rattle. You had better keep quiet, today. Tomorrow morning, if there is no sign of inflammation, I will take off the dressing and bandage and put on a plaster--one a third of the size that I took off will be sufficient; and as I will use a pink plaster, it will not be very noticeable, if you go outside the barracks.

"Where is your man? The colonel told me there were two patients.

"A nasty cut," he said, after examining Mike's wound. "It is lucky that it was not a little higher. If it had been, you would have bled to death in five minutes. As it is, it is not serious. You will have to keep your arm in a sling for a fortnight. You are not to attend parade, or mount a horse, until I give you leave."

On the ride from Versailles, Desmond had warned Mike to say no word as to the events of the night.

"I do not know what course the young lady's father may take," he said, "and until I do, the matter had better be kept a secret, altogether."

"I will keep a quiet tongue in my head, and no one shall hear anything, from me, as to how I got this slice on my shoulder. I will just say that it was a bit of a scrimmage I got into, with two or three of the street rascals; and the thing is so common that no one is likely to ask any further questions about it."

After the parade was over, O'Neil and O'Sullivan came up to Desmond's quarters.

"Now, Master Kennedy, we have come to receive your confession. We gave you credit for being a quiet, decent boy, and now it seems that you and that man of yours have been engaged in some disreputable riot, out all night, and coming in on two strange horses, which, for aught we know, have been carried off by force of arms."

Desmond laughed.

"As to the horses, you are not so far wrong as one might expect, O'Neil. We rode them this morning from Versailles."

"From Versailles!" O'Neil repeated. "And what, in the name of all the saints, took you to Versailles! I am afraid, Desmond, that you are falling into very evil courses.

"Well, tell us all about it. I shall be glad to be able to believe that there is some redeeming feature in this strange business."

Desmond laughed, and then said, more seriously, "Well, I have had an adventure. Other people were concerned in it, as well as myself. I have made up my mind to tell you both, because I know that I can depend upon your promises to keep it an absolute secret."

"This sounds mysterious indeed," O'Sullivan said. "However, you have our promises. O'Neil and I will be as silent as the grave."

"Well, then, you know how you were chaffing me, the other day, about finding Mademoiselle Pointdexter?"

"You don't mean to say that you have found her, Kennedy?" O'Neil exclaimed incredulously.

"That is what I mean to say, though found is hardly the word, since I was not looking for her, or even thinking of her, at the time. Still, in point of fact, I accidentally came across the place where she was hidden away, and after a sharp skirmish, in which Callaghan and I each had to kill two men, we carried her off, and delivered her safely to her father this morning."

The two young officers looked hard at Desmond, to discover if he was speaking seriously, for his tone was so quiet, and matter of fact, that they could scarce credit that he had passed through such an exciting adventure; and the three were so accustomed to hoax each other, that it struck them both as simply an invention on the part of their comrade, so absolutely improbable did it seem to them.

"Sure you are trying to hoax us, Kennedy," O'Sullivan said.

"You could not blame me, if I were," Desmond said, with a smile, "considering the cock-and-bull stories that you are constantly trying to palm off on me. However, you are wrong now. I will tell you the affair, just as it happened."

And he related, in detail, the story of the rescue of Mademoiselle Pointdexter, and the manner in which he had conveyed her to Versailles.

"By Saint Bridget, Kennedy, we were not far wrong when we called you a knight errant. Well, this is something like an adventure, though whether it will end well or ill for you I cannot say. Did you learn the name of the person who had the girl carried off?"

"No. I asked no questions, and indeed had but little conversation with her; for, as I have told you, I put her in a carriage, with the old hag who was in charge of her, and rode myself by the side of it, in case the old woman should try to escape."

"A truly discreet proceeding, Kennedy," O'Neil laughed. "I think, if I myself had been in your place, I should have taken a seat inside also, where you, of course, could at once have watched the old woman, and talked with the young one."

"I don't think that you would have done anything of the sort, O'Neil," Desmond said gravely, "but would have seen, as I did, that it was better that she should travel alone, with the old woman, till she reached her father's house. Scandal will be busy enough with her name, in any case, and it is as well that it should not be said that she arrived home, in a carriage, with a young officer of O'Brien's Irish regiment."

"By my faith, Kennedy, it seems to me that you are a Saint Anthony and a Bayard rolled into one. But, seriously, you are undoubtedly right. Well, it all depends upon who was the man who carried her off, as to whether you were fortunate or unfortunate in thus having thwarted his designs. If he is some adventurer, your action will gain you heaps of credit. If, on the other hand, it was one of the king's favourites, seeking to mend his fortunes by marrying, it is probable that you will have made a dangerous enemy--nay, more, have drawn upon yourself the king's displeasure. I should think it likely that, before attempting so desperate an action as the carrying off of the Baron Pointdexter's daughter, such a man would have assured himself that the king would not view the enterprise with displeasure.

"We may assume that he would not inform His Majesty of any particulars, but would put it, hypothetically, that as he was getting into sore straits, he thought of mending his fortunes by carrying off an heiress--not, of course, one of those of whose hands the king had the disposal; and that he trusted that, if he succeeded, His Majesty would not view the matter as a grave offence. From what I know of Louis, he would reply gravely: 'I should be obliged (duke or viscount, as the case might be) to express very grave displeasure, and to order you to leave the court for a time; but, as the harm would be done, and the young lady married to you, it might be that, in time, I should pardon the offence.'

"If this is how things have gone, you may be sure that the king will not view, with satisfaction, the man who has interfered with his favourite's plan for mending his fortunes."

Desmond shrugged his shoulders.

"The king's dissatisfaction would matter very little to me," he said, "especially as he could not openly manifest it, without making it apparent that he had approved of the scheme."

"It is not such a trifle as you think, Kennedy. Lettres de cachet are not difficult to obtain, by powerful members of the court; especially when the person named is a young regimental officer, whose disappearance would excite no comment or curiosity, save among the officers of his own regiment. The man who carried off Mademoiselle Pointdexter must be a bold fellow, and is likely to be a vindictive one. No doubt, his object was to keep the young lady a prisoner, until she agreed to marry him, and the loss of a pretty bride with a splendid fortune is no trifling one, and likely to be bitterly resented. Whether that resentment will take the form of obtaining an order for your confinement in the Bastille, or other royal prison, or of getting you put out of the way by a stab in the back, I am unable to say, but in any case, I should advise you strongly to give up your fancy for wandering about after dark; and when you do go out, keep in the frequented portions of the town.

"Jack Farquharson, who was at Versailles with the colonel last week, was speaking of Mademoiselle Pointdexter, and said that she was charming. Did you find her so?"

"I thought nothing about it, one way or the other," Desmond said, carelessly. "I only saw her face by torchlight, and she was, of course, agitated by what had happened; and indeed, as I was busy helping Mike to yoke the horses to the carriage, I had scarcely time to look at her. When we reached Versailles it was barely daylight. I handed her out of the carriage, and left her to enter by herself, as I thought it was better that she should meet her father alone. I do not think that I should recognize her, were I to meet her in the street."

"Most insensible youth!" O'Sullivan said, with a laugh; "insensible and discreet to a point that, were it not assured, none would believe that you had Irish blood in your veins. And so, you say you are going over to Versailles tomorrow?"

"Yes. I left a message with the servant who opened the door, to that effect. Of course, I shall be glad to know if the baron intends to take any steps against his daughter's abductor, or whether he thinks it best not to add to the scandal by stirring up matters, but to take her away at once to his estates."

"He is in a difficult position," O'Neil said gravely. "The young lady has been missing for a fortnight. No one knows whether she went of her own free will, or against it. Were her father to carry her off, quietly, it would excite the worst suspicions. Better by far lodge his complaint before the king, proclaim his grievances loudly everywhere, and tell the story in all its details. Whichever course he takes, evil-minded people will think the worse; but of the two evils, the latter seems to me to be the lesser."

"I suppose it would be," Desmond agreed, "though, for my part, I should be heartily glad if I never heard another word about it."

"You are too modest altogether, Kennedy. Whatever rumours may be current, concerning the young lady, there can be no doubt that you come out splendidly, in that you hear a cry of a woman in distress; you scale walls to get in to her assistance; you and your servant encounter five of her guards, kill four of them and bind the other; rescue the maiden, and carry her off, with flying colours, in the carriage of her abductor. My dear Kennedy, you will become an object of admiration to all the ladies of the court."

"That will be absolutely disgusting," Desmond said, angrily. "It is almost enough to make one wish that one had never interfered in the affair."

"Pooh, pooh, Kennedy! I am sure that either O'Sullivan or myself would give, I was going to say a year's pay, though how one would exist without it I don't know, to have been in your place. Why, man, if you had captured a standard in battle, after feats of superhuman bravery, you would not attract half the attention that will fall to you as a consequence of this adventure. Life in the court of His Most Christian Majesty is one of the most artificial possible. The women hide their faces with powder and patches, lace themselves until they are ready to faint, walk with a mincing air, and live chiefly upon scandal; but they are women, after all, and every woman has a spice of romance in her nature, and such an adventure as yours is the very thing to excite their admiration."

"I know nothing about women," Desmond growled, "and don't want to know any of them, especially the ladies at the court of Louis."

"Well, of course, Kennedy, if the baron proclaims his wrongs, and publishes the circumstances of his daughter's abduction and rescue, the seal of silence will be taken from our lips; especially as you will, almost to a certainty, be summoned to Versailles to confirm the lady's story."

"I am afraid that that will be so," Desmond said, despondingly. "However, it can't be helped, and I suppose one must make the best of it."

To most of the officers who dropped in, in the course of the day, to see Desmond and to enquire how he got his wound, he abstained from giving any particulars. It was merely said that he and Callaghan were suddenly attacked, by five ruffians, whom they managed to beat off. Much surprise was expressed that such attack should be made upon an officer and a soldier, on whom little plunder could be expected, and who would be sure to defend themselves stoutly. Several, indeed, expressed some incredulity.

"We do not doubt for a moment, Kennedy, that you were attacked by five men, as you say, and that you routed them, but there must have been some motive for the attack. These evening strolls of yours are suspicious, and I will warrant that there must have been a great deal at the bottom of it. Now, can you deny that?"

"I neither admit nor deny anything," Desmond said, with a smile; "enough that, at present, I have told you all that I feel justified in telling. I acknowledge that there is more behind it, but at present my mouth is sealed on the subject."

The colonel was among those who came in to see him. To him, Desmond said frankly that the affair was altogether out of the common, that it was likely that the whole facts would be known shortly, but that, as other persons were concerned, he could not speak of it until he had obtained their permission.

"Then I will ask no further," Colonel O'Brien said. "I have seen enough of you to know that you would not be concerned in any affair that could bring discredit upon the corps. I am curious to know the whole story, but am quite content to wait until you feel at liberty to tell me."

The next morning, Desmond took part in the usual work of the regiment, and then, mounting his horse, rode to Versailles. On his ringing the bell at the house occupied by the Baron de Pointdexter, the old servitor, whom he had before seen, opened the gate.

"The baron is expecting you, monsieur," he said, bowing deeply; and, at his call, another servant ran out and took Desmond's horse, and led it away to the stable, while Desmond followed the old man to the house.

The door opened as they approached, and the baron, a tall man, some fifty years of age, advanced hastily, holding out both hands.

"Monsieur Kennedy," he said, "you have rendered to me the greatest service that I have received during my life. No words can express the gratitude that I feel, for one who has restored to me my only child, just when I had come to believe that she was lost to me forever. It was surely her guardian saint who sent you to the spot, at that moment."

"It might have happened to anyone, sir," Desmond said; "surely any gentleman, on hearing an appeal for help from a woman in distress, would have done just what I did."

"Let us go in," the baron said. "My daughter has been eagerly waiting your coming, especially as she tells me that she does not think she said even a word of thanks to you, being overpowered by what she had gone through, and by her joy at her sudden and unexpected deliverance. Indeed, she says that she scarcely exchanged two words with you."

"There was no opportunity, Baron, for indeed, as soon as she told me that there was a carriage and horses in the stable, I was too much occupied in getting it ready for her to depart without delay, to think of talking."

They had now entered the house, and, as the baron led the way into the sitting room, the girl rose from a fauteuil.

"This, Monsieur Kennedy, is my daughter, Mademoiselle Anne de Pointdexter. It is high time that you were formally presented to each other.

"This, Anne, is the officer who rendered you such invaluable service."

"We meet almost as strangers, mademoiselle," Desmond said, deeply bowing, "for I own that I saw so little of your face, the other night, that I should hardly have recognized you, had I met you elsewhere."

"I should certainly not have recognized you, Monsieur Kennedy. What with my own fright, and, I may say, the condition of your face, I had but a faint idea of what you were really like; but I certainly did not think that you were so young. You had such a masterful way with you, and seemed to know so perfectly what ought to be done, that I took you to be much older than you now look."

"I joined the regiment but little more than three months ago," Desmond said, "and am its youngest ensign."

"Monsieur, I owe to you more than my life, for, had it not been for you, I should have been forced into marriage with one whom I despise."

"I cannot think that, mademoiselle. From what I saw of you, I should say that you would have resisted all threats, and even undergone hopeless imprisonment, rather than yield."

"There is no saying, Monsieur Kennedy," the baron said. "Anne is of good blood, and I know that it would have been hard to break down her will, but confinement and hopelessness will tell on the bravest spirit. However that may be, she and I are your debtors for life."

"Indeed, Monsieur Kennedy," the girl said, "I pray you to believe that I am more grateful to you than words can express."

"I pray you to say no more about it, mademoiselle. I deem it a most fortunate circumstance, that I was able to come to your assistance, and especially so, when I found that the lady I had rescued was one whose disappearance had made so great a stir; but I should have been glad to render such service to one in the poorest condition."

"My daughter said that you asked her no questions, Monsieur Kennedy, and you therefore are, I suppose, in ignorance of the name of her abductor?"

"Altogether."

"It was the Vicomte de Tulle, one who stands very high in the regard of the king, and who is one of the most extravagant and dissipated, even of the courtiers here. For some time, it has been reported that he had nigh ruined himself by his lavish expenditure, and doubtless he thought to reestablish his finances by this bold stroke.

"His plans were well laid. He waited until I had gone to Paris on business that would keep me there for a day or two. A messenger arrived with a letter, purporting to be from me, saying that I wished my daughter to join me at once, and had sent a carriage to take her to me. Anne is young, and, suspecting no harm, at once threw on a mantle and hood, and entered the carriage. It was broad daylight, and there was nothing to disquiet her until, on approaching the town, the carriage turned off the main road. This struck her as strange, and she was just about to ask the question where she was being taken, when the carriage stopped in a lonely spot, the door was opened, and a man stepped in.

"Before she had even time to recognize him, he threw a thick cloak over her head. She struggled in vain to free herself, but he held her fast. Again and again, she tried to cry out, but her mouth was muffled by the wrapping. She had heard the blinds of the carriage drawn, and finding that her struggles to free herself were vain, and receiving no answer to her supplications to be released, she remained quiet until the carriage stopped. Then she was lifted out, and carried into the house where you found her.

"The wrapping was removed, and the man who had taken it off, and, who by his attire, was a gentleman in the service of some noble, said, 'Do not be alarmed, mademoiselle. No harm is intended to you. My master is grieved to be obliged to adopt such means, but his passion for you is so great that he was driven to this step, and it will entirely depend upon yourself when your captivity will end.'

"'Your master, whoever he may be,' Anne said, 'is a contemptible villain.'

"'Naturally, you have a poor opinion of him at present,' the fellow said; 'but I am convinced that, in time, you will come to excuse his fault. It is wholly due to the depth of the feeling that he entertains towards you. There is a woman here who will wait upon you. I and my men will not intrude. Our duty is solely to see that you do not escape, which indeed would be an impossibility for you, seeing that the wall that surrounds the garden is well-nigh fifteen feet high, and the gate barred and locked, and the key thereof in my pocket.'

"He called, and the old woman whom you brought here with Anne entered, and bid her ascend to the room that had been prepared for her.

"In that respect, she had nothing to complain of. Of course, you did not notice it, as you had other things to think of, but it was handsomely furnished. There was a bed in an alcove, some flowers on the table, some books, and even a harpsichord--evidently it was intended that her imprisonment should be made as light as might be.

"Looking from the window, Anne saw that the room was at the back of the house, and had probably been chosen because some trees shut the window off from view of anyone beyond the wall. The next day, the old woman announced the Vicomte de Tulle. He bowed profoundly, and began by excusing the step that he had taken, and crediting it solely to the passion that he had conceived for her. You may imagine the scorn and reproaches with which she answered him. He was quite unmoved by her words.

"'Mademoiselle,' he said calmly, when she paused, 'you may be sure that I should not have undertaken this scheme, unless I had fully weighed the consequences. My plans have been so laid that whatever search may be made for you will be in vain. Here you are, and here you will remain until you listen to my suit. Every want shall be satisfied, and every wish complied with; but, whether it is one year or five, you will not leave this house until you leave it as my bride.'

"'Then, sir,' she said passionately, 'I shall be a prisoner for life.'

"'So you may think, at present, mademoiselle,' he said. 'And I expected nothing else. But, with time and reflection, you may come to think otherwise. Union with me is not so terrible a matter. My rank you know, and standing high, as I do, in the favour of His Most Gracious Majesty, your position at court will be such as might gratify the daughter of the noblest family in France. The study of my life will be to make you happy.

"'I shall now leave you to think over the matter. I shall not pester you with my attentions, and for another month you will not see me again. At the end of that time, I trust that you will have seen the futility of condemning yourself to further captivity, and will be disposed to make more allowance, than at present, for the step to which my passion for yourself has driven me.'

"It was just a month since she had been carried off, and, the very day when you rescued her, the old woman had informed her that the vicomte would do himself the pleasure of calling upon her the next day. For the first fortnight she had held up bravely, in the hope that I should discover the place where she had been hidden. Then she began to feel the imprisonment and silence telling upon her, for the old woman only entered to bring in her meals, and never opened her lips, except on the first occasion, when she told her that she was strictly forbidden to converse with her. After that she began to despair, and the news that her abductor would visit her, the next day, decided her to make an attempt to escape. She had no difficulty in letting herself down from the window by the aid of her bedclothes, but she found that what had been said respecting the wall and gate was true, and that she was no nearer escape than she had been, before she had left her room. She was trying, in vain, to unbar the gate, which, indeed, would have been useless could she have accomplished it, as it was also locked. But she was striving, with the energy of desperation, when the door of the house opened, and the men rushed out and seized her. As they dragged her back to the house, she uttered the cries that brought you to her assistance. The rest you know.

"As soon as I heard her story, I went to the palace and asked for a private interview with the king. The king received me graciously enough, and asked, with an appearance of great interest, if I had obtained any news of my daughter.

"'I have more than obtained news, Your Majesty. I have my daughter back again, and I have come to demand justice at your hands.'

"'I congratulate you, indeed, Baron,' the king said, with an appearance of warmth, but I saw his colour change, and was convinced that he knew something, at least, of the matter.

"'And where has the damsel been hiding herself?' he went on.

"'She has not been hiding herself, at all, Sire,' I said. 'She has been abducted, by one of Your Majesty's courtiers, with the intention of forcing her into a marriage. His name, Sire, is the Vicomte de Tulle, and I demand that justice shall be done me, and that he shall receive the punishment due to so gross an outrage.'

"The king was silent for a minute, and then said:

"'He has, indeed, if you have been rightly informed, acted most grossly. Still, it is evident that he repented the step that he took, and so suffered her to return to you.'

"'Not so, Your Majesty,' I said. 'I owe her return to no repentance on his part, but to the gallantry of a young officer who, passing the house where she was confined, heard her cries for aid, and, with his soldier servant, climbed the gate of the enclosure, and was there attacked by the man who had charge of her, with four others. The young gentleman and his servant killed four of them, and bound the other; and then, entering the house, compelled the woman who had been appointed to act as her servant to lead the way to her chamber. Fortunately, the carriage in which she had been taken there was still in the stables, with its horses. The gallant young gentleman at once got the carriage in readiness, placed my daughter in it, with the woman who had been attending on her. The servant drove, and he rode by the side of the carriage, and in that way brought her home this morning.'

"In spite of his efforts to appear indifferent, it was evident that the king was greatly annoyed. However, he only said:

"'You did quite right to come to me, Baron. It is outrageous, indeed, that a young lady of my court should be thus carried off, and I will see that justice is done. And who is this officer, who has rendered your daughter such a service?'

"'His name is Kennedy, Sire. He is an ensign in O'Brien's Irish regiment.'

"'I will myself send for him,' he said, 'and thank him for having defeated this disgraceful plot of the Vicomte de Tulle. I suppose you are quite sure of all the circumstances, as you have told them to me?'

"'It is impossible that there can be any mistake, Sire,' I said. 'In the first place, I have my daughter's account. This is entirely corroborated by the old woman she had brought with her, and whose only hope of escaping from punishment lay in telling the truth. In every respect, she fully confirmed my daughter's account.'

"'But the vicomte has not been absent from Versailles, for the past month. He has been at my morning levee, and on all other occasions at my breakfasts and dinners. He has walked with me in the gardens, and been always present at the evening receptions.'

"'That is so, Sire,' I said. 'My daughter, happily, saw him but once; namely, on the morning after she was captured. He then told her, frankly, that she would remain a prisoner until she consented to marry him, however long the time might be. He said he would return in a month, and hoped by that time to find that, seeing the hopelessness of her position, she would be more inclined to accept his suit.

"'It was on the eve of his coming again that my daughter, in her desperation, made the attempt to escape. She was foiled in her effort, but this, nevertheless, brought about her rescue, for her cries, as her guards dragged her into the house, attracted the attention of Monsieur Kennedy, who forthwith, as I have told you, stormed the house, killed her guards, and brought her home to me.'

"The king then sent for de Tulle, and spoke to him with great sternness. The latter did not attempt to deny my accusation, but endeavoured to excuse himself, on the ground of the passion that he had conceived for my daughter. Certainly, from the king's tone, I thought that he would at least have sent him to the Bastille; but, to my great disappointment, he wound up his reproof by saying:

"'I can, of course, make some allowances for your passion for so charming a young lady as Mademoiselle Pointdexter, but the outrage you committed is far too serious to be pardoned. You will at once repair to your estates, and will remain there during my pleasure.'

"The vicomte bowed and withdrew, and, an hour later, left Versailles. The king turned to me, as he left the room, and said, 'I trust, Monsieur le Baron, that you are content that justice has been done.'

"I was too angry to choose my words, and I said firmly, 'I cannot say that I am content, Your Majesty. Such an outrage as that which has been perpetrated upon my daughter deserves a far heavier punishment than banishment from court; and methinks that an imprisonment, as long as that which he intended to inflict upon her unless she consented to be his wife, would have much more nearly met the justice of the case.'

"The king rose to his feet suddenly, and I thought that my boldness would meet with the punishment that I desired for de Tulle; but he bit his lips, and then said coldly:

"'You are not often at court, Baron Pointdexter, and are doubtless ignorant that I am not accustomed to be spoken to, in the tone that you have used. However, I can make due allowance for the great anxiety that you have suffered, at your daughter's disappearance. I trust that I shall see you and your daughter at my levee, this evening.'

"As this was a command, of course we went, and I am bound to say that the king did all in his power to show to his court that he considered her to be wholly blameless. Of course, the story had already got about, and it was known that the vicomte had been ordered to his estates. The king was markedly civil to Anne, talked to her for some time, expressed his deep regret that she should have been subject to such an outrage, while staying at his court, and said, in a tone loud enough to be heard by all standing round:

"'The only redeeming point in the matter is, that the Vicomte de Tulle in no way troubled or molested you, and that you only saw him, for a few minutes, on the first day of your confinement.'

"I need not say that this royal utterance was most valuable to my daughter, and that it at once silenced any malicious scandal that might otherwise have got about.

"The king stopped to speak to me, immediately afterwards, and I said:

"'I trust that you will pardon the words I spoke this morning. Your Majesty has rendered me and my daughter an inestimable service, by the speech that you have just made.'

"Thus, although dissatisfied with the punishment inflicted on the Vicomte de Tulle, and believing that the king had a shrewd idea who her abductor was, I am grateful to him for shielding my daughter from ill tongues, by his marked kindness to her, and by declaring openly that de Tulle had not seen her, since the day of her abduction. I intended to return home tomorrow, but the king himself, when I went this morning to pay my respects, and state my intention of taking Anne home, bade those standing round to fall back, and was good enough to say in a low voice to me:

"'I think, Baron, that you would do well to reconsider your decision to leave tomorrow. Your sudden departure would give rise to ill-natured talk. It would be wiser to stay here, for a short time, till the gossip and wonder have passed away.'

"I saw that His Majesty was right, and shall stay here for a short time longer. It would certainly have a bad effect, were we to seem to run away and hide ourselves in the provinces."

Mademoiselle de Pointdexter had retired when her father began to relate to Desmond what had happened.

"I know little of life in Paris, Monsieur le Baron," Desmond said, "but it certainly seems to me monstrous, that the man who committed this foul outrage should escape with what is, doubtless, but a short banishment from court."

"I do not know that the matter is ended yet, Monsieur Kennedy. In spite of the edicts against duelling, I myself should have demanded satisfaction from him, for this attack upon the honour of my family, but I am at present Anne's only protector. It is many years since I have drawn a sword, while de Tulle is noted as a fencer, and has had many affairs, of which he has escaped the consequences owing to royal favour. Therefore, were I to challenge him, the chances are that I should be killed, in which case my daughter would become a ward of the crown, and her hand and estate be bestowed on one of the king's creatures. But, as I said, the matter is not likely to rest as it is.

"Anne has, with my full consent and approval, given her love to a young gentleman of our province. He is a large-landed proprietor, and a connection of our family. They are not, as yet, formally betrothed, for I have no wish to lose her so soon; and, in spite of the present fashion of early marriages, I by no means approve of them, and told Monsieur de la Vallee that they must wait for another couple of years.

"I need scarcely say that, after what has happened, I shall reconsider my decision; for the sooner she is married, and beyond the reach of a repetition of this outrage, the better. I imagine, however, that the young gentleman will be no better satisfied than I am, that the matter should have been passed over so lightly; and will take it into his own hands, and send a challenge immediately to the vicomte. He is high spirited, and has the reputation among us of being a good fencer, but I doubt whether he can possess such skill as that which de Tulle has acquired. It is not always the injured person that comes off victorious in a duel; and, should fortune go against Monsieur de la Vallee, it would be a terrible blow to my daughter, and indeed to myself, for I am much attached to him. She is worrying about it, already.

"Of course, it is impossible that the affair can be hidden from him. It is public property now; and therefore, I sent off one of my grooms, an hour since, with a letter to him.

"Hitherto, I had not written to him about my daughter's disappearance. Knowing he would, on hearing of it, at once hasten here, where he could do no good and would only add to my trouble, I thought it best to let matters go on as they were. I had been doing everything that was possible, and to have his troubles as well as my own on my hands would have driven me to distraction.

"The groom is to change horses at every post house, and to use the greatest possible speed. You may be sure that Monsieur de la Vallee will do the same, and that in six days he will be here. I have given him the merest outline of the affair, and have not mentioned the name of Anne's abductor. Had I done so, it is probable that Philip would have gone straight to de Tulle, and forced on an encounter at once. As it is, I trust that Anne and I, between us, may persuade him to take no step in the matter. It is the honour of my family, not of his, that has been attacked. Had he been betrothed to my daughter, he would have been in a position to take up her quarrel. As it is, he has no status, except distant relationship.

"And now, Monsieur Kennedy, I have the king's order to take you to the palace. He asked me several questions about you this morning. I said that I had not yet seen you, but that you were riding over here today, and he said:

"'Bring him to me when he comes, Baron. I should like to see this young fire eater, who thrust himself so boldly into a matter in which he had no concern, solely because he heard a woman's voice calling for help.'"

"I am sorry to hear it," Desmond said, bluntly. "From what you say I imagine that, in spite of what he has done, the king is far from gratified at the failure of his favourite's plan. However, I cannot disobey his commands in the matter."

Chapter 5: A New Friend.

The baron sent a servant to request his daughter to come down.

"I am going now, with Monsieur Kennedy, to the palace, Anne," he said, as she entered. "I do not suppose that we shall be absent very long. I have been talking matters over with him, and I think that he agrees with my view of them."

"But I have hardly spoken to him, yet, father!"

"You will have an opportunity of doing so, when we return. Monsieur Kennedy will, of course, dine with us. After the service that he has rendered to us, we have a right to consider him as belonging to us."

"Had I had an idea of this," Desmond said, as they walked up the hill towards the palace gate, "I should have put on my full uniform. This undress is scarcely the attire in which one would appear before the King of France, who is, as I have heard, most particular in matters of etiquette."

"He is so," the baron said. "He will know that you could not be prepared for an audience, and doubtless he will receive you in his private closet."

On ascending the grand staircase, the baron gave his name to one of the court chamberlains.

"I have orders," the latter said, "to take you at once, on your presenting yourself, to His Majesty's closet, instead of entering the audience chamber."

They were conducted along a private passage, of considerable length. On arriving at a door, the chamberlain asked them to wait, while he went inside to ascertain whether His Majesty was disengaged.

"His Majesty will see you in a few minutes, Baron," he said, when he came out. "The Duc d'Orleans is with him, but, hearing your name announced for a private audience, he is taking his leave."

In two or three minutes a handbell sounded in the room, and the chamberlain, who at once entered, returned in a moment, and conducted the baron and Desmond into the king's private apartment.

"Allow me to present, to Your Majesty," the former said, "Monsieur Desmond Kennedy, an officer in O'Brien's regiment, and an Irish gentleman of good family."

The king, who was now far advanced in life, looked at the young man with some surprise.

"I had expected to see an older man," he said.

"Though you told me, Baron, he was but an ensign, I looked to see a man of the same type as so many of my gallant Irish officers, ready for any desperate service.

"So, young sir, you have begun early, indeed, to play havoc among my liege subjects, for I hear that you, and a soldier with you, slew four of them."

"Hardly your liege subjects, Your Majesty, if I may venture to say so; for, assuredly, they were not engaged in lawful proceedings, when I came upon them."

A slight smile crossed the king's face. He was accustomed to adulation, and the simple frankness with which this young soldier ventured to discuss the propriety of the word he used surprised and amused him.

"You are right, sir. These fellows, who are ready to undertake any service, however criminal, for which they are paid, certainly do not deserve to be called liege subjects. Now, I would hear from, your own lips, how it was that you thrust yourself into a matter with which you had no concern; being wholly ignorant, I understand, that the lady whose voice you heard was Mademoiselle Pointdexter."

"The matter was very simple, Sire. Having joined the regiment but a few months, and being naturally anxious to perfect myself in exercises in arms, I have but little time to stir out, during the day, and of an evening I frequently go for long rambles, taking with me my soldier servant. I had, that evening, gone farther than usual, the night being fair and the weather balmy, and naturally, when I heard the cry of a woman in distress, I determined to see what had happened, as it might well be that murder was being done."

He then related all the circumstances of his obtaining an entrance into the gardens, of the attack upon him by the guard, and how he finally brought Mademoiselle Pointdexter to Versailles. The king listened attentively.

"It was an exploit I should have loved to perform, when I was your age, Monsieur Kennedy. You behaved in the matter with singular discretion and gallantry; but, if you intend always to interfere, when you hear a woman cry out, it is like that your time will be pretty well occupied; and that, before long, there will be a vacancy in the ranks of your regiment. Truly, Monsieur le Baron and his daughter have reason for gratitude that you happened to be passing at the time; and I, as King of France, am glad that this outrage on a lady of the court has failed.

"I am, perhaps, not altogether without blame in the matter. A short time ago, the Vicomte de Tulle told me that he hoped to better his fortune by a rich marriage. He named no names, nor said aught of the measures he intended to adopt. But I said it would be well that he should do so, for rumours had reached me that his finances were in disorder. Whether he took this as a permission to use any means that he thought fit I cannot tell; and I certainly did not suspect, when I heard of the disappearance of Mademoiselle de Pointdexter, that he had any hand in it, and was shocked when the baron came here and denounced him to me. I am glad, indeed, that his enterprise was thwarted, for it was a most unworthy one.

"You are too young, yet, for me to grant you military promotion, but this will be a proof of my approbation of your conduct, and that the King of France is determined to suppress all irregularities at his court."

And, taking a diamond ring from his finger, he handed it to Desmond, who went on one knee to receive it.

"You will please inform your colonel that, when he comes to Versailles, I request he will always bring you with him."

The audience was evidently finished, and the baron and Desmond, bowing deeply, left the king's cabinet. The baron did not speak, till they left the palace.

"Louis has his faults," the baron then said, "but no one could play the part of a great monarch more nobly than he does. I have no doubt, whatever, that de Tulle relied implicitly upon obtaining his forgiveness, had he succeeded in forcing Anne into marrying him; though, doubtless, he would have feigned displeasure for a time. He has extricated himself most gracefully. I can quite believe that he did not imagine his favourite intended to adopt so criminal a course, to accomplish the matter of which he spoke to him, but he could not fail to have his suspicions, when he heard of Anne's disappearance. However, we can consider the affair as happily ended, except for the matter of Monsieur de la Vallee, of whom I spoke to you.

"And now, sir, that the king has expressed his gratitude to you, for saving his court from a grave scandal, how can I fitly express my own, at the inestimable service that you have rendered us?"

"I should say, Baron, that it will be most welcomely expressed, if you will abstain from saying more of the matter. It is a simple one. I went to the assistance of a woman in distress; and succeeded, at the expense of this trifling wound, in accomplishing her rescue. The lady happened to be your daughter, but had she been but the daughter of some little bourgeois of Paris, carried off by a reckless noble, it would have been the same. Much more has been made of the matter than there was any occasion for. It has gained for me the approbation and thanks of the king, to say nothing of this ring, which, although I am no judge of such matters, must be a very valuable one, or he would not have worn it; and I have had the pleasure of rendering a service to you, and Mademoiselle de Pointdexter. Therefore, I feel far more than duly rewarded, for a service somewhat recklessly undertaken on the spur of the moment."

"That may be very well, as far as it interests yourself, Monsieur Kennedy; but not so far as I am concerned, and I fear I shall have to remain your debtor till the end of my life. All I can say at present is that I hope that, as soon as you can obtain leave, you will come as a most honoured guest to my chateau. There you will see me under happier circumstances. The life of a country seigneur is but a poor preparation for existence in this court, where, although there is no longer the open licentiousness that prevailed in the king's younger days, there is yet, I believe, an equal amount of profligacy, though it has been sternly discountenanced since Madame Maintenon obtained an absolute, and I may say a well-used, influence over His Majesty."

"I shall be happy, indeed, to pay you a visit, Baron, if my military duties will permit my absenting myself, for a time, from Paris. All I know of France is its capital, and nothing would give me greater pleasure than to have the opportunity of seeing its country life, in so pleasant a manner."

"Our pleasure would be no less than your own, Monsieur Kennedy.

"There is one thing I must warn you about, and that is, you must be careful for a time not to go out after dark. De Tulle has an evil reputation, and is vindictive as well as unscrupulous. Doubtless, he has agents here who will, by this time, have discovered who it was that brought his daring scheme to naught; and it is, to my mind, more than probable that he will endeavour to be revenged."

"I shall be on my guard," Desmond said quietly.

"You must be careful, indeed," the baron said. "Against open violence you can well defend yourself, but against a blow from behind with a dagger, skill and courage are of little avail. When you go out after dark, I pray you let your army servant follow closely behind you, and see that his sword is loose in its scabbard."

Desmond nodded.

"Believe me, I will take every precaution. It is not likely that there will long be need for it, for none can doubt that military operations will soon begin on a large scale, and we are not likely, if that is the case, to be kept in garrison in Paris."

When Desmond arrived that evening at the barracks, he found that the story of the rescue of Mademoiselle de Pointdexter was already known, and also that the Vicomte de Tulle had been the abductor, and had, in consequence, been banished from court. The baron had indeed related the circumstances to some of his intimate friends, but the story had varied greatly as it spread, and it had come to be reported that an officer had brought a strong body of soldiers, who had assaulted the house where she was confined, and, after a desperate conflict, had annihilated the guard that had been placed over her.

Desmond laughed, as this story was told to him, when he entered the room where the officers were gathered. The narrator concluded:

"As you have been to Versailles, Kennedy, doubtless you will have heard all the latest particulars. Have you learnt who was the officer, what regiment he belonged to, and how came he to have a body of soldiers with him, outside the town? For they say that the house where she was confined was a mile and a half beyond the walls."

There was no longer any reason for concealment. The matter had become public. The baron would certainly mention his name, and indeed his visit to the palace, and the private audience given to him and the baron, would assuredly have been noted.

"Your story is quite new to me," he said, "and is swollen, in the telling, to undue proportions. The real facts of the case are by no means so romantic. The truth of the story, by this time, is generally known, as Mademoiselle Pointdexter and her father have many friends at court. The affair happened to myself."

"To you, Kennedy?" was exclaimed, in astonishment, by all those present.

"Exactly so," he said. "Nothing could have been more simple. The evening before last I was, as usual, taking a walk and, the night being fine, I passed beyond the gate. Presently, I heard a scream and a woman's cry for help. None of you, gentlemen, could have been insensible to such an appeal. Callaghan and I climbed over a pretty high gate. Not knowing what force there might be in the place, we occupied ourselves, at first, by unbarring and shooting the lock of the gate. The bolts were stiff, and we made some noise over it, which brought out five men. These we disposed of, after a short fight, in which I got this graze on the cheek, and Callaghan his sword wound in the shoulder."

"How did you dispose of them, Kennedy?" the colonel asked.

"I ran two of them through. Callaghan cut down one, and shot another. The fifth man cried for mercy, and we simply tied him up.

"We then found Mademoiselle Pointdexter, and, learning from her that the carriage in which she had been brought there was, with its horses, still in the stable, we got it out, harnessed the horses, and put an old woman who was mademoiselle's attendant in the carriage with her. Mike took the reins, I mounted a saddle horse, and we drove her to her father's house at Versailles, saw her fairly inside, and then, as you know, got back here just as the regiment was forming up on parade."

"A very pretty adventure, indeed," the colonel said warmly, and loud expressions of approbation rose from the other listeners.

"And why did you not tell us, when you came in?" the colonel went on.

"I had not seen Baron Pointdexter, and did not know what course he would take--whether he would think it best to hush the matter up altogether, or to lay a complaint before the king; and, until I knew what he was going to do, it seemed to me best that I should hold my tongue, altogether.

"When I went to Versailles, today, I found that he had laid his complaint before the king, and that the Vicomte de Tulle, who was the author of the outrage, had been ordered to his estates. I may say that I had the honour of a private interview with His Majesty, who graciously approved of my conduct, and gave me this ring," and he held out his hand, "as a token of his approval."

"Well, gentlemen, you will agree with me," the colonel said, "that our young ensign has made an admirable debut, and I am sure that we are all proud of the manner in which he has behaved; and our anticipations, that he would prove a credit to the regiment, have been verified sooner than it seemed possible."

"They have, indeed, Colonel," the major said. "It was, in every way, a risky thing for him to have attempted. I do not mean because of the odds that he might have to face, but because of the trouble that he might have got into, by forcing his way into a private house. The scream might have come from a mad woman, or from a serving wench receiving a whipping for misconduct."

"I never thought anything about it, Major. A woman screamed for help, and it seemed to me that help should be given. I did not think of the risk, either from armed men inside--for I had no reason to believe that there were such--or of civil indictment for breaking in. We heard the cry, made straight for the house, and, as it turned out, all went well."

"Well, indeed," the colonel said. "You have rescued a wealthy heiress from a pitiable fate. You have fleshed your maiden sword in the bodies of two villains. You have earned the gratitude of the young lady and her father, and have received the approval of His Majesty--a very good night's work, altogether. Now, tell us a little more about it."

Desmond was compelled to tell the story in much further detail than before. The colonel ordered in a dozen of champagne, and it was late before the party broke up.

"You see, we were pretty nearly right in our guess," O'Neil said, as he and O'Sullivan walked across with Desmond to their quarters. "We said that we thought it likely she might have been carried off by one of the court gallants, who felt tolerably confident that, if successful, the king would overlook the offence. This fellow, thanks to your interference, did not succeed; and the king has let him off, lightly enough, by only banishing him from court. If it had been anyone but one of his favourites, he would, by this time, have been a tenant of the Bastille.

"I do not think, myself, that his punishment was adequate; but then, I am not a courtier, and should be rather glad than not, to be sent away to any estates I might have."

"But," Desmond remarked, "I suppose the punishment is a severe one to these men, accustomed to a round of pleasure and dissipation, and who consider it the highest of earthly honours to be in favour with the king. However, no one could be kinder than His Majesty has been, on the subject. At the reception last night, at which he ordered the baron and his daughter to appear, he showed her the most marked favour, and particularly put a stop to all scandals, by saying loudly that de Tulle had never seen her, after the first morning of her capture."

Six days later, when Desmond was engaged in the fencing room, Callaghan came in, and told him that a gentleman was at his quarters, wishing particularly to see him.

"What is his name?"

"Sure, and I don't know, your honour. He did not mention it, and it was not for the likes of me to ask him."

"Ridiculous, Mike! In future, when anyone comes and wishes to see me, you will say, 'What name shall I tell Mr. Kennedy?'"

He put on his uniform coat reluctantly, for he was engaged in an interesting bout with a professor, who was an old friend of the maitre d'armes. As he entered his room, a young man, who had been staring out of the window, and drumming impatiently with his fingers, turned. He was a stranger to Desmond.

"I am Desmond Kennedy, sir," the young officer said. "To what do I owe the honour of this visit?"

The other did not reply, but stood looking at him, in so strange and earnest a way, that Desmond felt almost uneasy.

"Sir," his visitor said at last, advancing to him and holding out both hands, "when I tell you that my name is Philip de la Vallee, you will understand what must strike you as my singular behaviour. I arrived last night at Versailles, and heard all that had happened. You can imagine, therefore, that my heart is almost too full for words, with gratitude and thankfulness."

Desmond was moved by the emotion of his visitor, and their hands met in a hearty clasp. Monsieur de la Vallee was a young man, of four or five and twenty, well proportioned, and active and sinewy from his devotion to field sports. He was about the same height as Desmond himself, but the latter, who had not yet finished growing, was larger boned, and would broaden into a much bigger and more powerful man.

"Henceforth, Monsieur Kennedy," de la Vallee went on, "I hope that we shall be as brothers, and more. Had it not been for you, my life would have been a ruined one. What agony have I been saved! It makes me mad, to think that I was idling at home, ignorant that my beloved had been carried away. I do not blame the baron for not informing me, and I acknowledge that the reasons he gave me were good ones. I could have done nothing, and should but have added to his troubles by my anxiety and anger. Still, he told me that, in another day or two, he would have felt that I ought no longer to be kept in the dark, and would have summoned me to Paris. I am thankful now that he did not do so, for I believe that my impotence to do anything would have driven me almost to distraction."

"I agree with you that the baron acted wisely," Kennedy said. "Had not chance, or Providence, taken me past the house where she was imprisoned, at the very moment when Mademoiselle Pointdexter cried for help, she might, for aught I can say, have remained a captive there for months, or even years."

"It was Providence, indeed, Monsieur Kennedy. Providence, not only that she should have cried at that moment, but that her cries should have reached the ears of one so ready and able to save her. And now, I pray you, call me Philip, and allow me to call you Desmond, as a pledge of our close friendship."

"With pleasure," Kennedy replied; and the compact was sealed with another close grasp of the hand.

"It is strange, Desmond, that while the king, who had but little interest in the matter, could present you, as I am told he did, with a diamond ring, the baron and I, who owe you so much, can do nothing to show our gratitude."

Desmond smiled.

"I can assure you that I need no such tokens," he said. "The thanks that I have received, from you both, are infinitely more grateful to me than any amount of rings and jewels."

"And now, my friend," Philip de la Vallee went on, "my own burning desire is to go to de Tulle, as soon as I have accompanied the baron and Anne to their home; first, to publicly chastise this villain noble; and then, of course, to fight him. Naturally, I have said nothing of this to the baron, but I feel, after what has happened, that in you I shall find an adviser, and a sympathizer."

"I sympathize with you, most heartily, Philip, and in your place should feel the same impulse; and yet, it would not be wise to give way to it. I say this on the ground that he is a notoriously good swordsman, and that, instead of your taking vengeance upon him, he might kill you.

"I feel that that argument would not have any influence with you personally, but, taking your position with regard to Mademoiselle de Pointdexter, it should have great weight. You can judge, from what you would have felt yourself, had you been aware of her disappearance, what she would feel, did she hear of your death in this quarrel. Were you her brother, I should say that you would be right--nay, that it would be your duty to endeavour to punish the outrage against the honour of your family. Were you openly betrothed to her, you would again have the right to punish her abductor; but, not being either her brother or her betrothed, neither reason nor public opinion would justify your doing so. Moreover, did you fight with him and kill him, you would incur the gravest resentment of the king; for, in fact, you would be impugning his justice, which has considered banishment from court to be a sufficient punishment for his offence. Not only was he a favourite of the king's, but he belongs, I understand, to a powerful family; who would, you may be sure, use their influence with the king to bring about your punishment, for the breach of the decree against duelling, and you would be fortunate if you escaped a long imprisonment."

The other was silent.

"I feel that you are right," he said, at last, "but, indeed, it is hard that I should not be able to avenge this outrage upon the lady who is to be my wife. I may tell you that, as soon as we return home, our formal betrothal is to take place, and ere long our marriage will be celebrated; but I shall feel lowered, in my own esteem, if I sit down quietly under this injury."

"I do not see that," Desmond said. "If you abstain from challenging de Tulle, it is from no fear of the consequences, but it is, as I have shown you, because, whatever the issue of the contest, it would be bad both for you and her. If you were killed, her life would be spoilt. If you killed him, you might languish for years in one of the royal prisons. The king prides himself on his justice, and, by all accounts, rightly so; and I am sure that he would feel the deepest resentment, were you or anyone to show, by your actions, that you considered he has favoured the transgressor."

"You are right, Desmond; and, at any rate for the present, I will put my intention aside; but should he ever cross my path, assuredly I will have a reckoning with him.

"But how is it that you, who are at least eight years younger than I am, should argue as an old counsellor rather than a young ensign?"

"I suppose, in the first place, it is from my bringing up. I lived with and was educated by a good priest, one not wanting in manliness and energy, but who often deplored the system of duelling, which is as strong with us as it is here, and denounced it as a relic of barbarism, and, at any rate, never to be put in use on account of a heated quarrel over wine, but only if some deadly injury had been inflicted, and even then better left alone. Of course, as an officer in one of His Majesty's regiments, I should be obliged to conform to the general usage; for, did I decline, I should be regarded as having brought dishonour on the corps. But my case differs altogether from yours.

"In the next place, knowing you were coming to Versailles, I thought over what course you would be likely to pursue, and considered it was probable you would lose no time in challenging de Tulle. I have thought the matter over, in every light, and made up my mind to endeavour to dissuade you from doing so, if the opportunity offered.

"So you see," he added with a smile, "I had prepared my array of arguments against it; and I cannot but think that the opinion of one interested, but not vitally so, on a point, is rather to be taken than that of a person smarting under an injury."

"And now, to turn to other matters. In three days we start for the south. The baron accompanied me here, and went to see your colonel, while I came to your quarters. His object was to ask him to grant you a month's leave of absence, with the provision, of course, that you should return at once, if the regiment was ordered on service."

"It is kind, indeed, of him," Desmond said, "but I doubt whether the colonel will assent. It is not a month since I was dismissed from drill, and took my place with my company, and I doubt whether he will consider that I am sufficiently versed in my duties, or that, after being so short a time in the regiment, I have any right to leave."

"What you say is right enough, under ordinary circumstances, but these are altogether extraordinary. Then, after what you have done, he will feel it but natural that we should wish to have you with us for a time. Moreover, I do not consider that our journey will be altogether unattended by danger. From what I have heard of de Tulle, he is a man who never forgives, and will pursue his object with the pertinacity of a bloodhound. He has failed in his first attempt, but there is no reason why he should not renew it, confident, perhaps, that if successful the king, though he may feel it necessary to feign much anger for a time, will finally forgive him and take him into favour again, especially as his family would bring all their influence to bear to bring this about. Doubtless, he will be kept perfectly informed of what is going on here. There are several forests to be traversed on the way, and these are, for the most part, the haunts of robber bands; and, should the carriage be found overturned, and the baron and his daughter missing, it would be put down as their work. Having the baron as well as his daughter in his power, de Tulle would find it easier than before to compel Anne to purchase her father's freedom, as well as her own, by consenting to his terms.

"Therefore, you see, the aid of a sword like yours would be valuable, and no doubt your servant, who is also a sturdy fighter, will accompany us."

"I can hardly think that de Tulle would venture upon so bold a stroke as that, and yet he might do so. Men of that kind are not accustomed to be thwarted, and it would be a satisfaction to his resentment at his former failure, as well as the attainment of the wide estates of which Anne is heiress."

At this moment there was a knock at the door, and the baron entered.

"My dear Monsieur Kennedy," he said, "I have succeeded. Colonel O'Brien has been pleased to say that you have been so assiduous, in learning your duties, that he considers you as capable of performing them as any of his subalterns; and that you have just brought so much credit on the regiment, that he is pleased to be able to grant the favour I asked. Here is your furlough, duly signed. Now it only rests with yourself, to accept or refuse my invitation."

"I accept it most gladly, Baron. It will give me the greatest pleasure to accompany you, and mademoiselle, and Monsieur de la Vallee, whom I now regard as a dear friend, to your home."

"That is settled, then," the baron said. "We start early on Thursday morning. It would be well, therefore, if you were to ride over on Wednesday evening, and occupy one of the many spare chambers there are in the house."

"I will do so willingly; and I shall ask the colonel to allow my servant to accompany me."

"That is already settled. I told Colonel O'Brien that I owed much to him also, and he at once acceded to my request, saying that, although the wound is healing, the surgeon said that it would be a fortnight, yet, before he will be fit for service; and, moreover, that it was a custom when an officer went on leave that he should, if he wished it, take his soldier servant with him."

"Thank you again, Baron. Mike is a faithful fellow, and a shrewd one. I am so accustomed now to his services that I should miss them, and his talk, very much."

"Have you heard, Mike," Desmond asked, when his servant came up to his room, after the baron and Philip de la Vallee had left, "that you are to go with me, to stay for a month, at Pointdexter?"

"I have, your honour. Sure, I was sent for to the colonel's quarters, and there I found a tall gentleman, whom I had never seen before, as far as I knew.

"'This is Mike Callaghan, Mr. Kennedy's servant,' the colonel said, and the baron stepped forward, and shook hands with me, for all the world as if I had been a noble like himself; and he said:

"'My brave fellow, I have to thank you for the aid you gave your master in rescuing my daughter, in which service you received the wound which still keeps your arm in a sling. Here is a token that we are not ungrateful for the service. If you will take my advice, you will hand it to an agent of mine here in Paris, who will keep it for you, and you may find it useful when the time comes for you to take your discharge.'

"So saying, he put a heavy purse into my hand, and said:

"'You will find my agent's name and address on a card inside the purse. I shall go round to him, now, and tell him that you are coming, and that he is to use the money to your advantage, and to hand it over to you whenever you choose to ask for it. Your master is coming down to stay for a month with me, and Colonel O'Brien has granted leave for you to accompany him.'

"I thanked him heartily, as you may believe, sir; though, as I said, I wanted no reward for obeying your orders, and for the share I took in that little skirmish. After I came out, I looked into the purse, which was mighty heavy, expecting to find a handful of crowns; and it fairly staggered me when I found that it was full of gold pieces, and on counting them, found that there were a hundred louis. Never did I dream that I should be so rich. Why, your honour, when I lave the regiment, which will not be for many a long year, I hope, I shall be able to settle down comfortably, for the rest of my life, in a snug little shebeen, or on a bit of land with a cottage and some pigs, and maybe a cow or two; and it is all to your honour I owe it, for if you hadn't given the word, it would never have entered my head to attack a gentleman's house, merely because I heard a woman scream."

"Well, I am heartily glad, Mike; and I hope that you will take it straight to the agent's, and not break in upon it, by treating half the regiment to drink."

"I will, your honour. It was given me to stow away for the time when I might want it, and though I don't say that my own inclinations would not lead me to trate a few of the boys, I feel that I ought to do what the gentleman told me."

"Certainly you should, Mike. If you once began to spend it in that way, it is not one louis, but five or more, that would disappear in a few hours. I am heartily glad that the baron has so handsomely rewarded you for the service, and if you like, I will go round with you this afternoon to his agent, and see the money safely deposited."

"Thank you, your honour. I sha'n't feel easy, as long as I have got it in my pouch. I should suspect everyone who came near me, and should never dare take my hand off it, lest someone else might put his in."

"You are a lucky fellow, Kennedy," O'Neil said, when Desmond told his two comrades of the arrangements that had been made. "And, if you go on like this, the regiment will believe that any good fortune that may fall to its lot is the result of your luck."

"I really do not like having leave given to me, when I have been such a short time in the regiment. It does not seem fair upon others."

"No one will grudge you that," O'Sullivan said. "It is not as if we were at home. Then, of course, everyone would like his turn. But here, although we are soldiers of France, we are as strangers in the land. Here in Paris we have many acquaintances, and a welcome at most of the receptions; but that is the end of it. It is seldom, indeed, that we are invited into the country houses of those we know. That sort of hospitality is not the fashion in France. Here, nobles may throw open their houses to all gentlemen by birth who happen to be presented to them, but at home they are rigidly exclusive; and, moreover, I am inclined to think they regard us Irishmen as detrimental and dangerous. Many Irishmen make exceedingly good matches, and we are regarded as having a way with us, with the girls, that is likely to interfere with the arrangements their parents have made for their marriages. Now, it seems to me that your baron must be a very confiding old gentleman, or he would never take you to stay in the society of the young lady who owes so much to you. Faith, it seems to me that you have the ball at your feet, and that you have only to go in and win. From what I hear, Mademoiselle Pointdexter is no older than you are yourself, and it is a glorious chance for you."

Desmond broke into a laugh.

"My dear O'Sullivan," he said, "it seems to me that it is the favourite dream of Irish soldiers of fortune, that they may improve their circumstances by marriage."

"Well, there is no easier or more pleasant way," his friend said, stoutly.

"Possibly I may come to think so, in another ten years," Desmond went on, "but, at present, I have no more thought of marrying than I have of becoming king of France. The idea is altogether absurd, and it happens to be particularly so, in the present case, since one of the objects of my going down to Pointdexter is that I may be present at the formal betrothal of this young lady, to Monsieur de la Vallee, a neighbour of theirs, whom I had the pleasure of meeting this afternoon, and to whom she is tenderly attached."

"By the powers, but that is unlucky, Kennedy!" O'Neil said; "and I have been thinking that your fortune was made, and that the regiment would soon lose you, as you would, of course, settle down as a magnate in Languedoc; and now, it seems that what we thought the proper sequence of your adventure, is not to come off, after all. Well, lad, I congratulate you on putting a good face on it, and hiding your disappointment."

"What nonsense you talk!" Desmond said, laughing. "It is you who have been building castles, not I, and it is your disappointment that they have fallen to pieces."

Chapter 6: An Ambuscade.

On the morning arranged, the cavalcade started from Versailles. The baron had instructed the stable keeper, where the carriage and horses had been placed, to notify the Vicomte de Tulle that he held them at his disposal. The woman, who had been brought to Versailles, had been dismissed, after having made before a magistrate a deposition, stating how Mademoiselle de Pointdexter had been held a close prisoner, and that, with the exception of herself, no one whatever had entered her apartment, except that the Vicomte de Tulle had paid her a visit, of some five minutes' duration, on the morning after she was brought there. A copy of this was left in the magistrate's hands for safekeeping, while the original was kept by the baron, who regarded it as a most important document, concerning, as it did, the honour of his daughter.

Anne had travelled to Paris in the family coach, and she again, with her maid, took her place in it. The baron, Monsieur de la Vallee, and Desmond rode on horseback behind it, two armed retainers rode in front, and two others, with Mike, took their places behind. The old servitor sat on the front seat, by the side of the coachman.

"I do not think, Desmond," Philip de la Vallee said, as the baron fell back to talk for a while with his daughter, "that he has the slightest thought of our being attacked by any of the agents of the vicomte; but I have made a good many enquiries about the fellow, in the past few days, and from what I have heard I am still more convinced that, before long, he is likely to renew his attempt to get possession of Anne. I hear that his circumstances are well-nigh desperate. He has mortgaged the income of his estates, which, of course, he is unable to sell, as they go with the title to the heir. He is pressed by many creditors, who, now that he has lost the favour of the king, will give him no further grace. Indeed, I understand that the king, who is always liberal, and who not infrequently makes considerable gifts to the gentlemen of the court, to enable them to support the necessary expenses, has already assisted him several times, and that it was only by such aid that he has been able to hold on as long as he has done.

"He is, in fact, a desperate man, and his only hope is in making a wealthy alliance. Therefore, putting aside his pique and anger at having failed, the temptation to again obtain possession of Anne is great, indeed. Once married to her he could, even if the king kept him in banishment, well maintain his position as a country magnate."

"But Mademoiselle de Pointdexter cannot come into the estates until her father's death."

"Not his estates, but those of her mother, who was also a wealthy heiress, and of which she will enter into possession either on coming of age or on marrying. So, you see, he can afford to disregard the enmity of her father, as well as the displeasure of the king, which probably would soon abate after the marriage took place. If I had known, when I left home, what had happened, and that if she was found we should be returning home, I would have brought with me a dozen stout fellows from my own estate. As it is, I sent off a messenger, yesterday, with an order to my majordomo to pick out that number of active fellows, from among the tenantry, and to start with the least possible delay by the route that we shall follow, of which I have given him particulars. He is to ride forward until he meets us, so that when he joins us, we shall be too strong a party for any force that the vicomte is likely to gather to intercept us."

"A very wise precaution, Philip; but we shall be far upon our way, before this reinforcement can come up."

"We shall be some distance, I admit. My messenger will take fully five days in going. He will take another day to gather and arm the tenants, so that they will not start until two days afterwards. Then, however, they will travel at least twice as fast as we shall, hampered as we are by the carriage. I should have suggested that Anne should ride on a pillion, behind me or her father, but I did not do so, because it would have been necessary to explain to him my reasons for suggesting the change; and, moreover, I felt sure that he would not agree to it, had I done so. Baron Pointdexter is one of the largest landowners in Languedoc, and although one of the kindest and best of men, he has his full share of family pride, and would consider that it was derogatory to his position for his daughter to be riding about on a pillion, like the wife or daughter of some small landed proprietor or tenant farmer, instead of in a carriage, as becomes her station. Therefore, I must accept the situation, carriage and all, and I can only hope that this villain will not attempt to interfere with us before my men join us.

"Fortunately, even if a courier take the vicomte word that the baron and his daughter have made their adieus to His Majesty, the fellow cannot hear of it for two days, however fast the messenger may travel. Of course, Tulle is nigh a hundred miles nearer Paris than Pointdexter, which lies between Florac and Sainte Afrique, both of which towns lie within the circle of the estate. I admit that, foreseeing the baron is likely to return to his estates without delay, the vicomte may have made his preparations, and be ready to start as soon as he gets the news. Nevertheless, he will have a ride of some eighty miles to strike the road on which we shall be travelling. He may then move north, until he finds some suitable place for a surprise; but, even allowing for his exercising the greatest speed, we should be halfway from Paris before we can possibly meet him, and my men should join us by that time."

"You have forgotten one contingency, which would entirely alter the state of things."

"What is that?" Monsieur de la Vallee asked sharply.

"We give this villain noble credit for resource and enterprise. What more likely than that he has left a couple of his retainers at Versailles, with orders that, should any messenger be sent off by a southern road from the baron, his journey is to be cut short, and any paper or letter found upon him carried with all speed to Tulle? In that case, the chances of our being met by a reinforcement are very small."

"Peste! You are right, Desmond. I never gave the matter a thought. Now that you mention it, nothing is more probable. It was the servant who accompanied me whom I sent off, but, as de Tulle would have been notified of my arrival, and the man started from the baron's house, it would be deemed certain that he was either going to Pointdexter or my own estate, and that the message he carried was a somewhat urgent one. Well, all we can do is to hope that the fellow has not thought of our taking such a precaution, and that my messenger will arrive unmolested. Still, I acknowledge that the idea makes me anxious, and I fear that we shall not get through without serious trouble. There are so many disbanded soldiers, and other knaves, in the forests that de Tulle would have no difficulty in hiring any number of them, and carrying his scheme out without the assistance or knowledge of his own tenants. The heavy taxation necessary to keep up the expenses of the court has driven numbers of people to despair, and many hitherto law-abiding folk are being forced to leave their holdings, and to take to unlawful courses.

"However, it is of no use our telling the baron our fears. He is obstinate, when he has once made up his mind to a thing, and nothing short of a royal command would induce him either to change his route, or to stop at one of the towns that we shall pass through, and wait until my band arrives. He would, indeed, consider his honour greatly attainted by allowing himself to make a change of plans, on the mere chance that our suspicions were justified."

Six days passed without anything occurring. Impatient as Philip de la Vallee and Desmond were to get forward, they could not hurry the slow pace at which they travelled. Mademoiselle Pointdexter was now suffering from the reaction after her month of captivity and anxiety. The baron therefore travelled with provoking slowness. Obtaining, as he did, relays of horses at each post, they could without difficulty have travelled at almost double the rate at which they actually proceeded, but stoppages were made at all towns at which comfortable accommodation could be obtained. Indeed, in some places the roads were so bad that the carriage could not proceed at a pace beyond a walk, without inflicting a terrible jolting upon those within it.

"There is one comfort," Philip said, when he had been bewailing the slowness of their pace, "my men should reach us at Nevers, at the latest, and you may take it as tolerably certain that any attempt to interfere with us will take place considerably south of that town. I should guess that it would be somewhere between Moulins and Thiers. If our escort does not come before we reach Moulins, I shall begin to think that your suggestion was correct, and that my messenger has indeed been intercepted and slain."

Desmond could not gainsay the truth of his friend's calculation, but he said:

"Possibly, Philip, instead of being attacked by the way, de Tulle's agents might rob him of his letter at one of the inns at which he put up. Did he know its contents?"

"Yes. I told him that it contained an order for the majordomo to ride, with a troop of twelve men, to meet us, and that he was to give what aid he could in getting them together as quickly as possible; so that, even if robbed of the letter, he might still be able to fulfil his mission. Not, I own, that I thought of that at the time, for the idea that he might be stopped never once entered my mind."

At Nevers, Desmond went round to all the inns in the town, to enquire if any body of men had put up at that place, but without success. When he related his failure to obtain any news to Philip, the latter said:

"Well, we must hope that we shall meet them before we arrive at Moulins. If not, I shall no longer have any hope that my messenger got through safely, and then we shall have to consider whether it will not be necessary to inform the baron of our fears, and to get him to change his route and make a detour, cross the Loire at Bourbon, make for Maison, and then journey down on the other bank of the Saone as far as Pont Saint Esprit, and thence over the mountains to Florac."

"That would certainly be the safest plan, always providing that we have not been watched ever since we left Paris. The vicomte might well take this precaution, in case we should deviate from the regular route."

"Sapriste! Desmond, you are always full of evil prognostications. Still, as usual, I cannot but allow that there is reason in them."

"You see, Philip, we have plenty of time, as we travel at a snail's pace, and in the evening when we stop, to think over the affair in every light. I always put myself in the position of the Vicomte de Tulle, and consider what steps I should take to ensure success in my next attempt to carry off Mademoiselle de Pointdexter."

"Then I am very glad that you are not in the position of de Tulle, for, if you were, I should consider that all was lost, and that there was not a chink or crevice by which we could escape. It is monstrous that a nobleman cannot travel from Paris to his estate, without being obliged to take as many precautions as the general of an army would have to do, against the attack of an active and formidable enemy."

"And will you tell the baron, Philip?"

"I hardly know what to do in that respect, for after all, we have no solid foundation whatever for our uneasiness, beyond the fact that the men I sent for have not met us. All our apprehensions are due solely to the fact that this fellow is utterly unscrupulous, and that his whole future depends on his carrying out his insolent designs successfully. If we had any solid facts to work on, I would urge the baron to change his route, but I fear that he would not only scoff at our views that there may be danger, but might be angry at my taking the step of sending for a party of my retainers, without his being in any way consulted in the matter. At any rate, I feel sure that he would refuse to change his route, without some very much stronger reason than we can give him."

"Then we must let matters go on as they are, Philip. It may be that really we have been alarming ourselves without sufficient cause. If the worst comes to the worst, we can make a good fight for it."

"It is certainly hard on you. You have performed one brave action for us, at the risk of your life, and now you are thrust into another danger, perhaps even greater than the first, and this in a quarrel in which you have no concern whatever."

Desmond laughed.

"Do you not see, Philip, that the adventure is good training for a soldier, and that, if I am on duty in command of a company, I shall be all the more useful an officer for having served a sort of apprenticeship in surprises, ambuscades, and alarms. The journey has been vastly more interesting than it would have been under other circumstances. We should have found it dull, without such matter of interest as this affair has given us, and, even should nothing whatever come of it, it will have served its purpose by beguiling our journey, which, in truth, riding at so slow a pace, would otherwise scarce have been amusing."

"Well, then, it seems that the only thing that we can do is to see that the servants all keep their pistols charged, and are prepared to do their duty in case of sudden attack. Of course, at present they have no idea that any special danger threatens us; but I shall tell them, before I start in the morning, that we fear the road is dangerous owing to a band of robbers reported to be in the forest, and that they must hold themselves in readiness for action, in case we fall in with any of them. Old Eustace and the coachman have both got arquebuses. I shall tell them that, should they be attacked, they are to fire at once, and then the coachman is to whip up his horses and drive at full speed, while we endeavour to keep off the assailants."

"That would be of use, if the assailants should be for the most part on foot, but I think it more likely that they will be mounted, and however fast this lumbering carriage might go, they could easily keep up with it. Fight as hard as we may, the carriage must be overtaken if they are in sufficient force to overpower us. I should think that it would be well that you should warn Mademoiselle de Pointdexter that we hear the road is not very safe, and that, if there is trouble, she is on no account to attempt to leave the carriage. As long as she remains there she will run but little risk, for you may be sure that de Tulle will have issued the strictest orders that no pistol is to be fired in its direction. I have also little doubt that he has ordered the baron's life to be respected, because his death would greatly add to the anger that would be excited by the attack, and would also put a barrier between him and mademoiselle, who would naturally regard him with even more hostility than before, as the author of her father's death. Therefore, I trust that in any case his life and hers will not be endangered, however numerous our assailants might be."

"Yes, I have no doubt that that is so, Desmond, though I am sure that, were I wounded and on the point of death, I would rather know that Anne had fallen by a chance shot, than that she was in the power of this villain."

The next morning, they started very early for Moulins, for the journey would be a longer one than usual, and the road through the forest would probably be so rough, that the pace must necessarily be very slow. At two o'clock, the men riding ahead noticed that a tree had fallen across the road, and one of them galloped back and informed the baron of it.

"That is strange," the latter said. "There have been no storms for the past two days. It must have fallen quite recently, for otherwise the news would have been taken to the nearest commune, whose duty it would be to see at once to its removal."

Philip de la Vallee had, as the servant was speaking, glanced at Desmond. To both, it seemed that this obstacle could scarcely be the result of an accident.

"I will see how large the tree is," the baron said. "Whatever be its size, it is hard if eight men and four horses cannot drag it off the road."

So saying, he cantered forward, followed by the retainer, whose comrade also fell in as they passed him.

"Look to your arquebuses," Philip said to the two men on the box, and at the same time called up Mike and the two men, from behind.

"A tree has fallen across the road," he said to them, "and it is possible that this may be an ambush, and that we may be attacked, so hold yourselves in readiness, look to your pistols, and see that the priming is all right in the pans."

Then they went to the door of the carriage.

"It is just possible that we are going to have trouble, Anne," Philip said. "Remember what I told you last night, and on no account move from your seat, whatever may take place."

As he spoke, there was a discharge of firearms in front, and at the same moment a score of horsemen broke from the trees, and rode down upon the carriage. Their leader was masked.

As they came up, the coachman and Eustace discharged their arquebuses, emptying two saddles. Then, drawing their swords, both leapt to the ground. In the meantime Philip, Desmond, and the three men dashed at their assailants. Philip made for their leader, who, he doubted not, was the Vicomte de Tulle, but the latter drew a pistol and fired, when he was within a horse's length of him. The young man swayed in his saddle, and fell heavily to the ground, while a piercing cry from the carriage rose in the air.

Desmond, after cutting down the first man he encountered, turned his horse and attacked the masked figure, who met him with a fury that showed he was animated by personal animosity. His skill in fencing, however, gave him but slight advantage in such an encounter, while Desmond's exercise with the sabre, in the regimental salle d'armes, was now most useful to him. Enraged at the fall of his friend, and seeing that there was but a moment to spare, for already some of the other assailants were coming to the assistance of their chief, he showered his blows with such vehemence and fury that his opponent had enough to do to guard his head, without striking a blow in return.

Seeing in a moment that he would be surrounded, Desmond made a last effort. The vicomte's weapon shivered at the stroke, but it somewhat diverted the direction of the blow, and instead of striking him full on the head, the sword shore down his cheek, inflicting a ghastly wound, carrying away an ear as well as the cheek from the eye to the chin. Then, wheeling his horse, he dashed at two men who were riding at him.

The attack was so sudden that one of their horses swerved, and Desmond, touching his charger's flank with a spur, rode at him and hurled horse and rider to the ground. A backhanded blow struck his other opponent full in the throat, and then he dashed into the wood, shouting to Mike to follow him.

The two servitors had both fallen, and the greater part of the assailants were gathered round the carriage. Mike was engaged in a single combat with one of the horsemen, and had just run his opponent through when Desmond shouted to him; so, turning, he galloped after his master.

They were not pursued. The fall of their leader had, for the moment, paralysed the band, and while three or four of them remained by the carriage--whose last defender had fallen--the others, dismounting, ran to where the vicomte was lying.

"That has been a tough business, your honour," Mike said, as he joined his master. "It is right you were, sir, when you told me that you were afraid that rascal would try and hinder us on our way. Sure it has been a bad business, altogether. Monsieur Philip is killed, and the baron, too, I suppose, and all the others, and Miss Anne has fallen into the hands of that villain again."

"I do not think that the baron has been hurt, Mike. I expect the orders were only to take him prisoner."

"Where are we going, your honour?" Mike asked, for they were still galloping at full speed.

"I am going to get into the road again, and try to find help, at Moulins, to recover the young lady. There is one thing, she is not likely to be molested by that fellow for some little time."

"Then you did not kill him, your honour?"

"No. I cut through his guard, but it turned my sword. But I laid his face open, and it will be some time before he will be fit to show himself to a lady. If, as I expect, I can get no help at Moulins, I shall ride on to Monsieur de la Vallee's place, gather some men there, and try to cut the party off before they get to Tulle. If I am too late, I shall see what I can do to rescue them. From la Vallee I shall go to Pointdexter. I have no doubt that we can get together a force, there, large enough to besiege de Tulle's castle."

After an hour's ride, they arrived at Moulins, and Desmond rode at once to the mairie. Being in uniform, he was received with every respect by the mayor, who, however, on hearing his story, said that he did not see how he could interfere in the matter. It seemed to be a private quarrel between two nobles, and, even if he were ready to interpose, he had no force available; "but at the same time, he would send out four men, with a cart, to bring in any they might find with life in them."

"Very well, sir," Desmond said, indignantly. "You know your duty, I suppose, and I know mine, and I shall certainly report to the king your refusal to give any assistance to punish these ill doers."

So saying, he left the room, and at once rode to some stables. Leaving his horse and Mike's there, he hired others, and then continued his journey south at full speed, and before evening rode into Roanne. He knew that it was useless, endeavouring to stir up the authorities here, as they would naturally say that it was the business of the mayors at Nevers and Moulins, since the attack had taken place between those towns. Ordering fresh horses to be got ready, he said to Mike:

"Do you go to all the inns on the left of the main street--I will go to all those on the right--and enquire if a troop of mounted men have come in. I am afraid there is no chance of it, but it is at least worth the trial."

At the first four or five places he visited, the answer was that no such party had arrived; then, seeing one of the civic guards, he asked him if he had seen or heard of a troop of men passing through the town.

"Such a troop arrived an hour ago, Monsieur l'officier. They stopped, as they passed me, and asked if Monsieur le Baron Pointdexter, accompanied by a carriage and some servants, had passed through the town. They put up at the Soleil, and I should think that they are there now, for they had evidently made a long journey, and their horses were too worn out to go farther."

Delighted at the unexpected news, Desmond hurried to the inn. It was a second-class establishment, and evidently frequented by market people, as there were large stables attached to it. The landlord was standing at the door. He bowed profoundly, for it was seldom that guests of quality visited the inn.

"What can I do for monsieur?" he enquired.

"You have a party of travellers, who arrived an hour ago. I have business with them."

"You will find them in this room, monsieur," the landlord said, opening a door.

There were some twelve men inside. The remains of a repast were on the table. Some of the men were still sitting there, others were already asleep on benches. One, who was evidently their leader, was walking up and down the room impatiently. He looked up in surprise when Desmond entered.

"You are the intendant of Monsieur de la Vallee, are you not?"

"I am, sir," the man said, still more surprised.

"I am a friend of your master. We have been expecting to meet you, for the past four or five days. He was travelling south with the Baron de Pointdexter and his daughter. We were attacked, this afternoon, on the other side of Moulins. The baron and his daughter were, I believe, carried off; the servants all killed. I saw your master fall, but whether mortally wounded or not I cannot say.

"I and my servant cut our way through the assailants, who were led by the Vicomte de Tulle, who had before carried off Mademoiselle de Pointdexter. I was on my way south to la Vallee, with but faint hope of meeting you on the road."

"This is bad news indeed, sir," the intendant said. "I trust that my master is not killed, for we all loved him. As to Mademoiselle Pointdexter, it was an understood thing that she, one day, would be our mistress.

"It is not our fault that we are so late. Our master's messenger was attacked, near Nevers, and was left for dead on the road. The letter he bore, and his purse, were taken from him. The night air caused his wounds to stop bleeding, and he managed to crawl to Moulins. Having no money, he was unable to hire a horse, and indeed could not have sat one. He went to an inn frequented by market people, and there succeeded in convincing an honest peasant, who had come in with a cart of faggots, that his story was a true one, and promised him large pay on his arrival at la Vallee.

"The pace was, as you may imagine, a slow one, but two days ago he arrived home, and told me the story. I had the alarm bell at the castle rung at once, and in half an hour the tenants came in, and I chose these twelve, and started an hour later. Fortunately, the master had told the messenger what was the purport of his letter, and we have ridden night and day since. I am at your service, monsieur."

"In the first place, let your men have a sleep. It is eight o'clock now. I will give them seven hours. At three in the morning, we will mount. There are not beds enough here, but if you get some clean straw scattered down in one of the sheds, the men can lie there. In the meantime, I will go round and hire fresh horses, leaving your own in pledge for their safe return.

"You had better pick out two of your men to ride on to Moulins. The mayor there promised to send out a cart, to fetch in any wounded who might be found at the scene of the conflict. If, on their arrival, they find that Monsieur de la Vallee is not among these, they must ride on till they get there--it is some three leagues from the town--and bring in his body, together with those of his servants. They must arrange to give them Christian burial there, but your master's body they will, of course, take on to la Vallee.

"His last wish, of course, would be that Mademoiselle de Pointdexter should be rescued from the power of the villain noble who has carried her off. Starting in the morning so early, we shall have no difficulty in cutting him off long before he arrives at Tulle. He will probably cross the Alier at the ferry at Saint Pierre le Moutier. I must look at a map, and see the road that he is likely to follow, but it is probable that he will make by country tracks till he strikes the main road from Moulins."

"Well, I should think, sir, that he would cross it near Aubusson, and then pass over the mountains by the road through Felletin, and come down upon Meimac, when he will be only two leagues from his castle near Correze. There is a good road from here to Aubusson, and we might take post on the road between that town and Felletin. At least, sir, we can avenge the murder of our dear master, though we have arrived too late to save him; and can rescue Mademoiselle de Pointdexter and her father."

The men, who had roused themselves and listened to the conversation with many ejaculations of fury and regret, now exclaimed that they were ready to ride on at once.

"There is no occasion for that, my friends," Desmond said. "The coach with mademoiselle can travel but slowly, especially along country roads."

"Perhaps the vicomte may take her on the saddle behind him," the intendant suggested.

"That he will not do," Desmond said. "In the fight I wounded him so sorely that he will, I think, have to be carried in a litter, and he will be in no condition for fast or long travelling, so that they certainly are not, at the present time, many leagues from the spot where they attacked us, and cannot reach Aubusson until the day after tomorrow. We might cut them off before they arrive there, but we do not know what road they may follow, and might miss them; whereas, from what you say, there can be no doubt that they would pass through Felletin."

"I think that he would be sure to come that way, sir, for if he followed the road on to Limoges questions might be asked. At any rate, sir, we might post a man at Aubusson, and another at Pont Gibaut, as he might make from that town to Felletin through the village of Croc. How many men has he with him?"

"That I cannot tell you. Some twenty mounted men, under his own leading, attacked the carriage. Two were shot by Eustace and the coachman. I disposed of two more, and my soldier servant of another. The two mounted men and the two servants probably killed two or three more, at least, before they themselves fell, so that the vicomte would only have some twelve mounted men with him. But there was another party in ambush, and I cannot say how strong they were; but probably, altogether, there would be twenty.

"There are ten of your men, after sending two off to Moulins. Now there is yourself, my servant, and I, so we shall be thirteen. With the advantage of surprise, I think that we may calculate upon an easy victory, especially as I imagine that the men employed in the affair are not de Tulle's own retainers, but some robber band that he hired for the purpose; and these, having no special interest in the matter beyond earning the pay, are not likely to make any very determined resistance."

Desmond now went back to the hotel where he had put up his horse. He found Mike awaiting him there, and the latter was delighted when he heard the news of the arrival of the party from la Vallee. Desmond's purse was but lightly furnished, and as he saw that the expenses might be heavy, he went to a jeweller's.

"I want to borrow fifty louis," he said, "on this ring. It is, I imagine, worth a good deal more, since it was a present to me from the king."

The jeweller examined the ring carefully.

"It is a valuable one, indeed, sir," he said, "and I would willingly lend you double as much upon it."

"Well, we will say seventy-five, then," Desmond said. "I think that will be ample for my purpose."

Having received the money, he returned to the inn, accompanied by Mike; and went round to the various stables in the town, where he hired fifteen horses. These were to be taken to the Soleil, at three in the morning, and the men who brought them were to take back the tired horses as security.

At that hour, the party started, and after a ride of some thirty-five miles reached

Clermont, where they stabled the horses for six hours. Late that evening they arrived at Aubusson, having accomplished a journey of some seventy miles. One of the men had been left at Pont Gibaut, with orders to take a fresh horse and ride on to Aubusson, if the party they were in search of passed through the town.

At Aubusson, Desmond took a fresh horse and rode back to Pont Gibaut, enquiring at all the villages along the road whether a party of twenty men had been seen to cross the road, at any point. Then he took four hours' sleep, and at daybreak started back again, making fresh enquiries till he arrived at Aubusson. He was convinced that the band had not, at that time, crossed the road on its way south.

At ten o'clock he started out with his party, followed the road by the side of the Crorrere river--here a mere streamlet--and halted in a wood about five miles from Felletin.

At six o'clock in the afternoon, a horseman was seen coming along, and was recognized as the man who had been left at Pont Gibaut. Desmond went out to meet him. He reported that, at twelve o'clock, a party of horsemen had come down on to the road a mile to the west of the town. He had followed at a distance, and they had turned off by the track leading to Croc. They had with them a carriage and a horse litter, and were travelling slowly.

Desmond and his men at once shifted their position, and took up a post on the track between Croc and Felletin. An hour later, the party of horsemen were seen approaching the wood in which they were hidden. Desmond drew up the men, all of whom were armed with pistols, as well as swords, in line among the trees. He waited until the carriage was abreast of them, and then gave a shout, and the men at once dashed upon the escort.

Taken completely by surprise, these made but a poor fight of it. Several were shot down at once. The vicomte, whose head was enveloped in bandages, leapt into the saddle of a horse whose rider had been shot, and, drawing his sword, rode at Desmond, who was making for the door of the carriage. Expecting no such attack, he would have been taken by surprise had not Mike, who saw his danger, shouted a warning, and at the same moment discharged his pistol. The ball struck de Tulle in the forehead, and he fell back dead.

His fall at once put an end to the conflict. The robbers, who had lost some eight of their number, at once turned their horses' heads and rode off at full gallop.

As Desmond drew bridle by the carriage, the door opened, and the baron leapt out.

"By what miracle have you effected our rescue, my dear Monsieur Kennedy?" he exclaimed. "My daughter told me that she saw you and your servant break your way through these brigands, and ride off. She has been suffering an agony of grief for Philip, whom she saw shot. Have you any news of him?"

"None, sir. I, too, saw him fall, but whether he was killed, or only wounded, I am unable to say. I have sent two men to bring him into Moulins, and I trust they will find that he is only wounded."

"My daughter saw you cut down that villain with a terrible blow. We have not seen him since, but we know that he was carried on a horse litter behind the carriage."

"At any rate, he will trouble you no more, Baron. My man shot him through the head, just as he was riding to attack me from behind."

"Thank God! We are saved from further persecutions! And now, tell me how you came to be here."

"It was simple enough, Baron. I found twelve men, with Monsieur de la Vallee's intendant, at Roanne. Philip, who feared that the vicomte would endeavour to make a further effort to repair his fortune, by carrying your daughter off on the road, sent a messenger to his intendant to ride at once, with twelve men, to meet us; and, had all gone well, they would have joined us fully two days' journey north of Nevers. The messenger was attacked on the way, robbed of his letter and purse, and left for dead. He managed to crawl to Nevers, and there, being too weak and ill to sit a horse, he hired a peasant's cart and made the journey, slowly and painfully, to la Vallee. As he knew the purport of the letter, two hours after his arrival there the intendant started, and rode, without drawing bridle, to Roanne. There, by great good fortune, I found them, though men and horses were alike done up. Knowing, however, that the vicomte, in his wounded state, and embarrassed with the coach, could proceed but slowly, I let them have seven hours' sleep, and in the meantime hired fresh horses for them; and we rode that day to Aubusson, and this morning moved down to within five miles of Felletin. I left a man on the road to Pont Gibaut, and he brought us word that you had left the main road, and were travelling through Croc, so we moved at once to intercept you; and you know the rest."

Chapter 7: In Paris Again.

"You have indeed done well, Monsieur Kennedy," the baron said, when Desmond finished his story.

"Now, let us see to my daughter. Her maid is attending on her. She fainted when the fight began. She is not of a fainting sort, but the trials of the last few weeks, and her belief that de la Vallee was killed, have very much upset her."

"No wonder," Desmond said. "It must have been terrible, indeed, to lose her lover, and to know that she was again in the power of that villain.

"And you, Baron; how did you escape the fate that befell the rest of your convoy?"

"We had ridden close up to the tree, when suddenly there was a discharge of firearms. The two men with me fell at once. I was unhurt, but as I turned my horse he fell dead, three bullets having pierced his chest. Before I could recover my feet, the rascals were upon me. They evidently intended to take me alive, for they were provided with ropes, and, binding my arms, hurried me back to the carriage.

"By the time we got there, all was over. My faithful Eustace and the coachman lay dead by the side of the carriage. They had fought stoutly, for three of the brigands lay beside them. Six others were scattered near, and the brigands were gathered round a fallen man, who I guessed was their leader.

"I found Anne in a state of the wildest grief. She told me that she had seen Philip shot by the vicomte, just as he was attacking him, and that you in turn had cut down the villain.

"For half an hour, nothing was done, and then one, who was evidently in authority over the others, left the troop and came up to the carriage.

"'Monsieur le Baron,' he said, 'the orders of my chief are that you are to be placed in the carriage, with your daughter and her maid. If you will give your word of honour that you will not attempt to escape, or to give the alarm as you go along, or to address a word to anyone whom we may encounter, your arms will be freed, and you will be treated with all respect. If, on the contrary, you decline to give this promise, my instructions are that your feet as well as your hands are to be tied, and that you are to be gagged and placed in the bottom of the carriage. You are also to answer for your daughter and her maid; that they, too, neither by word nor gesture, shall attempt to attract the attention of anyone in the villages that we may pass through."

"It was a hard condition, but I had no choice. The idea that I should suffer the indignity of being bound and gagged, like a common malefactor, made my blood boil. I should, in that case, no more be able to give the alarm than if I had been free; therefore I gave the promise, for at least it would be a comfort, to Anne, that I should be with her and able to talk to her.

"We stopped two nights on the road, being lodged at solitary houses on the way. A guard was placed at my chamber door, and another at my window, and even had I not given my word I could not have escaped.

"And now, Monsieur Kennedy, what do you propose?"

"I think, sir, that it would be best that you should start at once, in the carriage, for Pointdexter. Monsieur Philip's intendant and his men will ride as your escort, but I do not think that there is the slightest probability of your being interfered with; for now that the vicomte is dead, these men--who were not, I think, his retainers, but a band of robbers whom he had hired for the occasion--will have no further motive for attacking you.

"I myself shall return to Aubusson, send back the horse on which I rode there, hire another, and make straight for Moulins, where I still hope that I may find Monsieur de la Vallee alive."

"Did you see the vicomte, after you were attacked?"

"No. I heard one of the men tell the fellows who were guarding us that your stroke had cut off one of his ears, and laid his cheek bare from the eye to the chin. I fancy that he was too badly hurt to come to us, but in any case he would not have cared to show himself, in so terrible a plight."

"We must admit that, with all his faults, he was brave," Desmond said; "for, in spite of his pain and weakness, and of the fact that his head was enveloped in bandages, he sprang from his litter, leapt into one of the saddles we had emptied, and, single handed, made for me, until my man cut his career short with a bullet.

"As you go through Croc, it might be well that you should send one of the villagers off to his castle, to tell them that their master is lying dead here, when doubtless they will send out a party to fetch in his body."

By this time, Mademoiselle de Pointdexter had recovered from her faint. She held out her hand to Desmond, as he stood bareheaded beside the door.

"You have rescued me again, Monsieur Kennedy," she said; "for, though life seems worthless to me now, you have saved me from far worse than death. That you have so saved me, for my father's sake as well as my own, I thank you with all my heart."

"I would have you still hope, mademoiselle. We know that Monsieur de la Vallee fell, but many men fall from their horses when wounded, even when the wound is not vital. I am riding at once to Moulins, and trust to find him still alive. Therefore, I pray you do not give up all hope."

"I dare not let myself hope," she said. "It would be but to suffer another blow. Still, I feel that I have so much to be thankful for that, grievous as my sorrow is, I shall try to bear it, with the help of the Holy Virgin."

The party now separated. The baron mounted one of the horses left behind by the brigands, and with the men from la Vallee started for Pointdexter; while Desmond, with Mike Callaghan, rode back to Aubusson.

There they slept for a few hours, and then obtained fresh horses and started for Moulins, where they arrived late in the evening. They alighted at the Soleil, where Desmond had ordered the two men, who had gone on from Roanne, to bring the body of Monsieur de la Vallee.

"The gentleman is not here, sir," the landlord said, as he came to the door. "He was brought into the town by the men sent out by the mayor. As, by his dress, he was evidently a gentleman of quality, they took him straight to the Couronne."

"Was he alive?"

"Yes, sir; but, as I hear, the surgeons are unable to decide yet whether he will live. The men you sent here arrived the day after he was brought in. They told me that you would return, and put their horses here, but they are now in attendance on the wounded gentleman, who, it seems, is their lord."

"Thank God, he is alive!" Desmond exclaimed. "I have news for him that will do more than the surgeons can to restore him to himself."

Leaving Mike to see the horses stabled, he hurried away to the other hotel. He sent up his name, and one of the surgeons came down.

"Monsieur de la Vallee is very ill," he said, "although his wound is not necessarily mortal. This morning we succeeded in extracting the ball, but he is in a terribly weak state. He is unable to speak above a whisper, and does not seem to care to make any effort. It would appear that he even does not wish to live."

"I have news that will put fresh life into him."

"Then by all means go in and see him, sir. We have thought that he is fast sinking; but if the news you bring can rouse him into making an effort to live, he may yet recover. I will go in and give him a strong restorative, and tell him that you are here."

In three or four minutes, he came to the door of the chamber, and beckoned to Desmond to enter.

"The sound of your name has roused him from the lethargy, into which he seemed sinking," he whispered. "When I told him that I could not allow you to enter, until he had taken the draught that I gave him, he swallowed it eagerly."

Desmond went up to the bedside, and took the hand which lay on the coverlet. The pressure was slightly returned, and Philip's lips moved, but he spoke so faintly that Desmond had to lean over him, to hear the words.

"I am glad, indeed, that you are safe and sound. I have been reproaching myself, bitterly, that I should have brought you into this fatal business. As to the rest of it, I dare not even think of it; but I shall die all the easier for knowing that you have escaped."

"I escaped for a good purpose, Philip. I have good news for you. Monsieur le Baron and mademoiselle are on their way to Pointdexter, under the guard of your men."

"Is it possible, Desmond, or are you only saying it to rouse me?"

"Not at all, Philip. You do not suppose that, even for that purpose, I would hold out false hopes to you; or tell an untruth on a matter so vital to your happiness."

Philip's eyes closed, but his lips moved, and Desmond knew that he was returning thanks to God for this unlooked-for news.

"How did it happen?" Philip said, after a silence of some minutes.

His voice was much stronger than before, and there was a faint touch of colour in his cheeks. The surgeon nodded approvingly to Desmond, and murmured, "I think that he will live."

"It is too long a story to tell you in full, now," Desmond said. "Seeing that all was lost, that you were down, and that further resistance was absolutely fruitless, Mike and I cut our way out; the more easily since I had struck down their leader, de Tulle, and most of his band had crowded round him. At Roanne I found your men, who had just arrived there. It matters not now why they had been detained. I got fresh horses for them and rode for Correze, placed an ambush, and turned the tables upon them. Mike shot the vicomte, and we easily defeated his followers, and rescued the baron and his daughter. I sent them to Pointdexter under charge of your intendant and followers, and rode hither, hoping against hope that I might find you still alive. Your two men, who came on here, could have told you that I had escaped."

"I did not allow them to speak to monsieur," the surgeon said, "or even to see him. They are below, greatly grieved at being refused entry; but I told them that any agitation might be fatal to their master, and that they could do nothing for him if they came up; for indeed, up to the time when we extracted the ball, he was unconscious.

"And now, monsieur, I think that it were best you should retire. I shall give Monsieur de la Vallee a soothing draught. A night's rest will be of vital importance to him. And now that you have relieved his mind of the load that has evidently weighed upon him, I think there is little doubt that he will soon fall asleep."

"I will go and have supper," Desmond said, "for I have ridden fifty miles since I last ate, and then it was but a piece of bread with a draught of wine. After that I will, with your permission, return here, and if you tell me that he sleeps, will take my place by his bedside till morning."

"To that I have no objection," the surgeon said. "I and a colleague have, one or other, been with him since he was brought in; and I shall be glad of a rest, myself."

Desmond returned to the Soleil, where he had left Mike. The latter, who had just finished his supper, was delighted to hear that de la Vallee was likely to recover.

After satisfying his own hunger, Desmond returned to the Couronne. He went upstairs, and, taking off his riding boots, stole to the door of his friend's chamber. It stood a little ajar, and, pushing it open noiselessly, he entered.

The surgeon, who was sitting at the bedside, rose at once.

"He is asleep already," he whispered, "and is breathing quietly. I think it likely that he will not stir until tomorrow morning. I shall be here at six. If he wakes, and there is any change, send for me at once."

After he had left the room, Desmond took his place on the fauteuil by the bedside. For a time, he thought over the singular chain of adventures that he had gone through. Gradually, in spite of his efforts, his eyelids drooped. De la Vallee had not moved, and, being dead tired by the exertions of the past four days, he fell into a deep sleep, from which he did not awake until daylight streamed into the room.

Shocked at having thus given way, he looked anxiously at de la Vallee, and was relieved to find that he was lying exactly in the same position, and had evidently slept without once waking. Half an hour later, Philip opened his eyes, looked wonderingly at him, and then said:

"So, it was not all a good dream, Desmond! You are really here, and your news is true?"

"Certainly, it is true, Philip. By this time Mademoiselle de Pointdexter and her father are far on the way home. They were to have travelled on to Argentan, and then through Aurillac, striking the Lozere at Entraigues and proceeding along its banks to Mende, and thence by a road over the hills to Villefort, where they would be twenty miles from Pointdexter. The carriage was to be left behind at their first halting place. Mademoiselle was then to ride, and her maid to be carried behind one of your men, by which means they would travel more than twice as fast as they would do, if encumbered by the carriage. The baron said that he would spare no pains to get home as quickly as possible, and would send a man on, some hours ahead of him, to see that fresh horses were in readiness for the whole party at each town they came to."

"Now tell me all about it, Desmond. I feel another man. Your good news, and a long night's sleep, have done wonders for me. Now, please tell me all about the affair."

Seeing that Philip was so much stronger that he could hear, without being overexcited, the story of the rescue, Desmond related all the details to him.

"You have indeed done wonders," Philip said. "You do not seem to know what fatigue is. How strange that you, whose name I had never heard until ten days back, should have rendered to Baron Pointdexter and myself two such inestimable services.

"And so, after all your exertions and fatigue, you have been keeping watch at my bedside all night?"

"I am ashamed to say that I have not been keeping watch, Philip," Desmond replied with a smile. "I had intended to, but you were sleeping so quietly, and everything was so still, that I went off and slept, as soundly as you have done, until within half an hour of the time when you opened your eyes; but I am sure that I should have awoke at once, had you moved."

"Then I am glad that I did not move, Desmond, for you must sorely need a long sleep, after having passed three days and almost three nights in the saddle."

The surgeons now arrived, and were delighted at the change that had taken place in their patient.

"And when shall I be fit to travel, doctor?"

"Ah, well, we will talk of that in another fortnight's time. You need absolute quiet, for were you to move, before your wound is fairly healed, inflammation might set in, and that would throw you back for a very long time. You have had a very narrow escape, and you are fortunate, indeed, to have got off with only a trifling detention."

"But I might be carried in a horse litter?"

"Certainly not, at present," the surgeon said decidedly. "Possibly, in ten days, you might without danger be so carried, providing they take you in short stages and with easy-paced horses; but I should say that it would be still better, were you to be carried on men's shoulders. There is never any difficulty in hiring men, and you could get relays every eight or ten miles, while it would be difficult to get horses accustomed to such work."

"You don't think that I should be able to ride, doctor?"

"Certainly not in less than a month, probably not in six weeks."

"Then I must be carried," Philip said. "I should work myself into the fever you talk of, if I were to be kept here.

"What are your plans, Desmond?"

"I have not thought of them, yet. At any rate, I shall stay with you till you are well enough to start."

"I could not think of that, Desmond."

"You have no say in the matter, Philip. In the first place, you will get on all the faster for my being with you. In the next place, ten days of my leave are already expired, and were we to go on straight to Pointdexter, I should only have a few days there before starting back for Paris, and I must therefore postpone my visit to some future time. I can stay here ten days, accompany you some four days on your journey, and then turn back again."

"A nice way of spending a month's holiday!" Philip grumbled.

"It will be a holiday that I shall long look back to," Desmond said quietly, "and with pleasure. I do not say that I should not have enjoyed myself at the baron's chateau, for that I should have done; but the adventures that I have gone through will remain in my mind, all my life, as having gained the friendship of yourself, the baron, and his daughter."

"Friendship seems to me too mild a word for it, Desmond. You have earned a gratitude so deep that it will be a pain to us, if we cannot show it in deeds."

"And now, Philip," Desmond said, changing the subject abruptly, "I suppose that you will be, at once, sending off one of your men with the news that you are in a fair way towards recovery. Mademoiselle de Pointdexter is suffering at the thought that you were probably killed. I did my best to give her hope, but without much success. Your two retainers have been fretting greatly that they were not allowed to see you, but I think that now they can be brought up, and you can choose one of them to act as your messenger. He will, of course, ride post, and can arrive at Pointdexter very soon after the baron, if indeed he does not get there first. If he starts at once, and changes horses at each place, he may be there by tomorrow at noon, if not earlier; for it is not more, I believe, than a hundred and twenty miles to Pointdexter. If you will dictate a letter for him to take, I will write it for you."

"It must be a short one," the surgeon said, "just a few words. Monsieur de la Vallee has talked more than is good for him."

Half an hour later the messenger started, carrying a note with a few words from Philip to Anne, and a longer letter from Desmond to the baron. Four days later answers were received. The messenger had arrived at Pointdexter two hours before the travellers reached home, and Anne's joy at the news that, not only was Philip alive, but might in a short time be with her, was deep indeed. The baron wrote to Desmond, as well as to Philip, again expressing the deep gratitude of himself and his daughter, greatly regretting that he should not have the opportunity, at present, of thanking him personally. With the letter the messenger brought a bag of money, concerning which he wrote:

"You have, I know, dear Monsieur Kennedy, expended a considerable sum of money in hiring relays of horses, for yourself and Monsieur de la Vallee's men; and this, of course, is a debt you cannot object to my repaying. Without knowing the exact sum, I have roughly calculated the probable amount, and forward it to you by the messenger who will bring you this letter."

Desmond had no hesitation in accepting the money. The baron had evidently taken considerable pains to calculate the sums that he must have laid out, in order not to hurt his feelings by sending a larger sum than he had spent, for the amount contained in the bag was but a few louis over his disbursements. He at once rode over to Roanne and redeemed his ring, which had proved of more value to him than he had ever anticipated.

At the end of the ten days, Philip was strong enough to walk across the room, and the surgeon gave permission for him to start, if, instead of being carried all the way, he would be taken to Lyons, which was but twenty miles distant, and there take boat down the Rhone to Viviers. Desmond went with him to Lyons, and saw him comfortably bestowed on board a craft going down the river, and there left him in charge of his own retainers. Then, accompanied by Mike, whose wound was now well healed, he rode back to Paris by comparatively easy stages, arriving there on the day before his leave was up. He reported himself to the colonel.

"So you have not been to Pointdexter after all! I received a long letter a week ago from the baron, sent by special messenger, giving me a full account of your doings, which reads like a chapter of romance. He mentioned that he had also written to the king, denouncing the conduct of the Vicomte de Tulle; and stating that, in the fight between his own rescuers and the vicomte's band, the latter was killed, and doing full justice to the part you played in the affair. I had a message from His Majesty yesterday, ordering that you should, as soon as you returned, go at once to

Versailles, in order that he might question you further on the affair.

"I have another piece of news for you. We have received orders to march in three days' time, which is a fortunate circumstance for you, for there can be no doubt that, however gallantly and well you have behaved in this affair, and in whatever light His Majesty may view it, you have incurred the enmity of de Tulle's family and connections, and the air of Paris would not be healthy for you, for a time. I need not say that I have read the baron's letter to your comrades, and that they fully shared with me the admiration I feel at your conduct."

"Had I better start at once for Versailles, sir?"

"I think so. The king is not pleased at being kept waiting. He is sure to ask you when you arrived. You had better take one of my horses. I will order it to be brought round, and shall be at your quarters by the time you have put on your full uniform."

The king had just returned from hunting when Desmond arrived at the palace, and gave his name to one of the ushers. Five minutes later, he was conducted to the king's dressing room.

"This is a serious business, young sir, in which you have been engaged," the king said shortly to Desmond, as he entered.

"I am aware of that, Sire, and yet I am well assured that every officer in Your Majesty's service would have acted as I did, under similar circumstances."

"The Baron de Pointdexter has written to us fully on the matter," the king said, "but we wish to hear the account from your own lips. When did you return to Paris?"

"But two hours since, Sire."

"Then you have lost no time in presenting yourself here. Now, tell us the whole matter, omitting no detail."

Desmond told the story fully. He was interrupted once by the king.

"How was it that Monsieur de la Vallee's people were at Roanne?"

Desmond then related the fears that he and Philip had entertained, lest the vicomte should make another attempt to carry off Mademoiselle Pointdexter, and how, without the baron's knowledge, Philip had sent off a messenger to his intendant for a body of his men to meet them on the way; how the messenger had been intercepted and desperately wounded, and how, in consequence, instead of their being met by the party at Nevers, or north of that town, they had only reached Roanne after the attack had been made on the travellers, near Moulins.

The king asked no more questions, until Desmond finished his story.

"You did well, sir," he then said; "and the conduct of the Vicomte de Tulle was outrageous, and we should have visited him with our heaviest displeasure, had he not already received his deserts. It is intolerable that a noble gentleman, with his daughter, cannot travel along the highroads of our kingdom without being thus assaulted. It was the more scandalous when the vicomte was banished from our court for a similar attempt. The fact that he had enjoyed our favour would in no degree have mitigated--indeed it would have increased--our anger at his conduct, since it would have seemed as if he had relied upon it for immunity for his action. Surely, such a belief would have been an erroneous one. The law must be observed, and the higher placed a man is, the more is he bound to set an example of obedience to it.

"We thank you, sir, for having thwarted so daring and villainous a scheme. We have not yet sent an answer to the Baron de Pointdexter, because we wished your report of the matter before doing so. We shall now cause him to be informed of our indignation at the plot against his person and that of his daughter, and our satisfaction that they have escaped from it.

"You have begun your career well, indeed, young sir. Your regiment is about to start for the frontier. We shall direct your colonel to report to us, from time to time, as to your conduct, and shall see that your promotion is in accordance with your actions, and shall request him to offer you any opportunity that may occur for distinguishing yourself."

Desmond rode back to Paris well satisfied with the result of the interview. He had not been slow in noticing that, although the king's approval of his actions had been warmly expressed in words, there was a certain coldness in the tone in which they were spoken, which showed that, although the king's sense of justice constrained him to praise, he was at heart sore at the death of one who had been a favoured companion in his sports and amusements.

On his return, he found his two friends waiting for him, at his quarters. They gave him a hearty greeting.

"You are a perfect paladin, Kennedy," O'Neil said; "and, though we are all proud of you, we cannot help feeling a little envious that such adventures have all fallen to the lot of our junior ensign. It is evident that, if you were not born with a silver spoon in your mouth, fortune determined to make up in other ways, by giving you such chances as do not fall to the lot of anyone else."

"Yes, I think I have every right to consider myself exceptionally fortunate."

"You may have been fortunate, Kennedy," O'Sullivan remarked. "The thing is, that you took advantage of the opportunities. You threw yourself into the first adventure that came your way, rescued a lovely damsel in distress, and her gratitude and that of her father attracted the king's notice, and gained that ring on your finger. In the next place, after escaping from the ruffians who attacked the coach--principally, as it seems, by cutting down their leader, and so occupying the attention of his followers--you instantly took the resolution to attempt to rescue him and his daughter, and succeeded in doing so. Another man might have stopped at Moulins, congratulating himself that he had escaped from the trap, and lamenting that he could do nothing towards again rescuing this damsel from her abductors. Of course, it was a piece of good fortune, meeting de la Vallee's men at Roanne; but I have no doubt that, if you had not done so, you would still have got to Pointdexter, gathered a force, and intercepted the vicomte's party."

"It would have been a very near thing, O'Sullivan. Changing horse at every post, I might have got to Pointdexter from Roanne in twenty-four hours; but I doubt whether, even allowing that no time was lost in getting the men together, I could have got to Tulle before them. They had but one hundred and fifty miles to travel, I should have had still farther; and, as they would have had three days' start, they should have been there before me; for I heard from the baron that, in addition to the four horses in the coach, they had four others, ridden by troopers, fastened to it where the road was bad."

"What would you have done if they had got to the vicomte's chateau--it is, I believe, a strong place--before you could intercept them?"

"I cannot say what I should have done. I thought the matter over and over again as we rode. It seemed absurd to think of attacking a chateau with only twelve men; and besides, it would have been a very serious business to assault a noble in his own castle. There would almost certainly be twenty or thirty men there, at the least, and the ringing of the alarm bell would have brought all his vassals within five miles round to his aid, at once. I have no doubt that I should have attempted something, but in what way I could form no idea, until I saw the place."

The two young men laughed.

"I believe that you would have succeeded somehow, Kennedy," O'Neil said. "After what you have done, I have an almost unlimited faith in you, and if you told me you could see no other plan than carrying off His Gracious Majesty, and taking him down to Tulle and forcing him to order this rascal vicomte to deliver up his captives, you would accomplish it."

Desmond laughed.

"The plan might be as good as another, though I own that it had not occurred to me; but it would certainly necessitate my having him held prisoner until I had got safely out of France, otherwise my fate would assuredly be to be broken on the wheel."

"Yes; I don't think His Gracious Majesty would have forgiven such an indignity, even if put upon him for a good purpose. It is almost treason even to dream of such a thing."

Desmond laughed.

"It was a purely imaginary case; but you see, not having been accustomed, as you are, to a country where the king is regarded almost as a god, I am afraid I have not that awe of him that is generally entertained here. I have, naturally, a great respect for the king whom I serve, and whose pay is a matter of the greatest importance to me; but after all, although in his service, he is not my lawful king."

"Then you would not even imagine such a thing as to take your lawful king, James, prisoner, however much the fate of someone in whom you were interested was concerned?"

Desmond did not answer at once.

"I don't know," he said at last, "what I should do, in such a case. For King James, as lawful king of my country, I have the deepest respect, and would freely venture my life in his service; but for him as a man, irrespective of his crown, I own that my admiration is not extreme, and that I should not hesitate to join in any plan for putting pressure upon him, on behalf of anyone in whom I was extremely interested, as I certainly am now in Mademoiselle de Pointdexter and Monsieur de la Vallee."

"You are a curious fellow, Kennedy," O'Neil said, with a smile, "and I should be very much puzzled if I were called upon to predict what your fate is likely to be. It seems to me that you have an equal chance of becoming a French marshal, or being broken on the wheel. Here you are, not yet seventeen. You have, as I doubt not, somewhat interfered with the king's plans, and caused him the loss of one of his personal friends. You have twice rescued a noble lady from the hands of her abductors. You have brought disgrace and death upon a member of one of the most powerful families in France. You have earned the gratitude and friendship of one of the leading nobles of Southern France, that of the fiance of his daughter, and of the daughter herself. As soon as this affair spreads abroad, you will be the object of general remark and attention. You have rendered the regiment to which you belong proud of you, its junior ensign, and made Paris emphatically too hot to hold you.

"If all this is done before you are seventeen, what may we expect when another ten years have passed over your head?"

"You had better wait for the ten years to pass, O'Neil," Desmond laughed; "by which time, perhaps, you and O'Sullivan will both have learned wisdom, and will see that, because a man happens to have gone through a very exciting adventure without discredit, it by no means proves him to be anything in the smallest degree out of the way."

Chapter 8: To Scotland.

Two days later the regiment was paraded, but no order had been received for their start, and their destination was still uncertain. The officers stood in a group, awaiting the arrival of the colonel, who entered, accompanied by Colonel Wauchop and several other Irish officers. As there had been no notice of an official inspection, there was a general feeling of surprise at the appearance of the visitors. The colonel rode up to the group of officers.

"Gentlemen," he said, "I must ask you all to accompany me to the common room. I have news of importance to give you."

He and those with him dismounted, and, followed by the wondering officers of the regiment, went into the large room where they gathered in the evening.

"The news that I am about to give you is of an important and happy nature. His Most Gracious Majesty has decided to send an expedition to Scotland, where the whole country is ready to rise in favour of our lawful king."

A cheer broke from his hearers.

"Many Scottish and Irish gentlemen," the colonel went on, "have been selected to accompany it. Among them is my friend, Colonel Wauchop, and the officers with him. The expedition will consist of six thousand French troops. I regret to say that no Irish regiments will accompany it."

A groan of disappointment followed this announcement.

"We must hope," the colonel said, "that Irish troops are not employed, only because it is intended that another expedition will sail to Ireland, in which case we may be sure that some of us will have an opportunity of fighting, again, on our own side of the water. Moreover, between France and Scotland there has long been a close connection and friendship, and the employment of French troops would, therefore, better suit the Scots than would be the case with Irishmen. Another reason perhaps is, the King of France does not like to spare his best troops, when he has sore need of them in Flanders and Spain.

"However, a number of Irish officers will accompany the expedition, for the purpose of drilling and commanding the new levies, for which work they will be far better suited, by their knowledge of English, than French officers would be. Therefore, the various Irish regiments are all to furnish a certain number of lieutenants. Generals Hamilton, Sheldon, Dorrington, and Lords Galmoy and Fitzgerald, and our friend Colonel Wauchop will be in command of the newly-raised force, having with them many Scotch officers now in the service of France.

"The secret of the expedition has been well kept, but I have known it for a fortnight, and have prepared a list of the fifteen officers who are to go. I may say that, in order to avoid partiality, I have, with one exception, selected them by lot. Those who are to go will doubtless consider themselves fortunate. Those who are to stay are still more lucky, if, as I hope, the regiment will form part of a similar expedition sent to Ireland."

He then read out the list of the officers chosen. O'Sullivan and O'Neil were both among them, and the name of Desmond Kennedy was the last read out.

"You will, gentlemen, start in an hour's time, taking the northern road through Montvidier and Arras. In each of these towns you will be joined by officers from other regiments. Colonel Wauchop will accompany you. I do not name the port from which you are to sail, and no word must be said, by you, as to the route you are to travel; but you can no doubt judge for yourselves, by the road that you are taking, what port is your destination. The French troops will be already there, and the fleet is all in readiness.

"You all have horses. You can each take your soldier servant with you, but those who do so must either hire or purchase a horse for him. All further details you will learn from Colonel Wauchop, and the paymaster will have orders to issue two months' pay to each of you, in advance. The distance will be about a hundred and fifty miles, and you will perform it in five days."

Colonel Wauchop then addressed a few words to the officers, all of whom were under the rank of captain.

"Gentlemen," he said, "you have an honourable task before you. For years we have been waiting for the day when our swords might aid to place our king upon the throne. At last it has come. I need not say that the struggle will be a severe one, and that your courage will be taxed to the utmost, but you have proved that in a score of desperate fights.

"The task before you will need tact to no ordinary degree. The Scotch are as peppery a race as the Irish are, and it will be necessary in no way to hurt their feelings, or to excite among them the smallest degree of discontent at being drilled and led by men who are not of their own race.

"And now, as we have much to do before starting, I will leave you to make your arrangements. The rendezvous for us all is in your barrack yard, and at nine o'clock we shall be here."

The colonel now left the room, and the officers eagerly and excitedly talked over the startling news that they had just heard. The greater part of those who had been selected for the service were delighted to go, while the others were equally pleased, at the thought that they might shortly be fighting for King James on the soil of Ireland.

"Sure, your honour, I wish it had been in the ould country instead of Scotland," Mike said, when he heard the news.

"I cannot say that I agree with you, Mike. In Ireland, we should find tens of thousands of brave hearts ready to join us, but they are unarmed, undrilled, and undisciplined, and would be of comparatively slight assistance to us against the English troops. Defeat would bring down fresh persecutions, fresh confiscations, and greater misery upon the land."

"Sure we would beat them, your honour."

"We might, Mike; but you must remember that we failed to do so, even when the people were armed. No doubt we shall take a certain amount of muskets and ammunition with us, but the power of England is more assuredly fixed in Ireland now than it was then--the influence of the old Irish families is broken, and even if we armed all who joined us, it would be but an armed rabble and not an army.

"In Scotland it is altogether different. The Scottish clans would join us under their chiefs, to whom they give absolute obedience, and they would turn out armed and ready for action. Thus, then, I think that, allowing that Ireland is as loyal as Scotland, the choice has been a wise one."

"Sure, you know best, your honour; but I will warrant that as soon as Scotland rises, Ireland will be in a blaze from one end to the other."

"That may well be, Mike; but there will then be a chance of success, since the English forces will be fully occupied by our descent in the north, which will threaten London, while Ireland can be left to itself until the main question is settled."

"It is mighty lucky, your honour, that I should have stuck to the horse we got when we rescued Miss Pointdexter."

"I am very glad, too, Mike, for otherwise I should have had to buy one, and it is likely enough that I may want all the money I have, before this campaign that we are starting upon is over."

O'Neil and O'Sullivan, at this moment, burst into the room.

"It is glorious that we three should all be going, Kennedy!" the latter exclaimed. "It is just your luck, for you are the only ensign named, while the regiment will be left with only four lieutenants. Of course, I should be still better pleased if we were going to Ireland. Still, for anything we know that expedition may not come off, and, so that we are fighting for the king, it's all one whether it is in Scotland or at home."

Having seen that all was ready for departure, Desmond went to the colonel's quarters to say goodbye. Several of the officers who were going were already there, and the colonel motioned to him to stay until they had left. When they had done so, he said:

"Perhaps you guessed, Kennedy, that you were the one exception I mentioned to the rule I adopted, of fixing by lot upon those who were to go."

"No, indeed, sir," Desmond said, in surprise; "I thought it an extraordinary piece of good fortune that I should be the only ensign to go, when there were so many others all senior to me. Indeed, I thought for a moment of saying that I would resign, in favour of one who was older and more experienced than myself; but then it struck me that if I did, some of the junior lieutenants might feel themselves obliged to do the same, in favour of their seniors."

"I should not, in any case, have permitted a change to be made. I had decided that, in order to avoid jealousy, chance should decide the matter. Indeed, you are the only ensign going with the expedition. I informed Colonel Wauchop and General Hamilton of the reason for which I specially included you.

"So long as it was supposed that the regiment was on the point of marching to

Spain, I considered that, if you took my advice and did not leave the barracks after nightfall, no harm would befall you. But the case is altered, now that it may remain here for some time, for no doubt it will take part in any expedition sent to Ireland. I have heard, within the past forty-eight hours, that the friends of de Tulle have made very strong representations to the king. They have urged that your proceedings, involving what they call the murder of their kinsman, were of the nature of civil war; and that, if his conduct had been reprehensible, it was for the Baron de Pointdexter to lay the matter before His Majesty and ask for redress.

"I hear, however, the king received their remonstrances coldly, told them that de Tulle had brought his fate upon himself, that it was the duty of every gentleman to endeavour to rescue a lady, so feloniously carried off, and that he approved of the readiness and energy with which you had taken steps to do so.

"On finding, then, that they have failed in their hope of having you sent to one of the royal prisons, from which you would probably never have come out alive, I have no doubt whatever that these people will endeavour to take the matter into their own hands, and that, with the means at their disposal, they will find no difficulty in procuring persons who would undertake to assassinate you. As I have said, if you had at once started for the army, we might have looked after your safety until you crossed the frontier, but here in Paris you would not be safe for an hour, and could scarce venture between the barracks and your lodging, unless under a strong guard. Under such circumstances, I consider that I was justified in placing you on the list of the officers who would accompany the expedition.

"I explained to General Hamilton and Colonel Wauchop, who both happened to be with me, my reasons for wishing to include so young an officer in the ranks of those selected for the service. The officers heartily agreed with me, having, of course, heard the story, or, at any rate, the main facts of your rescues of Mademoiselle de Pointdexter."

"I am indeed greatly obliged to you, Colonel. I know that it is a dangerous thing to incur the enmity of one of those powerful families, and, though I should certainly have taken every precaution in my power, I felt that I should be in constant danger until we fairly embarked upon a campaign."

At nine o'clock the party started. It numbered some fifty officers, Scotch and Irish. The baggage had started half an hour before. It was to join the carts, with the baggage of the other officers, outside the northern gates; and was under an escort of dragoons, whose officer had powers given him to requisition fresh horses at each town through which he passed, and so to push on to the port with but two halts.

Once off, there was no longer any necessity for keeping their destination a secret, and the officers were informed that, as they had already guessed, Dunkirk was the harbour from which they were to sail.

The journey was a pleasant one. All were in the highest spirits. A short distance behind them marched a body of infantry, composed entirely of noncommissioned officers, of whom O'Brien's regiment furnished thirty. All were picked men, and, marching each day as far as the party of officers rode, arrived at Dunkirk on the fifth day after starting, and were at once embarked on the ships of war.

Colonel Wauchop and the officers of O'Brien's regiment were told off to the Salisbury, which was a ship that had been taken from the English, and was now loaded with military stores, arms, and munitions for the use of those who were expected to join them on landing. After seeing that the officers were all properly accommodated, the colonel went ashore, and when he returned it was at once seen, by the expression of his face, that something was wrong.

"I have very bad news," he said. "King James, who arrived here two days ago, has been taken suddenly ill, and until he is partially recovered we cannot sail, for it is absolutely necessary that he should be with us. This may mean the delay of a week or ten days, and may defeat all our arrangements. The English Government have spies here, as well as elsewhere; and their fleet has, for the last week, been hovering off the coast. They may not have known the purpose of the assembly of troops here, for this has been kept strictly secret; and few even of the French officers of the expedition knew, until they arrived here, for what reason the regiments had been ordered to Dunkirk. But the arrival of King James, of course, showed what was the intention, and, as soon as the news reaches London, you may be sure that the English fleet will be sent to intercept us."

It was, indeed, ten days before James was sufficiently recovered to be embarked--a delay which probably cost him his kingdom, for there can be no doubt that, on landing, he would have been joined at once by all the great clans, and by no small proportion of the able-bodied men of the country.

The consequences were so evident, to all engaged in the expedition, that despondency took the place of the enthusiasm with which they had embarked. The fact that the expedition, after being so carefully and secretly prepared, should at its outset meet with so serious a misfortune, was considered an omen of evil. At last, however, James embarked, under a salute by the guns of the ships of war; and as the sails were hoisted and the anchors weighed, the spirits of all again rose.

They had sailed but a few miles when it became evident that the Salisbury was the slowest ship in the fleet, for, although she had every stitch of canvas set, she lagged behind the rest, and the other vessels were obliged to lower some of their sails, in order to allow her to keep up with them.

"I begin to think, Kennedy," O'Neil said, "that the good fortune that has hitherto attended you has spent itself. O'Sullivan and I both regarded it as a good omen that you should be the one ensign selected to go with us, but this miserable delay at Dunkirk, and the fact that we are on board the slowest tub in the fleet, seems to show that Dame Fortune is no longer going to exercise herself in your favour."

"It looks like it, indeed," Desmond agreed. "Still, I can't hold myself responsible for either the king's illness, or for our being allotted to this heavy-sailing craft; and, perhaps, even if fortune should not favour me any longer, she will do something for some of the others.

"She has always been favourable to Colonel Wauchop. He has been through innumerable engagements. Though many times wounded, he has never been seriously so, though scores of other officers have fallen in enterprises in which he has taken part. In his case, fortune has not been fickle, and, as he is the chief officer on board, we must hope that she has not deserted him on this occasion. I think there is a certain amount of luck in the fact that we carry a large amount of guns and ammunition. If that had not been the case, it is likely that, rather than delay, the squadron would sail on at full speed, and have left us to follow as best we might."

A constant watch was maintained at the masthead of the ship, but no signs were seen of the English fleet, until, on the 23rd of March, six days after sailing, they reached the mouth of the Firth of Forth, and were congratulating themselves that they had brought the voyage to a successful termination.

At daybreak next morning, however, just as they were about to enter the estuary, they beheld the masts of a great fleet coming out to meet them. This was the squadron of Sir George Byng, which had for some days been on the coast, having been despatched as soon as the news reached London of the gathering of ships and troops at Dunkirk, and of the arrival of the Pretender there. The French admiral at once signalled to all the ships to put about, and he lay off until the English fleet were near enough to discern its composition, which was far superior in force to his own. Seeing the impossibility of landing the troops and stores, and the slight chances of success in giving battle, he hoisted the signal for all to make their way back to Dunkirk, keeping as much as possible together, in order to defend themselves if overtaken, or if intercepted by another hostile fleet.

In vain, James begged that a few boats might be given him, with which to land with his chief followers. The French admiral replied that his instructions would not justify him in doing so, and that he had been ordered to specially protect the person of the young king, whose safety was of the highest concern to his sovereign.

It was with the deepest feeling of disappointment, and depression, that the Scotch and Irish officers heard that it was determined to sail for Dunkirk again. Had the troops on board the ships been of their own nationality, they would have ordered them to disobey the admiral's commands, and to insist upon the fleet, if it succeeded in evading the pursuit of the enemy, making another effort to effect a landing. As, however, all the soldiers were French, with the exception of the two or three hundred noncommissioned Irish officers, they were powerless, and were half mad with rage and grief.

"This looks bad for us," O'Sullivan said gravely to his two friends. "I think that the French ships will outsail the English, but there is little chance that this unwieldy craft will do so; in which case, my friends, it is likely that we shall all see the inside of an English prison, and that probably not a few of us will be executed. The colonel should be safe, for he came over with the Brigade after Limerick, and therefore by that treaty was allowed to enter the service of France; but it is different with the rest of us. We have all joined since those days, and are therefore not covered by the treaty, and so are liable to be tried as traitors."

O'Neil shrugged his shoulders.

"Well, we knew that when we joined," he said. "However, I hardly think they are likely to proceed to such an extremity. Very many of our Brigade have been taken prisoners, at Blenheim and other places, and they have always had the same treatment as other prisoners of war."

"That may be," O'Sullivan replied; "but this is a different matter. It is not a question of war on foreign soil. We were going to attack the throne of Anne, to promote civil war, and to overthrow the Government. The attempt once made can be made again, and you may be sure that the news of our sailing has created a tremendous scare throughout the country. However, we are in for it, and there is no use grumbling against fate. Already, you see, the rest of the fleet are leaving us--faster, I think, than the English fleet are gaining on us--and I trust they will get safely away into Dunkirk.

"The fact that we so nearly succeeded will, perhaps, act as an inducement to Louis to renew the expedition; and the loss of a colonel, fifteen lieutenants, and thirty noncommissioned officers will not seriously affect anyone except ourselves."

"However," Desmond put in, "I think that, after all, things may not be as bad as you think. In the first place, our execution would have an extremely bad effect in Scotland and Ireland, and would add to the general hostility to the present Government. In the next place, Louis has many English prisoners in his hands, and might threaten reprisals. Lastly, there is always a chance of escape."

"Your first two arguments are good, Kennedy," O'Neil said, "but I cannot say as much for the last. The chances of escape from an English prison must be small indeed."

"Nevertheless there must always be chances," Desmond said. "If you will take my advice you will at once go below, and conceal your money."

"Where are we going to conceal it?" O'Sullivan said. "You may be sure that we shall be searched."

"Well, you took my advice, in changing the silver in which you were paid into gold, though you lost pretty heavily by the transaction. We did it to prevent lugging about a heavy bag of silver. Now, it has its advantages. You could not hope to conceal silver, but we may, at least, hide a few pieces of gold. Mike is a handy fellow, and I have no doubt will be able to help us. At any rate, let us go below and see what can be done."

Mike was summoned to the cabin.

"Now, Mike," Desmond said, "I suppose, in a campaign, a good many of you carry what money you may have about you, and I dare say some of you hide it so that, if you are taken prisoners, you may have means of adding to your prison fare."

"We do, your honour; and, by the same token, I have a score of crowns in between the soles of my boots. It does not always succeed, for if your boots happen to be good, the chances are that someone takes a fancy to them. Still, on the whole, that is the best place there is, for they are sure to feel all the lining of your clothes."

"Well, we want to hide some gold, Mike. In another hour we shall have the English within shot of us, and, of course, fighting is out of the question. Do you think that you will have time to hide a dozen gold pieces in each of our boots?"

Mike looked doubtful.

"To do the thing properly, your honour, one should take off the lower sole, take some leather out of the upper one, put some money in, and then sew it up again; but it would take more than an hour to do one pair."

He thought for a moment.

"The quickest way would be to get out the inside lining of the sole, then to cut out enough leather for the money to lie in, then to put in the lining again. It would not be soft walking on a twenty-mile march, but I think, if I get the lining in tight, with a few little nails to keep it from dropping out, if anyone takes the trouble to turn the boots upside down, I might manage it."

"Well, let us commence at once, then, Mike. We have all got riding boots, and can put them on before we are taken prisoners. Do you take the linings out, as you say, and then we will help to cut out some of the leather of the upper sole."

They were quickly at work. Mike cut out enough of the thin lining to admit of a hole being made, large enough to hold ten louis in each boot, and he and the two officers then set to work, to cut out a sufficient depth of leather for the coins to lie side by side. Half an hour sufficed for this.

The coins were put in. Mike had, in the meantime, obtained a handful of pitch and melted it at the galley fire. This he ran in over the gold, and then replaced the pieces of lining with hot pitch.

"There, your honours," he said, when he had finished. "I call that a neat job, and it would be hard, indeed, if the spalpeens find that there is anything amiss. And, with these heavy boots, the extra weight won't betray that there is anything hidden.

"Don't put them on till the last moment. Give them time to cool, for if any of it oozes out, you will stick your stockings so tight to it that you won't get your foot out without laving them behind."

Leaving their high boots in the cabin, the three young men went on deck. The leading vessel of the British fleet was not more than a mile astern, while the French fleet was three miles ahead, having gained more than a mile since the chase began. Mike had been given four louis, which he said he could hide in his mouth.

Five minutes later, there was a puff of smoke from their pursuer's bow. The ball struck the water close to them.

"Shall I hold on, Colonel?" the captain of the ship asked Colonel Wauchop.

"There is no use in your doing so. That ship will be alongside in an hour, and it might only cause a useless loss of life were we to keep on. If she were alone I should say, let her come alongside, and with your crew and our officers and men we might, if we had luck, take her by boarding; but, with the whole fleet close behind us, it would be madness to think of such a thing, as we have but twelve guns, and those of small weight."

Accordingly, the topsails were run down, and the courses brailed up, and the ship lay motionless till the English frigate came up. Signals had been exchanged between the English vessels, and as they came along six of them dropped boats, each with some twenty men in it. While these rowed towards the prize, the fleet pressed on, under all canvas, in pursuit of the French squadron.

The English officer in command of the boats received the swords of the French officers, and the noncommissioned officers were all sent below into the hold. All sail was at once got on to the vessel again, and she followed in the wake of the fleet. The English lieutenant then took the names of the prisoners.

"You are all Irish," he said, seriously. "I am sorry, gentlemen, that this should be so, for I fear that it will go harder with you than if you were French, when, of course, you would be merely prisoners of war."

"We should be prisoners of war, now," Colonel Wauchop said. "We are in the service of the King of France, and were but obeying his orders, along with our French comrades."

"I hope they may see it in that light, in London," the officer said courteously; "but I doubt whether, at the present moment, they will take a calm view of the subject. However, I hope they will do so, especially as no shot has been fired by you, and they cannot charge you with resisting capture. At any rate, gentlemen, I will do my best to make you comfortable while you are under my charge. I must ask a few of you to shift your quarters, so as to make room for me and the three officers with me; beyond that you will continue, as before, to use the ship as passengers."

When darkness set in, the pursuit was discontinued. The French fleet was fully ten miles ahead, and it was evident that there was no chance, whatever, of overtaking it; while there was a risk of its doubling back during the night, and again making its way north. The greater part of the sails of the men-of-war were therefore furled, while the frigates and corvettes made off, on either hand, to establish themselves as sentries during the night, and to give warning should the French fleet be seen returning. An hour and a half after the pursuit had ceased, the Salisbury joined the fleet, and the officer in command went on board the admiral's ship, to report the number of prisoners taken and the nature of her cargo.

The officers had, at his invitation, dined with him and his officers in the cabin. All political topics had been avoided, and no one who had looked in would have supposed that the majority of those present were the prisoners of the others. The Irish temperament quickly shakes off a feeling of depression, and the meal was as lively as it had been during the voyage north.

The lieutenant, however, omitted no precaution. A dozen men kept guard over the prisoners below, and as many more, with loaded muskets, were always stationed on deck. The Irish officers saw that, among many of the sailors, there was a strong feeling of sympathy with them. The fleet had been largely recruited by impressment; and by the handing over, to the naval authorities, of numbers of men imprisoned for comparatively slight offences; and, as was natural, these had but small feeling of kindness towards the government who had so seized them; while many shared in the feeling of loyalty towards the house of Stuart, which was still so prevalent among the population.

At daybreak, the cruisers all returned. None had seen any signs of the French squadron, and Sir George Byng, leaving the majority of the fleet to maintain watch, sailed with his prize for Harwich. Here the prisoners were handed over to the military authorities; while the admiral started for London, in a post chaise, to carry the news of the failure of the French to effect a landing, and of their return to Dunkirk,-

-news that was received with exuberant delight by the supporters of Government, and the commercial portion of the population, who had been threatened by ruin. The run upon the banks had been unprecedented, and although the House of Commons had relaxed the regulations of the Bank of England, the panic was so great that it could not have kept its doors open another twelve hours.

The treatment of the prisoners was now very different from what it had been on board ship. Not only were they confined to prison, but, to their indignation, irons were placed on their legs, as if they had been common malefactors. The only mitigation allowed to them was that their servants were permitted to attend upon them. Their clothes had been rigorously searched, and their boots taken off, but no suspicions had been entertained that coin had been hidden in those of Desmond and his friends.

Two days later an order was received from Government, and the officers were marched up to town, ironed as they were, under a strong guard, and were imprisoned at Newgate. Callaghan and the other servants remained in prison at Harwich.

"Things are looking bad, Kennedy," O'Neil said dolefully, for the three officers had, at their own request, been allotted a cell together.

"They don't look very bright, but we must make allowance for the awful fright that, as we hear, has been caused by the expedition. Possibly, when they have got over the shock, things may be better."

"I will never forgive them for putting irons on us," O'Sullivan said passionately. "If they had shot us at once, it was, I suppose, what we had a right to expect; but to be treated like murderers, or ruffians of the worst kind, is too bad."

"Well, we were rid of the irons as soon as we got here. No doubt these were only put on to prevent the possibility of any of us escaping. I am sure, by their looks, that some of our escort would willingly have aided us, only that it was impossible to do so; and, knowing how large a number of persons would sympathize with us, I cannot blame them so very much for taking steps to prevent our escape."

"I never saw such a fellow as you for finding excuses for people," O'Sullivan said, almost angrily. "You look at things as calmly as if they concerned other people, and not ourselves."

Kennedy smiled.

"If an opinion is to be worth anything, O'Sullivan, it must be an impartial one; and it is best to look at the matter calmly, and to form our plans, whatever they may be, as if they were intended to be carried out by other people."

O'Sullivan laughed.

"My dear fellow, if you had not gone through those adventures, I should have said that you had mistaken your vocation, and were cut out for a philosopher rather than a soldier. However, although your luck did not suffice to save the Salisbury from capture, we must still hope that it has not altogether deserted you; and anyhow, I am convinced that, if it be possible for anyone to effect an escape from this dismal place, you are the man."

Newgate, in those days, stood across the street, and constituted one of the entrances to the city. Its predecessor had been burnt, in the great fire of 1666, and the new one was at this time less than forty years old, and, though close and badly ventilated, had not yet arrived at the stage of dirt and foulness which afterwards brought about the death of numbers of prisoners confined there, and in 1750 occasioned an outbreak of jail fever, which not only swept away a large proportion of the prisoners, but infected the court of the Old Bailey close to it, causing the death of the lord mayor, several aldermen, a judge, many of the counsel and jurymen, and of the public present at the trials.

The outward appearance of the building was handsome, but the cells were, for the most part, small and ill ventilated.

"This place is disgraceful," O'Neil said. "There is barely room for our three pallets. The air is close and unwholesome, now, but in the heat of summer it must be awful. If their food is as vile as their lodging, the lookout is bad, indeed."

"I fancy the cells in the French jails are no better," O'Sullivan said. "No doubt, in the state prisons, high-born prisoners are made fairly comfortable; but the ordinary prisoners and malefactors, I have been told, suffer horribly. Thank goodness I have never entered one; but even the barrack cells can scarcely be called inviting."

"You are learning philosophy from Kennedy," O'Neil said, with a laugh.

"I don't know that I shall feel philosophic, if we are served with nothing but bread and water. However, the turnkey told us that, until we have been tried and condemned, we are at liberty to get our food from outside--certainly a mockery, in most cases, considering that we all were relieved of any money found upon us, when we arrived in Harwich. It is a comfort that we are, as he said, to take our meals together, and the money we have in our boots will alleviate our lot for some time. Probably, it will last a good deal longer than we are likely to be here."

When they joined their companions, in the room in which they were to dine, all were astonished at seeing an excellent dinner on the table, with eight bottles of wine.

"Is this the way they treat prisoners here?" Colonel Wauchop asked one of the jailers, of whom six remained present.

The man smiled.

"No, indeed. It has been sent in from a tavern outside, and with a message that a like meal will be provided, as long as you are here. One of us was sent across, to enquire as to the person who had given the order. The landlord said that he was a stranger to him, but that he had paid him a fortnight in advance, and would call in and renew the order, at the end of that time."

"Well, gentlemen," the colonel said, "before we begin to eat, we will drink the health of our unknown benefactor. Not only is the gift a generous and expensive one, but it cannot be without danger to the donor, for none but a strong adherent of King James would have thought of thus relieving our necessities."

It was plain that the authorities suspected that some message might have been sent in to the prisoners, concealed in the viands. The bread had been cut up into small squares, the crust had been lifted from two pasties, the meat had evidently been carefully searched; and the turnkeys placed themselves round the table so that they could narrowly watch every one of the prisoners, as they ate, and notice any movement that would seem to indicate that they had come across some pellet of paper or other substance.

Every day, the servants at the tavern brought in similar fare, and this continued as long as the prisoners were in the jail; and it was a matter of deep regret, to all, that they were never able to discover the name of the person to whom they were so much indebted.

Chapter 9: An Escape From Newgate.

After being allowed to remain an hour at the table, the prisoners were again marched off to their cells.

"I wish we had Mike with us," Desmond said, as he and his comrades discussed the possibility of escape. "He is a shrewd fellow, and would probably be allowed greater freedom in moving about the prison than we are; but I was sure that we should see no more of him after we left Harwich.

"Of course, the first question is, are we to try bribery, or to work our way out of this cell?"

"I think that it would be dangerous to try bribery," O'Sullivan remarked. "Our turnkey is a sour-faced rascal. I am convinced that, if we were to try to bribe him, he would denounce us at once. Not from any principle, you know, but because he would think that it would pay him better to do so, and so obtain promotion and reward, rather than to accept our money and run the risk of being detected and hanged."

"I don't blame him," O'Neil said. "He is, as you say, a sour-looking rascal, but I don't think that he is a fool, and none but a fool would run that risk for the sake of the money that we could give him; for, in any case, we should have to retain a portion of our store, in order to obtain disguises and maintain ourselves till we could find means of crossing the channel."

"Then let us put that idea altogether aside, O'Neil, and give our whole attention to the manner in which we are to escape."

"The manner in which we are to try to make our escape!" O'Neil repeated, with a laugh.

"Well, put it that way if you like. Now, in the first place, there is the window, in the second the door, and lastly the walls and floor."

"The door would withstand a battering ram," O'Sullivan said. "I noticed, as I went out, that it was solid oak some four inches thick, with two bolts as well as the lock, and, moreover, if we could get through it we should be no nearer escaping than we are at present. What with the corridors and passages, and the turnkeys and the outer gate, that course seems to me impossible.

"Let us come to the second point, the window."

They looked up at it. The sill was fully six feet from the ground. The window was a little over a foot wide, with a heavy bar running down the centre, and cross bars.

"The first point is to see where it looks out on," Desmond said. "I will stand against the wall, and as you are the lighter of the two, O'Neil, you can stand on my shoulder and have a good look out, and tell us what you see.

"Give him your hand, O'Sullivan.

"Put your foot on that, O'Neil, and then step on my shoulder."

O'Neil was soon in his place.

"You need not hold me," he said. "The wall is very thick, the bars are placed in the middle, and there is just room for me to take a seat on the edge, then I can see things at my ease."

He sat looking out, for a minute or two, before he spoke.

"Well, what can you see?" O'Sullivan asked, impatiently.

"This room is on the outer side of the prison," he said. "I noticed, as we came in, that it was built along on both sides of the gate; and, no doubt, this side stands on the city wall."

"Then what do you see?"

"I see the ground, sloping steeply down to a stream that runs along the bottom of it. There are a good many small houses, scattered about on the slope and along by the stream. Over to the left, there is a stone bridge across it. Near this is a large building, that looks like another prison, and a marketplace with stalls in it. Houses stand thickly on either side of the road, and beyond the bridge the opposite side of the slope is covered with them. Among these are some large buildings.

"If we were once out, there would not be much chance of our being detected, if we had something to put over our uniforms; but, of course, they would betray us to the first man we met."

"Yes, of course," O'Sullivan said; "but we might possibly obtain plain clothes at one of those small houses you speak of, though that would be risky."

"We might leave our coatees behind us, and go only in our shirts and breeches; and give out that we had been attacked, and robbed of our money and coats by footpads," Desmond said.

"That is a good idea," O'Neil agreed. "Yes, that might do, especially as, after dark, they would not be likely to notice that our breeches were of a French cut."

"But it seems to me that we are beginning at the wrong end of the business. It is of no use discussing what we are to do, when we escape, till we have settled upon the manner in which we are to get out. Let us talk over that first.

"Are the bars firmly in, O'Neil?"

O'Neil tried, with all his strength, to shake them.

"They are as firm as the walls," he said. "There is no getting them out, unless we have tools to cut away all the stonework round them."

"I suppose there is no chance of cutting through them?" O'Sullivan asked.

"There is not," O'Neil said. "We have not got such a thing as a knife about us. If we had, we could never saw through these thick bars; it would take a year of Sundays."

"You are rather a Job's comforter. Now, do you get down, and let Kennedy and myself have a chance of a breath of fresh air, to say nothing of the view."

A few minutes satisfied O'Sullivan, but Desmond, when he took his place, sat there considerably longer; while the other two, throwing themselves on their pallets, chatted gaily about Paris and their friends there.

"Well, what conclusions do you arrive at?" they asked, when he leapt down from his seat.

"They are not very cheering," he replied, "and I recognize fully that we cannot possibly make our escape, without aid from without."

"That is the same as to say that we cannot make our escape at all."

"Not exactly. We have found one unknown friend, who supplied us with our dinners. There is no absolute reason why we should not find one who would supply us with means of escape. There must be a great number of people who sympathize with us, and whose hearts are with King James. I have seen several men come from the market, stand and look up at this prison, and then walk off, slowly, as if they were filled with pity for us. Now, I propose that one of us shall always be at the window."

"Oh, that is too much!" O'Sullivan said. "That ledge is so narrow that I could hardly sit there, even holding on by the bars; and as to stopping there half an hour, I would almost as soon be on the rack."

"There will be no occasion for that," Desmond said. "We can easily move one of the pallets under it, pile the other straw beds upon it, and, standing on these, we could look out comfortably, for our shoulders would be well above the ledge."

"I don't see that we should be nearer to it, then, Kennedy."

"We should have gained this much: that directly we saw any person looking up, with a sympathizing air, especially if of a class who could afford to do what is necessary for us, we could wave our hands and attract his attention. If disposed to help us, he might give some sign. If not, no harm would be done. We might, too, tie a handkerchief to the bars, which in itself might be taken for an indication that there are followers of the Stuarts here."

"But supposing all this turned out as you suggest it might, how could even the best disposed friend do anything to help us?"

"That is for after consideration. Let us first find a friend, and we shall find a way to open communication with him. We have no paper, but we could write the message on a piece of linen and drop it down. As far as we can see, from here, there is nothing to prevent anyone coming up to the foot of the wall below us."

For the next four days, nothing whatever happened. They could see that the white handkerchief at the bars attracted some attention, for people stopped and looked up at it, but continued their way without making any gesture that would seem to show that they interested themselves, in any way, in the matter.

On the fourth day, Desmond, who was at the window, said in a tone of excitement:

"There is a man down there who, after looking fixedly in this direction, is making his way towards us. He does not come straight, but moves about among the houses; but he continues to approach. I can't make out his face yet, but there is something about him that reminds me of Mike; though how he could be here, when we left him in the prison at Harwich, is more than I can say."

O'Neil and O'Sullivan in turn looked through the window. Not being so much accustomed as he was to Mike's figure and walk, they could not recognize in the man, in the dress of a country peasant, the well-set-up soldier who attended on Desmond. Both admitted, however, that in point of figure it might well be the man.

"If it is," Desmond said, "all our difficulties are at an end, and I will wager that we shall be free in three or four days. Now, how are we to communicate with him?"

"I have a piece of paper in my pocket. It is only an old bill, and they threw it down, contemptuously, when they searched me," O'Neil said. "I picked it up again. I hardly know why, except perhaps that the idea occurred to me that, some day, I might get a chance of paying it. But as we have no ink, nor pen, nor charcoal, I don't see how it can benefit us."

He drew the bill from the pocket of his coatee. Desmond took it, and stood looking at it in silence for a minute. Then an idea occurred to him.

"I have it!" he exclaimed, presently. "O'Neil, see if you can get a piece of this gold wire off my facings. I want it five or six inches long, so that when it is doubled up and twisted together, so as to be an inch long, it will be stiff enough for our purpose."

Somewhat puzzled, O'Neil did as he was requested. Desmond straightened out the fine wire wrapped round the centre thread, doubled, and again doubled it, and finally twisting it together, reduced it to a length of about an inch, and the thickness of a pin. The others looked on, wondering what was his intention.

He held the paper out before him, and began pricking small holes through it, close together. He continued to work for some time, and then held it up to the light. The others understood the nature of his work, and they could now read:

Come ten tonight under window. Bring long thin string. Whistle. We will lower thread. Tie end of string to it. Will give further instructions.

He tore off the portion of the bill on which the message was written, twisted off two of the buttons of his coatee, folded them in the paper, and took his place at the window again. The man who had been watching was standing some sixty feet from the foot of the wall. His back was towards them. Presently he turned, carelessly looked up at the window, and then, as if undecided what to do, took off his cap and scratched his head.

"It is Mike, sure enough," Desmond exclaimed, and, thrusting his hand through the bars, waved it for a moment.

Then, taking the little packet, he dropped it. Mike put on his hat again, turned round, then looked cautiously to see that no one was noticing him, and strolled, in an aimless and leisurely way, towards the wall. Desmond could no longer see him, but felt sure that he would find the missive.

Presently he came in sight again, walking quietly away. He did not look round; but when nearly at the bottom of the hill turned, lifted one hand, and disappeared behind some houses.

"He can't read," Desmond said, "but I have no doubt he will get someone to do it for him."

A vigilant watch was kept up, but nothing was seen of Mike, till late in the afternoon, when he emerged into one of the open spaces. They had now taken the handkerchief down from the window, and, directly they saw him, Desmond waved it, showing that they were watching him. He threw up his arm, turned, and disappeared again.

"He has made out my message," Desmond said. "We may expect him here at ten o'clock."

While he had been watching, his two comrades had, under his instructions, been unravelling a portion of one of their blankets. When enough thread had been obtained, the strands were tied together and doubled, and Desmond had little doubt that it was sufficiently strong to draw up the string Mike would bring with him. He now took another portion of the bill, and pricked upon it the words:

At nine tomorrow night, bring, if possible, fine steel saw, two files, and small bottle of oil. Fasten these to string we will lower with further instructions.

He then opened his coatee, took out some of the white wool with which it was padded, formed this into a loose ball, in the centre of which the note was fastened, and all being in readiness, waited patiently, until, just as the city clock struck ten, they heard a low whistle. The ball had already been attached to the end of the thread, and Desmond at once lowered it down.

Presently, they heard another whistle and, hauling at it again, they found that the ball had gone, and attached to the end of the thread was a very light silken cord, which they drew in. There was another low whistle, and all was silent.

"So far, so good," Desmond said. "We are fairly on our way to liberty. How long do you suppose it will take us to cut through these bars?"

"It would take us a long while to file through them all," O'Neil said, "but with a fine steel saw, I should think that a couple of nights' work should do it. But of course that is mere guesswork, for I have not the least idea how fast even the best saw could cut through iron."

"Well, there is no particular hurry, for we know that no day has been fixed yet for our trial. So, whether it is one night or six, it does not matter much."

On the following evening at nine o'clock the whistle was heard, and another ball lowered down at the end of the string. The instructions this time were:

When we are ready, we will show a handkerchief at window. Bring with you, at nine that evening, rope strong enough to bear us, and have disguises for three ready for us at foot of wall. Herewith are ten louis to purchase three disguises.

The cord brought up a small packet, which contained two very fine small steel saws, two files, and the oil. They did not lose a moment in setting to work, and, oiling the saws, one began to cut through the central bar, just above the point where the lowest cross bars went through it, as they determined to leave these to fasten the rope to. There was not room for two of them to work together, and they agreed to take it by turns, changing every quarter of an hour.

To their great satisfaction, they found that the saw did its work much more quickly than they had expected, and by the time each had had a turn the bar was cut through; and by morning the side bars had also all been cut. They did not attempt to cut the main bar higher up, as, had they done so, it would have been difficult to keep the portion cut out in its place.

When it was light, they filled up all the cuts with bread, which they had managed to secrete in the palms of their hands at dinner. This they kneaded into a sort of putty, rolled it in the dust of the floor until black, and then squeezed it into the interstices.

"There is no fear of their noticing it," O'Neil said, when they had finished. "I cannot see the cuts myself from the floor, though I know where they are; and unless they were to climb up there, and examine the place very closely, they would not see anything wrong."

"Shall we hang out the flag today, Kennedy?"

"I think we had better wait till tomorrow. He will be hardly expecting to see it, today, and may not be ready with the rope and disguises."

The next morning the signal was hung out. They saw nothing of Mike, but as he would be able to make out the handkerchief from a considerable distance, they had no doubt whatever that he had observed it, but thought it prudent not to show himself near the prison again. As soon as it was dark they recommenced work, and had cut through the main bar, and cautiously lowered the grating to the ground, before the clock struck nine. Then, on hearing Mike's signal, they lowered the cord, and soon brought up a rope which, although small, was more than strong enough to support them.

"We had better tie some knots in it," Desmond said. "They will help us to avoid sliding down too rapidly. If it was a thick rope, I think we could manage without them; but, not being sailors, I do not think that we could grasp this tightly enough."

"How close shall we put them, Kennedy?"

"About two feet apart. Then we can come down hand over hand, helping our arms by twisting our legs round it.

"Now," he went on, when they had finished the knots, "who will go down first?"

"You had better do so," O'Sullivan said. "You are the lightest of us, and, I fancy, the strongest, too."

"Very well. I don't think that it will make any difference, for the rope is strong enough to hold the three of us together. However, here goes. We may as well leave our coatees behind us. They might get us into difficulties, if we took them."

So saying, he took off his coat, fastened the end of the rope securely to the bars that had been left for the purpose, and, holding it firmly, made his way through the opening and swung himself over. With his muscles strengthened by military exercises and sword practice, he found it easier work than he had expected. The depth was some sixty feet, and in a couple of minutes his feet touched the ground.

Mike had been hanging on by the rope to steady it, and as Desmond descended, he seized him by the hand and shook it enthusiastically, murmuring brokenly, "My dear master, thank God that you are free!"

"Thanks to you also, my dear fellow. Now, hold on again. My friends O'Neil and O'Sullivan shared my cell with me, and are following me."

He added his weight to that of Mike, and it was not long before O'Neil came down; but not so quietly as Desmond had done, for his strength had failed him, and the rope had slipped rapidly through his fingers, and Mike and Desmond narrowly escaped being knocked down by the suddenness with which the descent was made. He stood for a minute, wringing his hand, and swearing in an undertone in English, Irish, and French.

"By the powers," he said, "it has taken the skin off the inside of my hands, entirely! A red-hot poker could not have done it more nately!

"Mike, you rascal, what are you laughing at? I have a mind to break your bones before thanking you."

O'Sullivan succeeded better, but was completely exhausted when he joined his friends.

"Now, Mike, where are the disguises?"

"Here they are, your honour. They are just like my own. Loose coats, rough breeches, white stockings and buckled shoes, and soft hats with wide brims. I thought that you would pass better, like that, than in any other way; for if you were dressed up as citizens, your tongues might betray you, for somehow they don't speak English as we do; and whenever I open my mouth, they discover that I am an Irishman."

Desmond laughed.

"There would be no difficulty about that. Now, let us put on our disguises at once, and be off. Sometimes the turnkeys take it into their heads to look in during the night, and we had to keep one on watch while we were at work, and take to our beds when we heard a footstep approaching.

"I see you have brought shoes. I forgot to mention them. Our jack boots would have attracted attention, so we have left them behind us, after getting our stores of money from their hiding places."

They were soon dressed.

"What are we supposed to be, Mike?"

"You are sedan chair men, sir. Most of the chairs are carried by Irishmen, who seem to be stronger in the leg than these London folk. You will have to cut your hair short, and then you will pass without observation."

"Where are you taking us to?" Desmond asked, as they descended the hill.

"I have got a lodging in a house out in the fields. I said that I was an Irishman who had come to London in search of employment, and that I expected three friends to join me, and that we intended to hire chairs and carry the gentry about, for here they seem too lazy to walk, and everyone is carried; though it is small blame to them, for dirtier streets I never saw. They are just full of holes, where you go in up to the knee in mud and filth of all kinds. Faith, there are parts of Paris which we can't say much for, but the worst of them are better than any here, except just the street they call Cheapside, which goes on past Saint Paul's, and along the Strand to Westminster."

"What have you brought these sticks for, Mike?"

For he had handed, to each, a heavy bludgeon.

"Sure, your honour, 'tis not safe to be in the streets after nightfall. It is like that part of Paris where no dacent man could walk, without being assaulted by thieves and cutthroats. Dressed as we are, it is not likely anyone would interfere with us in the hope of finding money on us, but they are not particular at all, at all, and a party of these rascals might try to roll us in the mire, just for fun. So it is as well to be prepared."

However, they met with no interruption, passed out through Holborn Bars, and soon arrived at the house where Mike had taken a lodging. They were not sorry, however, that they were armed, for, several times, they heard outbursts of drunken shouting and the sound of frays.

Mike had hired two rooms. In one of these were three straw beds, for the officers. He himself slept on a blanket on the floor of the other room, which served as kitchen and sitting room.

Now, for the first time, they were able to talk freely.

"Mike, we have not said much to you, yet," Desmond began, "but I and these gentlemen are fully conscious that you have saved us from death, for we hear that Government is determined to push matters to the extremity, and to have all the officers captured condemned to be hanged."

"Bad cess to them!" Mike exclaimed, indignantly. "If I had two or three of them, it's mighty little they would talk of execution, after I and me stick had had a few minutes' converse with them.

"As to the getting you out, I assure you, your honour, there is little I have done, except to carry out your orders. When I first saw the prison, and the little white flag flying from the window, I said to myself that, barring wings, there was no way of getting to you; and it was only when I got your first letter that I saw it might be managed. Faith, that letter bothered me, entirely. I took it to the woman downstairs, and asked her to read it for me, saying that I had picked it up in the street, and wondered what it was about. She was no great scholar, but she made out that it was writ in a foreign language, and seemed to her to be a bit of an old bill. When I took it up to my room, I looked at it every way. I knew, of course, that it was a message, somehow, but devil a bit could I see where it came in.

"I fingered it for an hour, looking at it in every way, and then I saw that there were some small holes pricked. Well, I could not ask the woman what they meant, as I had told her I picked it up; so I went across to an Irishman, whose acquaintance I had made the day before, and who had recommended me, if I wanted work, to hire one of these chairs and get a comrade to help me carry it. I could see that he was a man who had seen better days. I expect he had come over in the time of the troubles, and had been forced to earn his living as he could; so I went to him.

"'I have got a message,' I said, 'pricked on a piece of paper. I picked it up, and am curious-like to know what it is about.'

"So he held it up to the light, and read out your message.

"'I think,' says he, 'it is some colleen who has made an appointment with her lover. Maybe she has been shut up by her father, and thought it the best way to send him a message.'

"'That is it, no doubt,' says I; 'and it is plain that it never came to his hand.'

"The next day, I went to him again with the second letter.

"'It's lying you have been to me,' he said. 'It is some plot you are concerned in.'

"'Well,' says I, 'you are not far wrong. I have some friends who have suffered for the Stuarts, and who have been laid by the leg, and it's myself who is trying to get them out of the hands of their persecutors.'

"'In that case, I am with you,' he said, 'for I have suffered for the cause myself; and if you want assistance, you can depend upon me.'

"'Thank you kindly,' says I. 'Just at present it is a one man job, but maybe, if I get them out, you will be able to give us some advice as to how we had best manage.'

"So that is how it stands, your honour."

"And now, tell us how you got away, Mike. You may guess how surprised we were, when we first made you out, believing that you were safe under lock and key at Harwich."

"The matter was easy enough," Mike said. "It took me two or three days to get to understand the position of the place, with water all round it except on one side; and it was plain that, if I were to start running, it is little chance I should have if I did not hit upon the right road. Luckily, they were mounting some cannon the day after you were taken away. We were ordered to go out and lend a hand, so it was not long before I learnt enough to know which road I ought to take. I was always a good runner, your honour, and many a prize have I carried off, at fairs in the old country, before troubles began. So it seemed to me that, if I could have anything of a start, I ought to be able to get off.

"There was nearly half a mile betwixt the town and the place where the narrow ground, at whose end it stood, widened out into the country. If I could only hold my own, as far as that, I could take to the woods and lanes and save myself.

"A guard of soldiers, with muskets and bayonets, went out with us, and at the end of the second day I managed to slip off, and hide behind a pile of cannonballs. The rest assembled at a spot about fifty yards away, to be counted before they marched to prison again. As soon as the others had got there, and the guards had gathered round, I went off as hard as I could tear. And a good start I should have got, if it hadn't been that a sentry on a fort close by fired his piece at me. Still, I had a good hundred yards' start.

"The guards set to, to run after me, and when they got in sight of me fired their guns; but they were flurried, and the bullets flew past without one of them touching me. Then I felt pretty safe. If they stopped to load their muskets, I should get clean away. If, as I expected, they would not stop for that, they would not have a chance with me, carrying their muskets and cartridge boxes and belts. I had taken off my coatee and boots, while I was waiting for the start, and went up the hill like a deer.

"I did not look round, till I got to the top. Then I found that I had gained a hundred yards of them. I doubled down a lane, at once, and then struck through some orchards; and ran, without stopping, maybe a couple of miles.

"I never heard any more of the soldiers, and knew that, for the present, I was safe, though maybe they would send some dragoons to scour the country when the news came in. I went on at a jog trot till it was quite dark; then I sat down to think what I should do next.

"I had got my four louis with me, for they hadn't found them when they searched me. The first thing was to get some duds, and I walked along till I saw a light in a cottage, which I entered. There were two women there. I told them at once that I wanted clothes, and was ready to pay for them; but that, if they would not give them to me for money, I should take them without paying. Though I could see that they doubted the payment, and regarded me as a robber, they brought out the clothes, which belonged, one of the women said, to her husband. I took what I wanted.

"'Now,' I said, 'how much shall I pay you for these?'

"They were still terribly frightened, and said that I was welcome. However, I put one of my louis down on the table. This was certainly more than the clothes ever cost, so I said:

"'Here is a gold piece, but I want a shilling in change, to buy food with.'

"At first, they evidently hardly thought that I was in earnest. Then at last, when they found that I really intended to give the money, they brightened up, and not only gave me a shilling in change, but offered me some bread and cheese, which I was glad enough to take.

"Then I put the clothes on over my own, not wishing to lave anything behind that would show searchers that it was I who had been there. I told the woman that the coin was a French one, but that it was worth about the same as an English guinea. I advised them to put it away, for the present, and not to try and change it for a few weeks, as enquiries might be made as to how they had obtained it.

"I had no difficulty on my way up to London. I avoided the main road till I got to Colchester, and after that walked boldly on, having money to pay for victuals. When I got to town, I changed another of my louis at a money changer's. He asked me where I had got it, and when I said that it was no business of his, but that it had been paid me by a French Huguenot gentleman, who had lately arrived, and for whom I had been doing some work; and as there are many of these Huguenots in

London, he was satisfied, and changed it for me.

"I then fell across the Irish porter I told you of. He told me whereabouts I could get lodgings, and advised me to apply to one of the men who let out a number of sedan chairs, to hire one out to me by the week.

"Well, your honour, once I had taken the lodging, I thought no more of the chair, but went about the business for which I had come to London. I had not been an hour in the town before I made the acquaintance of half a dozen, at least, of my countrymen, and found out which was the prison in which you were kept. At first, I thought of going there and giving myself up, on condition that I might be employed as your servant. Then I thought, perhaps they would not keep their word to me, but would send me back to Harwich; and then the thought struck me that I might, some way or other, get your honours out of prison.

"When I first saw the place, it seemed to me that it was impossible. The place was mighty strong, the windows all barred, and I had no means of finding out where you were lodged. I spent a whole day in prowling round and round the jail, but sorra an idea came into my thick head, though I bate it wid my fists till it was sore; for, says I to myself, there is no lock so strong but it can be picked, if you do but know the right way. It was the second day, when I espied a little bit of white stuff at one of the windows. It might be a signal, or it might not, and even if it was, there was no reason why it should be yours, except that, I said to myself:

"'Mr. Kennedy is not the boy to sit quiet in prison, if he can see any possible way of slipping out of it. His head is crammed full of ideas. So I will walk near and investigate the matter.'

"As I came close, I could make out that there was someone behind the bars, but I could not see who it was. Of course, I did not come straight to the spot, but went about promiscuously.

"For anything I could tell, there might be someone in the towers watching me. Then I saw a hand drop a little white parcel, and I found it without much trouble and went off with it. It was as much as I could do, to keep myself from running like a madman, for I felt somehow sure that it was you who had dropped it, but of course, it was not until I got it read for me that I was certain.

"After that, your honour, it was all easy enough. You told me what to do, and I did it. There was a little difficulty about the saw, but I got it through one of the chair men, who told me, when I asked him, that he had the acquaintance of some cracksmen--more shame to him--and that he could get such a thing as I wanted through them. I was not surprised, for I had already heard that many of the chair men worked in connection with the bad characters, letting them know which way they were coming with people from an entertainment, and carrying them down lanes where there was little chance of the watch interfering.

"It went against the grain to have dealings with such a man, for I was born of honest people, but if the ould gentleman himself had offered me a couple of saws, and I knew that I would have to give him a thousand years extra of purgatory, I would have closed with the bargain. Those two saws cost me another louis, and cheap enough, too.

"After that, it was all plain sailing, and the money you lowered to me was much more than sufficient for all the other things. And now, what is your honour going to do next?"

"That is more than I can tell you, Mike. We must talk it over."

This was a matter that they had already discussed, in their cell, after they had once made their preparations for flight. Closely watched as they were, when with the other officers, it would have been impossible to communicate their plans to them; but, even if they could have done so, they could see no possible way in which the others could share in their escape. Doubtless the doors of their cells were also strong and heavy, and, could all these difficulties have been overcome, there would have been passages, corridors, and staircases to traverse, with the certainty of meeting with some of the night watchmen who patrolled them, and they would finally have had to force the door into their cell.

They were, therefore, reluctantly obliged to abandon the hope of liberating their friends, and decided that, once away, they must endeavour to cross to France without delay. The king would doubtless have been, before now, informed by his agents in London of the determination of the English Government to bring all the prisoners to execution, but nevertheless, it would be their duty to obtain an audience, and implore him to take steps to save them. They would therefore, on their arrival in Paris, at once see General Hamilton, and other officers of rank, and beg them to accompany them to Versailles to act as spokesmen, and to influence the king in their favour.

Chapter 10: Kidnapping A Minister.

In spite of the war between the two countries, communications were frequent. Smuggling boats brought over, with their cargoes of wine and brandy, Huguenot fugitives; and, by the same means, secret agents carried back news of events in Paris to the Government. Having decided upon making for the coast without delay, Desmond and his friends next discussed the port to which they had best travel, and which seemed to offer the fairest opportunities. They agreed that Weymouth seemed to be most advantageous, as it was from there that the communications with Brittany were chiefly maintained.

At the same time, it was evident that considerable difficulty would be experienced in discovering the men engaged in such traffic, and in making an arrangement with them, and it was all-important that no time should be lost, for there was no saying when the trial might come on.

"If we could but get hold of Godolphin," Desmond said, next morning, "we might get an order, from him, to embark in one of the boats that carry his agents."

The others laughed.

"Yes; and if you could get hold of Anne, you might persuade her to sign an order for the release of our comrades."

Desmond did not answer, but sat thinking for a few minutes.

"It is not so impossible as you seem to imagine," he said, at last. "Doubtless, like everyone else, he goes in a sedan chair to the meeting of the council, and returns in the same manner. There are two ways in which we could manage the matter. Of course, he has his own chair, with his chair men in livery. We might either make these men drunk and assume their dress, or attack them suddenly on the way; then we should, of course, gag and bind them, and carry him here, or to some other place that we might decide upon, and force him to give us an order for the boatmen to take us across the channel, at once. Of course, we should have horses in readiness, and ride for the coast. We should have a twelve hours' start, for it would be that time before our landlady came in as usual, with our breakfast, when Godolphin would, of course, be released."

The two officers looked at each other, astounded at the audacity of the scheme that Desmond had quietly propounded. O'Sullivan was the first to speak.

"Are you really in earnest, Kennedy?"

"Quite in earnest. I do not see why it should not be done."

"Well, you are certainly the coolest hand I ever came across," O'Neil said. "You are proposing to seize the first minister in England, as if it were merely an affair of carrying off a pretty girl quite willing to be captured. The idea seems monstrous, and yet, as you put it, I do not see why it might not succeed."

"I hardly think that it could fail," Desmond said quietly. "De Tulle managed to carry off the Baron de Pointdexter's daughter from the court of Versailles, and did so without any hitch or difficulty. Surely three Irishmen could arrange an affair of this sort as well as a French vicomte."

"If it is to be done," O'Sullivan said, "I think the second plan is best. You might fail in making the chair men drunk, or at any rate sufficiently drunk to allow them to be despoiled of their clothes; whereas you could have no difficulty in silencing a couple of chair men by a sudden attack--a sharp rap on the head with these bludgeons ought to settle that affair."

"Quite so," Desmond agreed; "and while Mike and one of us were so employed, the other two might throw open the doors of the chair, and gag Godolphin before he was conscious of what was happening."

"It all seems simple enough, Kennedy, and, if it were a citizen, one would think nothing of the undertaking. But it is nothing short of high treason for us thus to make free with the person of the chief minister of England."

"That is a matter that does not concern me at all, O'Neil. If we were captured now, we should be executed for high treason with the others; and if we carried off Anne herself, they could not do much more to us.

"Now, it seems to me that if you are both agreed that we should carry out the plan, the first thing to be done is to arrange for horses; or, better still, for a light cart to carry the four of us. I should think that Mike would, among his acquaintances, be able to hear of a man with a couple of fast horses and such a cart as we require, who would agree to drive us to the coast, arranging a change of horses on the way. He could offer ten louis, which would be a sum that a man of that kind would be well satisfied with."

"I will see to that, your honour. I have no doubt that I can find such a man without difficulty. When would you want him?"

"Tonight, certainly, with the arrangement that, if we do not come to the appointed spot, we shall be there tomorrow night. Recollect ten louis is all we can afford, but if he wants any more, he must have it.

"Well, we will leave that to you."

Then he went on to the others:

"We had better go down to Saint James's. Mike can go out and buy us three shock wigs, with which we can cover our hair and look our parts better. We had better separate when we get there, and watch the entrances to the palace, gazing about like rustics; then we can get into a conversation with any servant that we see, and try and find out from which door members of the council usually issue, and at about what hour. We could succeed without that, because we should notice the chairs waiting for them. Still, it is as well that we should get all the information we can. There will be, doubtless, personages leaving who have been with the Princess Anne. They might go out by another entrance, and therefore we should miss our man."

"You will have more than the two chair men to deal with, your honour, for there are sure to be two link men with the chair."

"Well, it will be as easy to dispose of four men as of two, Mike."

"Every bit, your honour, and the more of them the more divarsion."

An hour later they set out, now so well disguised that no one would have dreamt that the three Irishmen were officers in a French regiment; and before noon Desmond succeeded in obtaining, from a scullion employed in the palace, the particulars that he required. On saying that he had but just come to London, and wanted to get a sight of the great people, the present of a shilling sufficed to extract the information from the boy; and Desmond then rejoined his companions, and they at once returned to their lodgings, where they found Mike awaiting them.

"I have managed it, your honour, but it will cost twelve louis. I went to the man from whom I got the saws, and he said at once that the affair could be managed easily, and, sure enough, he took me to the shop of a man who, he said, sometimes acted with cracksmen. The fellow was sharp enough to see, at once, that it was something special that we wanted the horses for, but after some bargaining he agreed to do it for twelve gold pieces, and, if necessary, to get a change of horses twice on the road. He will be ready with his cart at twelve o'clock, a hundred yards or so outside the last houses on the south side of the Old Kent Road. I could not tell him which port you would go to, but he said from there he could go to Dover, or turn off so as to make for Southampton or Weymouth. It is to be twelve pounds if it is to Dover or Southampton; fifteen pounds if it is to Weymouth."

"That is satisfactory," Desmond said. "Now we have nothing else to do till ten o'clock tonight, when, as the boy said, the council generally ends; though we will be there an hour earlier, in case they should leave before. Now I think we had better find out where Godolphin's house is, and fix upon the best spot for the attack, and how we shall each station ourselves."

This part of the business offered no difficulties. They found that the minister would probably be carried through Saint James's Park, and they fixed upon the spot where they would await his coming.

Mike was to attack the first porter. O'Sullivan was to follow close behind him and, at the same moment, fell the rearmost man. O'Neil and Desmond, who were to conceal themselves among trees on opposite sides of the path, were to spring out and strike down the link bearers, and then enter the chair and bind and gag the minister.

Mike was sent out to buy a pot of black paint, with which to efface the gildings of the chair, and to reduce its appearance to that ordinarily used by the citizens. He was ordered to get a supply of rope, and some wood, to make gags for the men they were to stun.

The others were to post themselves at the spot agreed on, while Desmond was to remain at the entrance to the palace by which ministers would issue, to note Lord Godolphin's chair, and, when he was fairly on his way, to follow it for a short distance to make sure that it was being taken through the park, and then to run on and warn the others to be in readiness.

On their return to their lodging, they ate the dinner that Mike had got in for them, and, as they drank their wine, laughed and joked over their enterprise; for, now that they were fairly embarked upon the scheme, the two officers were as eager as Desmond in the matter, and were much more excited over the prospect than he was.

Before nine o'clock, they and Mike were posted in the park, and Desmond was at the entrance to the palace. Here seven or eight chairs, with their bearers and link men, were assembled. As most of the porters were hired men, Desmond readily entered into conversation with them, and expressed his desire to see the great persons and learn which were their chairs, so that he should know them as they entered them.

In half an hour there was a stir, and a servant, coming out, shouted:

"His Grace the Duke of Somerset's chair."

This was at once brought up to the door. Next came a call for the chair of Mr. Henry Boyle, who was followed by Harcourt, the attorney general, then the chair of My Lord Godolphin was summoned.

Desmond and three or four others, who had gathered to see the members of the council come out, had been ordered off by the sentries as soon as the first chair was called, but remained near enough to hear the names. To his satisfaction, Godolphin's chair was carried off in the direction they had anticipated, and he at once ran on and joined his companions.

Presently, the lights carried by the two link men were seen approaching, and, as the chair came abreast of him, he shouted:

"Now!"

Almost simultaneously, the four heavy cudgels alighted on the heads of the four men, levelling them senseless to the ground; and O'Neil and Desmond sprang to the chair, and wrenched the door open, while O'Sullivan and Mike bound the four men, and thrust the gags into their mouths. Lord Godolphin had been thrown from his seat by the sudden fall of his bearers, and was seized and bound before he was conscious of what had happened. Then his captors assisted the others in carrying the fallen men to some distance from the path.

A couple of minutes sufficed to cover the gilding and armorial bearings upon the chair. The torches were still burning on the ground. One of these was stamped out. Desmond took the other. Mike and O'Sullivan went between the poles, and adjusted the leathern straps over their shoulders, and started.

Emerging from the park at Charing Cross, past the old church of Saint. Martin's in the Fields, and keeping round the walls to Holborn Bars, they made their way to their lodging, and Godolphin was carried into their room, which was on the ground floor. Mike and O'Neil then took the chair away, and left it in a narrow alley, where it was not likely to attract attention until the morning.

Not until they returned was anything said to their prisoner. It had been agreed that O'Neil, as the senior, was to be spokesman of the party.

"Lord Godolphin," he said, "I regret that circumstances have obliged us to use force towards you, but our necessities compel us to leave the country at once, and it has appeared to us that in no way could we get away so expeditiously as with the aid of your lordship. We will now set you free. I must tell you, beforehand, that if you attempt to raise your voice and give the alarm, we shall be constrained to blow out your brains."

Mike now released him from the bonds, and removed the gag from his mouth, but for a time the minister was incapable of speech, being choked by anger at the treatment he had met with.

"You will repent this outrage," he burst out, at last.

"I think not, sir," O'Neil said, quietly. "At any rate, we are quite ready to take our chance of that. In order that you may feel at ease with us, I have no hesitation in telling you who we are. We are the three French officers who, as no doubt you have heard, yesterday escaped from Newgate, and we are anxious to get out of the country as soon as possible. It will be also a guarantee to you that we have no designs on either your pockets or your person."

Angry as he still was, it was evident, by the expression of the treasurer's face, that the information was a relief to him, for indeed he had supposed that he had been carried off by political enemies, and was very uncertain as to what would befall him.

"What is it that you require, then?" he asked, after a pause.

"Merely this, sir. That you will give us an order, upon an agent through whom you communicate with France, to take us across the channel immediately."

"Well, gentlemen," Godolphin said, more calmly, "I must say your coolness surprises me. Your escape yesterday was, of course, reported to us; and the manner in which you obtained that rope, by which you descended, is a mystery that the jail authorities are wholly unable to solve.

"If you obtain the order you desire, will you give me your word of honour that it shall be used in a manner in no way hostile to the interests of this country, but solely, as you say, for the purpose of conveying you across the channel?"

"That promise we give willingly. We must ask you to pledge your honour, as a gentleman, that the order you give us will be a genuine one--a matter that we cannot ascertain until we arrive at the address given. We are willing to play fairly with you, sir, but if you do not do the same, we shall certainly return to London, though in some different guise, and, if so, I warn you that no guards will save you from our vengeance."

"You need not threaten, sir," Lord Godolphin said calmly. "I will give you the order, to the person to whom such communications are addressed, and it shall be couched in the same words as usual."

Desmond placed a sheet of paper, pen, and ink before him. He, dating it from the Treasury, wrote:

To John Dawkins, Mariner, High Street, Rye. Urgent.

On the receipt of this, you will at once convey the bearer, and three persons with him, and land them in some convenient spot in France.

He then added his signature.

"Now, gentlemen, what next?" he said, looking up.

O'Neil looked at his companions, and then they spoke for a moment together.

"We are about to start at once, my lord," he said, "and it was our intention to have left you bound and gagged, until the morning, when the woman of the house would have assuredly found you and released you. But, as you have acceded to our request at once, we will, if you give us your word of honour that you will raise no alarm, and say no word of this business until eight o'clock tomorrow morning, let you depart at once."

"Thank you for your courtesy, gentlemen, and for your confidence in my honour. I am, indeed, anxious to return home at once. If I do not do so, there will be a hue and cry for me, and by the time I return in the morning all London will know that I am missing. I naturally should not wish this adventure to become a matter of common talk: in the first place, because the position in which you have placed me can scarcely be called a pleasant one; and secondly, because the success of your enterprise might lead others to make similar attempts on my person, or that of my colleagues. Even now, I fear that my servants, when sufficiently recovered, will go to my house and give the alarm."

"I do not think that that is likely to be the case, my lord," O'Neil said, "as we took the precaution of gagging and binding them, and laid them down some distance from the roadside. If, on your return home, you find they have not arrived, you have but to send a couple of your servants out to release them. You can give them strict orders that no word is to be said of the affair, and make them to understand you were attacked in error, and that the ruffians who took part in the outrage at once released you, upon discovering your identity."

"Very good, sir," Godolphin said, with a grim smile. "I must really compliment you all on your fertility of resource and invention. And now, is there anything else that I can do for you?"

"There is one small favour," Desmond said. "Your lordship has doubtless twenty guineas in your possession. You would greatly oblige us if you would give us them, for so many louis. These you will have no difficulty in exchanging, whereas the exhibition of French money, on our part, might excite suspicion."

Lord Godolphin placed his hand in his pocket, drew out a heavy purse, and, opening it, counted out twenty guineas. O'Neil took these up, and handed to him twenty louis pieces.

"One more question, gentlemen. What has become of my sedan chair?"

"It is in an alley, hard by," O'Neil said, "and as we are ourselves going in your direction we will carry it to your door."

"You are obliging, indeed, sir. If it had been found, the escutcheon on the panels would have shown that it was mine."

"I fear, my lord, that you will have to have it repainted; for, before starting with you, we took the precaution to put black paint over the gilding and panels. Still, the lining and fittings would show that it belonged to some person of wealth and importance. As you have been so obliging to us, we will gladly escort you, with it, to your door."

"I shall be glad, indeed, of that, gentlemen, for I certainly should not care about travelling alone through these lanes and alleys, which have by no means a good reputation."

"We are ready to start at once, my lord," O'Neil said. "We have a long journey to perform, and, although there is now no need for extraordinary speed, we shall be glad to be off."

They were ready at once, having settled with their landlady before starting out in the evening, telling her that they had heard of a job and should start early in the morning. Mike and Desmond fetched the empty chair, and they then started, Godolphin walking with the other officers in front.

"This is the most surprising adventure that ever happened to me," Lord Godolphin said; "and it is a pity that officers who possess the wit to plan an escape from Newgate, and to ensure a speedy flight from the country by carrying me off, are not in the service of Her Majesty."

"We may yet be in the British service some day, my lord," O'Sullivan laughed; "but I may tell you that my friend, and myself, disclaim any credit in contriving the matter of which you spoke, that being solely the work of our young comrade, who is at present the youngest ensign in our regiment."

"Then he must be a shrewd fellow, indeed," Godolphin said, "likely to do service in any position to which he may attain."

They walked sharply. Several times rough men came and peered at them, but Godolphin was wrapped in a cloak, and the appearance of those with him showed that hard knocks, rather than booty, would be the result of interfering with them. On reaching Lord Godolphin's house they placed the sedan chair on the steps.

"Goodnight to you, gentlemen, and good fortune!" Lord Godolphin said. "The lesson has not been lost, and I shall take good care, in future, to have a strong escort."

They then crossed Westminster Bridge, and made rapidly for the spot where the cart was waiting for them.

"You are an hour after your time," the man said. "I had begun to think that something had gone wrong with you."

"That is not the case," O'Neil said; "but we have certainly been detained longer than we anticipated."

"Where are we going to?"

"To Rye."

"That will suit me very well," the man said. "I have friends along that road, and shall have no trouble about horses."

They started at once, at a rattling pace, the animals, though but sorry-looking creatures, being speedy and accustomed to long journeys. It was evident, from the man's manner, that he believed his passengers were cracksmen who had just successfully carried out an enterprise of importance. He expressed surprise that they had brought no luggage with them.

They did not care to undeceive him. Mike had brought with him a bottle of good brandy, and a drink of this soon removed the vexation the man had felt at being kept waiting for them.

Twice during the journey they changed horses, each time at small wayside inns, where some password, given by the driver, at once roused the landlord into activity. But a few minutes were spent in the changes, and the fifty miles to Rye were accomplished in seven hours--a very unusual rate of speed along the badly kept roads of the period. When the car drew up in the High Street of Rye, the four occupants were scarce able to stand, so bruised and shaken were they by their rapid passage over the rough road.

They handed the twelve pounds agreed upon to the driver, adding another as a token of their satisfaction at the speed at which he had driven them, and then enquired for the house of William Dawkins. It was close by, and upon knocking at the door, it was opened by the man himself.

"I have a message to deliver to you, in private," O'Neil said.

The man nodded, and led the way indoors, where the letter was handed to him.

"That is all right," he said. "My craft is always ready to set sail, at an hour's notice, and if the wind holds fair I will land you on the French coast before nightfall. I see that your business is urgent, or you would not have put on disguises before leaving London. I suppose you have brought other clothes to land in?"

"We have not," O'Neil said. "We came away in such a hurry that we did not think of it until on the road, and then we thought that we might procure them here."

"There will be no difficulty about that," the sailor said. "I will go out, and warn my men that we shall sail in half an hour, and then I can get any garments that you desire; for, doubtless, you do not wish to attract comment by the purchase of clothes that would seem unfitted to your present position."

"That is so," O'Sullivan said, "and we shall gladly embrace your offer. We should like three suits, such as are worn by persons of fair position in France, and one proper for a serving man."

"I cannot get you quite French fashion, sir, but they do not differ much from our own; and with a cloak each, I have no doubt that you would pass without attracting attention--that is, of course, if you speak French well."

"As well as English," O'Neil said. "Here are seven pounds in gold, which will, I should think, be sufficient. If not, we are provided with French gold, for use after landing there."

"I have no doubt it will suffice, sir. If not, I will pay what is the excess, and you can settle with me afterwards."

In three-quarters of an hour after their arrival at Rye, they were dressed in their new disguises and on board the little lugger, which at once started down the river, which was at that time much more free from shoals and difficulties than it is at present.

"Your boat seems fast," Desmond remarked, as, having cleared the mouth of the river, she put out to sea.

"She is fast, sir; the fastest thing that sails out of Rye. She needs be, for the gentlemen who come to me are always in a hurry."

"I suppose you have no fear of English cruisers?"

"Not at all. I have the order you brought with you, and have only to show it to any English ship of war that overhauls us, for them to let us go on at once. I am careful when I get near the French coast, for although their big craft never venture out far, there are numbers of chasse marce patrolling the coast. However, even if caught by them, it would be but a temporary detention, for I am well known at Etaples, which is always my port, unless specially directed to land my passengers elsewhere."

The wind was fresh and favourable, and at six o'clock in the afternoon they entered the little port. Some gendarmes came down to the wharf.

"We need have no fear of them," William Dawkins said. "Their lieutenant is paid handsomely for keeping his eyes shut, and asking no questions."

"So you are back again," the officer said. "Why, it is not a week since you were here!"

"No, it is but six days since I sailed."

"And you have four passengers?"

"That's the number, sir. The Irish gentlemen are desirous of entering the service of France."

The officer nodded.

"Well, gentlemen, you will find plenty of your countrymen in Paris; and, as everyone knows, there are no better or braver soldiers in His Majesty's service."

The friends had already enquired, from William Dawkins, whether there was any passage money to pay, saying that they had forgotten to ask before starting.

"Not at all. I am well paid by Government. My boat is always retained at a price that suits me well, and I get so much extra for every voyage I make. No, sir, thank you; I will take nothing for myself, but if you like to give half a guinea to the crew, to drink success to you, I will not say no."

The party made no stay at Etaples, but at once ordered a chaise and post horses. Then, changing at every post house, and suffering vastly less discomfort than they experienced in the journey to Rye--the roads being better kept in France than they were on the English side of the channel--they arrived in Paris at eleven o'clock next day.

Chapter 11: On the Frontier.

On entering the barrack yard, they found that the regiment had marched, ten days before, for the frontier, and that Lord Galmoy's regiment had taken their place. They went at once to his quarters and told him that, having effected their escape, they had travelled with all speed to inform the king of the determination of the English Government to bring the Irish officers to execution, and to implore him to intervene in their favour.

"I will go with you to Versailles, at once," Lord Galmoy said; "but, as you have no uniforms, and the king is very strict on matters of etiquette, three of my officers will lend you their suits and swords. While they are being fetched, sit down and share my meal, for doubtless you have not waited to eat on the road."

He then gave the necessary instructions, and half an hour later the three officers, now in uniform, started with him on horseback for Versailles. The king had just returned from hunting, and it was an hour before Lord Galmoy could obtain an audience with him. He had, on the road, told the others he felt sure that the king, who was well served by his agents in London, had already heard of the intention of the English Government, but as to whether he had sent off a remonstrance he was of course ignorant.

"I shall press the matter strongly upon him, and point out the deep feeling that will be excited, throughout his Irish and Scotch troops, if nothing is done to save the prisoners.

"Louis is a politic monarch," he said, "and, knowing our worth and that of his Scotch soldiers, I think that he will, on my representations, bestir himself. Wauchop has many times performed brilliant services, and deserves well of France. However, we shall see."

When they were admitted to the audience, Lord Galmoy introduced the three soldiers of O'Brien's regiment as coming that morning to Paris, having effected their escape from Newgate. As he repeated their names, the king looked sharply at Desmond.

"Ah, ah!" he said, "so our young ensign is in the thick of adventures again. These we will hear presently.

"Well, my lord, why have they come here so hurriedly after their arrival?"

"They came to inform Your Majesty that the English Government have determined to execute Colonel Francis Wauchop, and the twelve officers of their regiment who were on board the Salisbury, captured on the coast of Scotland."

Desmond, who was watching the king's face closely, saw that this was no news to him, and that he was annoyed by its being now brought to his notice; for doubtless the fate of a colonel, and a dozen young officers, was a matter that affected him little; and that, had the matter not been forced upon him, he would not have troubled about it, but, when it was too late, would have professed entire ignorance of the intentions of the English Government.

He only said, however, "It is incredible that there can be an intention to execute officers in our service, captured upon a warlike expedition."

"It is but too true, sir. Against Colonel Wauchop they have no ground for severity. By the convention of Limerick, he and all other officers were formally permitted to enter Your Majesty's service; but the young lieutenants have, of course, joined long since that time, and therefore cannot benefit by the terms of the convention; and could, with a show of justice, be executed as English subjects, traitors serving against their country."

"We are afraid that our remonstrance would have but little effect with the English Government."

Lord Galmoy smiled slightly, for it was notorious that negotiations had gone on between King James and his councillors, and several of the members of the English Ministry, Marlborough himself being more than suspected of having a secret understanding with the little court at Saint Germain.

He only said, however, "Your Majesty has in your hands the power of compelling the English Government to alter their determination in this matter."

"How so, my lord?" the king asked, in much surprise.

"You have, sire, many prisoners, Frenchmen of the reformed religion, who had entered the service of the Protestant princes--your enemies--and who were taken in Dutch and Flemish towns we have captured. These stand in the same relation towards Your Majesty as the Irish officers towards England. You have, then, but to inform the government there that, if they in any way harm the Irish officers and noncommissioned officers in their hands, you will at once execute a similar number of these French Protestant officers, whom you have hitherto treated as prisoners of war. Then, possibly, an exchange might be effected.

"Your Majesty will, I think, pardon me for saying that, unless steps are taken to save these officers' lives, the matter is likely to have a very bad effect on the Irish and Scotch regiments, whose ardour will not be improved by the knowledge that in case of a reverse they will, if not killed in the field, be executed as traitors; for nearly half of the men who are now serving have joined since the formation of the Brigade, and are not protected by the terms of the Limerick treaty. They are devoted to Your Majesty's service, and are ready to lay down their lives freely for the cause of France; but it would not be fair that they should also run the risk of execution, if they are by misfortune made prisoners."

"There is much in what you say, Lord Galmoy, and you certainly point out a way by which these officers can be saved. A messenger shall start, in an hour's time, with a letter to the English Government. It shall be delivered at their headquarters in Flanders by noon tomorrow, with a request that it shall be forwarded by special messenger to the British minister; and we will have a proclamation posted in Paris, and in the various camps of the army, saying that we have warned the English Government that, unless the officers and men captured off the coast of Scotland are treated as prisoners of war, we shall retaliate by treating all French officers taken in foreign service in the same way; and that we have furthermore offered to exchange an equal number of such officers and men, in our hands, for those held by the British Government."

"I thank Your Majesty, most respectfully and heartily, in the name of all the foreign officers in your service. Even should, unfortunately, the English Government refuse to pardon or exchange their prisoners, it will be seen that Your Majesty has done all in your power to save them, and there will be a general feeling of reprobation, throughout Europe, at the conduct of the English Ministry."

"We beg these officers to wait in the anteroom, while we dictate our despatch and proclamation to our secretary. We would fain question them as to how they effected their escape from their prison, and how they have made so speedy a journey here."

Lord Galmoy bowed, and retired with the others.

"We have done well," he said, "better indeed than I had hoped. Now, having succeeded in saving our countrymen's lives, which I doubt not would have been otherwise sacrificed, I shall return at once to Paris, for there is an inspection of my regiment this afternoon."

"We have been fortunate, indeed," O'Neil said, when Lord Galmoy had left. "I have no doubt the king had heard that the English Government had resolved to execute the prisoners, but I question whether he would have stirred in the matter, had it not been for Galmoy's representation."

"I am sure, by his manner, that he had received the news before," Desmond said, "and, as you say, had not intended to interfere. It was the suggestion that he might threaten retaliation, and that the effect of his not moving in the matter would be very bad among his Irish troops, that decided him to interfere. He may have felt that any mere protest made by him would have had little effect, and it is not his nature to expose himself to a rebuff; but, directly he saw that he had an effective weapon in his hands, he took the matter up as warmly as we could wish."

In point of fact, the king's threat had the desired effect, and two months later the imprisoned officers and men were exchanged for an equal number of Huguenots.

In a quarter of an hour, the three officers were again summoned to the king's presence. With him was a tall dark officer, of distinguished mien, whom O'Neil and O'Sullivan both recognized as the Duke of Berwick, one of the most famous generals of the time. He had been in command of the French forces in Spain, from which he had been recalled suddenly, two days before, in order that the king, who had a great confidence in him, might consult him as to the general plan of operations, in that country and in the north, before despatching him to join the army in Flanders. This was commanded by the Duke of Burgundy and the Duke of Vendome jointly; and as both were headstrong and obstinate, and by no means agreed as to the operations to be undertaken, the king had determined to send Berwick there, in order that he might, by his military genius and influence, bring matters to a better state between the two dukes, and arrange with them some definite plan by which the tide of fortune, which had hitherto gone against the French, might be arrested.

The king appeared now to be in a good humour.

"And now, young sirs," he said, "I have an hour at leisure, and would fain hear a true account of your adventures, omitting nothing.

"I have no doubt, Monsieur Kennedy, that your ready wit had no small share in the matter."

"With your permission, Sire, I will tell the story," O'Neil said, "for Mr. Kennedy is not likely to place his own share of the work in its due prominence."

The king nodded, and O'Neil gave a detailed account of the manner in which they had made their escape, and succeeded in getting themselves conveyed across the channel in a vessel in the Government service, explaining that both affairs were due entirely to Desmond's initiative and ingenuity. The king listened with great interest, and even laughed at the story of the capture of Lord Godolphin.

"You have all three behaved extremely well," he said.

"You, Monsieur Kennedy, have again shown that you possess unusual shrewdness, as well as daring.

"What think you, Duke, of this young subaltern, who is, we may tell you, the hero of whom you have doubtless heard, who twice rescued Mademoiselle de Pointdexter from the hands of her abductor?"

"I was told the story yesterday, Sire, and was filled with admiration at the boldness and resource of her rescuer, who was, I heard, an ensign in O'Brien's regiment; but certainly I did not expect to find him so young a man. He has, indeed, a fertility of invention that fills me with surprise. The other officers deserve praise, for having so willingly followed the leadership of their junior, and their generosity in assigning to him the whole merit of their undertaking is highly commendable. It is no easy thing, Sire, to find in young officers--especially, if I may say so, among the cadets of good family, who form for the most part the staff of your generals--men ready to exercise their own discretion when in difficulties, and to carry out with due diligence the orders committed to them."

"O'Brien's regiment has marched to the northern frontier. The vacancies in the ranks of its officers have been filled up from those of other regiments. I should, with Your Majesty's permission, be glad to take these three officers on my own staff, as, leaving Spain privately in accordance with Your Majesty's orders, I have brought with me only Captain Fromart, my secretary, and one young aide-de-camp. I should be glad if you would promote Mr. Kennedy to the rank of lieutenant."

"We quite approve of both requests," the king said graciously; "and indeed," he added with a smile, "shall not be altogether sorry to see Lieutenant Kennedy employed outside our kingdom, for, after making war on his own account with one of our nobles, and kidnapping the first minister of England, there is no saying what enterprise he might next undertake. And should he join any of those who trouble the country with their plots, we should feel compelled to double our guards, in order to hold ourself secure from his designs.

"Well, gentlemen, since the Duke of Berwick has appointed you his aides-de-camp, the least we can do is to see that you are properly fitted out for the expedition. You have, of course, lost your uniforms, horses, and money in our service, and it is but just that we should see to your being refitted. If you will wait in the anteroom, you shall each receive an order on our treasury for a hundred louis d'ors."

The three officers bowed deeply in acknowledgment to the king, and, bowing also to the Duke of Berwick, returned to the anteroom, where presently one of the royal attendants brought to them the three orders on the treasury, and also begged them, in the name of the Duke of Berwick, to wait until his audience with the king should be over.

They were all highly delighted with the change in their position. The posts of staff officers were, as the duke had said, considered to belong almost of right to members of noble families, and it was seldom that officers of the line could aspire to them.

"Did I not tell you, Kennedy, that your luck would bring good fortune to us all! And, by the powers, it has done so! Faith, if anyone had said a month ago that I should by now be on the Duke of Berwick's staff, I should have laughed in his face, if indeed I had not quarrelled with him for mocking at me. And now here we are, with money to buy horses and outfit, and with no more drilling recruits and attending parades."

"But not an end to work, O'Sullivan," Desmond Kennedy said. "You won't find much idle time, when you are serving with the duke."

"No. He has the name of being a strict commander, sparing neither himself nor his soldiers; and I have heard that his staff have a very hard time of it. However, I am not afraid of hard work, when it is done on horseback, and there are many more chances of promotion on the staff than there are in marching regiments. Well, I don't mind being taken prisoner a dozen times if this is what comes of it, providing always that you are taken with me, Kennedy, and are there to help me out of the scrape."

"We should have to have Mike prisoner, too," Desmond laughed, "for without his help we should be in Newgate at present."

"I don't believe it. I am sure that, even if he hadn't turned up, you would have managed somehow."

In a short time, the duke came out.

"I am likely to be detained here another week, before I start for Flanders. That will give you time to procure your outfit of horses and equipments and arms. You will require two horses each, and these should be good ones. I doubt whether, if you get proper outfits, the sum that His Majesty has given you will suffice to buy two horses. I have, however, in my stables here, plenty of good animals that have been taken from the enemy, and one will be given to each of you. Therefore, it will be only necessary for you to purchase one.

"I am staying here, and should be obliged, when you have taken a lodging, if you would send me your address. I shall then let you know where and when you are to join me. Is there anything else that you would ask me?"

"I would ask, sir, that I might take my servant with me," Desmond said.

"Certainly; and you can do so without further question. One man, more or less, will make no difference to O'Brien's regiment, and it would be a pity that you should not have him with you, for it is evident that he is at once faithful, and possesses a large amount of shrewdness."

After thanking the duke for the present of the horses, the three officers, having drawn their money, left the palace and rode back to Paris. They went first to the barracks, and returned the horses and uniforms, with many thanks, to the officers who had lent them; had an interview with Lord Galmoy, and informed him of their new appointments.

"You have well won them," he said, "and I wish you every good fortune. Assuredly, you are more likely to rise under the Duke of Berwick than as subaltern in the Irish Brigade, though promotion is not slow there, owing to the vacancies that battle always makes in their ranks."

They went out and took a lodging together, and then went to a military tailor, who promised them their undress and full dress suits in four days. Then they ordered military saddles, bridles, and equipments.

On the next day, after visiting half the stables in Paris, they purchased three horses for themselves, and Desmond bought, in addition, a serviceable animal for Mike, with a cavalry saddle and accoutrements, and ordered a uniform for him. Each provided himself with a sword and a brace of pistols.

Mike was greatly pleased when Desmond communicated his promotion and appointment to him.

"You will look grand, your honour, as a general's aide-de-camp, with your handsome uniform and your horses and all that, and 'tis glad I am that we are going to Flanders, for, from all I have heard from men who have fought in Spain, little pleasure is to be had in campaigning there. The food is vile, the roads are bad. You are choked with dust and smothered with heat.

"As to their making you lieutenant, if you had your dues, it would be a colonel they should have made you, or at any rate a major."

"There is plenty of time, Mike," Desmond laughed. "A nice colonel I should look, too, leading a thousand men into battle. If I obtain a majority in another fifteen years, I shall consider myself lucky."

Desmond did not share Mike's gratification that they were to campaign with the army of the north, instead of with that in Spain. However, as he would be fighting against English troops in either country, he concluded it would not make much difference, especially as, being an aide-de-camp, he would not himself have to enter into actual conflict with them.

His friends were heartily glad that their destination was not Spain, for all had, like Mike, heard much of the hardships suffered by the troops in that country.

"I know from what you have said, Kennedy, that if you had had your choice you would have taken Spain, but, putting aside the heat there, it is but poor work, by all accounts. You are well-nigh starved, you can't get at your enemy, who knows all the mountains and the paths over them, is as difficult to catch as one of their fleas, harasses you while you are on the march, and shirks fighting as the old one shirks holy water. There has only been one fight which could be called a battle since the war began; and as for the sieges, it means that you lose a lot of men, and have little credit when you take a place, especially as the moment you go out one way the enemy enter on the other side, and there is all the work to be done over again."

"I admit that we shall see a great deal more of war in the north," Kennedy said, "and Marlborough and Eugene on the other side, and the Dukes of Berwick and Vendome on ours, are such skilful commanders that there will be far greater interest in the operations, than in carrying on what is little more than a partisan war in Spain."

"Not only that," O'Neil put in, "but there will be a possibility of getting decent food. While in Spain there are few great towns, and these a long distance from each other; in Flanders there are towns every few miles, and you are sure of decent quarters and good cooking."

"Why, O'Neil, I did not know that you were particular as to your food," Desmond laughed.

"I can starve as well as another, Kennedy, but when I get good food and good wine and good lodgings, I own that I prefer it vastly to the fare that our troops have to put up with, in Spain. I can see no reason why, because you are going to risk your life in battle, you should put up with all sorts of miseries and inconveniences beforehand, if they can be avoided.

"As to fighting against the English, there are English both in Spain and Flanders, and in both armies they form but a small proportion of the force, though I grant willingly that they are the backbone of both armies. If you look at the thing sensibly, you will see that we have gained no slight advantage by Berwick's going to Flanders, instead of returning to Spain."

Three days after their preparations were completed, an orderly brought a note from the Duke of Berwick. It was brief and to the point.

The rendezvous is at six o'clock tomorrow morning, in front of La Louvre.
(Signed) Berwick.

All were glad that the summons had come. They had discussed the future from every point of view, and were already growing impatient, short as their stay had been in Paris.

Five minutes before the hour, they were at the rendezvous. As the clock struck, the duke rode up with two officers and an escort of six troopers. He looked at their accoutrements and horses, and nodded his head approvingly.

"You will do very well," he said. "I can tell you that the gloss of your uniforms will not last long, in Flanders."

The other officers were Captain Fromart, who acted as the duke's secretary, and Lieutenant d'Eyncourt. Mike fell in with the escort, behind which also rode the body servant of the duke, and the two cavalry men who were the servants of his officers.

Once beyond the limits of the town, the party broke into a trot. The duke rode on ahead, evidently in deep thought, and the five officers followed in a group.

"I see, messieurs," d'Eyncourt said, "that only one of you has brought a servant with him."

"We only arrived in Paris a week ago," O'Neil said. "Our own regiment had left, and we did not care to ask for two soldiers from another regiment, as these might have turned out badly. We thought it better, therefore, to delay until we joined the army, and wait till we could obtain a couple of good men from one of the cavalry regiments there. As it is, Monsieur Kennedy's servant can look after the three of us, and, I have no doubt, two of the soldiers of the escort will not object to earn a few livres by looking after our horses on the way."

"I think you are right," the other said. "If one gets a good man, a soldier servant is invaluable. If, as is often the case, he is a bad one, well, one is far better without him. It is curious how men who have been smart soldiers, when in the ranks, are apt to go to the bad when they become servants. They have more time on their hands, are free from most of the parades, have no sentry duty to perform, and the consequence is that they become slovenly and careless, and in nine cases out of ten give way to drink at every opportunity. If Mr. Kennedy's servant is really a good one, you will be better off, with a third of his services, than you would be with the whole of that of an ordinary soldier servant.

"You have just returned from England, have you not? The duke told Captain Fromart that you were among those who were captured in the Salisbury, but that you had made your escape. He gave no particulars, for indeed, the duke is not given to much speech. As a general he is splendid, but it would be more pleasant for his staff if he were to unbend a little."

"Yes, we managed to give them the slip," O'Neil said, "thanks to Monsieur Kennedy and his servant. Did you return from Spain with the general, Captain Fromart?"

"Yes. There was nothing doing at the moment, and he gave us the option of accompanying him or staying behind. We vastly preferred the trip, as we considered it, for of course we had no idea that the duke was about to be sent to Flanders. You hear a good deal of the climate of Spain. It is said to be lovely. I vow that it is detestable. The heat, when it is hot, is terrible, and when it is not hot, there is a bitter wind that chills you to the bone. A great portion of the country is but half populated, and you can go a day's march without coming to a village. The roads are villainous. There is nothing to buy, and it is as much as the transport can do to get, I will not say enough bread, but a bare sufficiency to maintain the troops. Moreover, the duke has been constantly thwarted in his plans by the Spaniards, who are ready enough to make promises, but never take a single step towards their fulfilment. The duke's temper is of the shortest, and he has quarrelled openly with most of the leading Spaniards, and has threatened, four or five times, to throw up his command and return to France. He did do so a year ago, but affairs went so badly, without him, that the cause of France was seriously imperilled by his absence, and it was at the urgent request of Philip that he returned; for at that time the English general, Peterborough, was striking dismay all over the country, and if the duke's advice had not been taken, all our officers acknowledge that we should speedily have crossed the Pyrenees."

"And do the population incline towards Philip or the Austrian?"

"As a rule, they incline towards the party which seems likely to win. They would shout in Madrid as loudly for the Archduke Charles as for Philip. Catalonia and Valencia are the exceptions. There the balance of feeling is certainly in favour of the Austrian, but this is principally because they are afraid of Peterborough, whom they regard as almost supernatural, and fear he would take vengeance upon those who deserted his cause. But there is no accounting for them; cities have held out as stoutly for one candidate as for the other, without any apparent reason, so far as we can observe.

"We fight for Philip because he is Louis's grandson, and it is important in the interest of France to stand closely allied with his party. But as for the Spaniards with us, I can tell you that we have but little trust in them."

"But some of them are good, are they not?"

"We do not consider any of them of much account. But then the Spaniards on the other side are no better. They seem to have lost all their military virtues, ever since their best troops were demolished at Rocroi by Conde. That and the destruction of their fleet by the English, and the drain of their resources both in men and money, entailed by the long war in Holland, altogether deprived the people of their martial spirit. The war is to some extent between the English and us, because, of the allies England, Holland, and Austria, neither the Austrians nor the Dutch take any great share in the struggle. The Dutch are wholly engrossed with the defence of their fens, the Austrians are fully occupied in Italy and on the Rhine frontier, and it is only the English, who, fortunately, are not very numerous, who are against us, for the Portuguese can scarcely be counted in the business, being, if anything, slower and more stupid than the Spaniards themselves.

"However, at present the prospect is good. Peterborough has gone. Galway's army has been almost destroyed; though, to do them justice, the English regiments fought magnificently, and if they had been seconded by the Portuguese the result might have been altogether different."

"Then you found Spain much less rich than France?"

"There is no comparison," Captain Fromart said. "It ought to be fully as rich, but the plains lie almost uncultivated. The people seem wholly without energy, and the ruling class are always intriguing, and seem to pay little attention to their estates. You see but few castles and chateaux, such as are dotted over France. I do not say that, at the present moment, France can be considered a prosperous country in material matters. The expenses of the wars have been enormous, to say nothing of the Court. The people are ground down by taxation, and the misery in some parts of the country is extreme; but left to themselves the people will work, and work hard. Our soil will grow anything, and after twenty years of peace, France would altogether recover herself."

"And yet the alliance of Spain is considered as of vital importance to France!"

"Of great importance, certainly. Spain has still soldiers who can fight well, as they have proved in Italy; and were the levies at home equally well drilled and disciplined, they would no doubt turn out good soldiers. But these are, at present, almost undrilled. They desert in numbers and return to their homes, after the slightest reverse, and prefer to act as partisans under leaders of their own choosing. But with Philip once firmly seated on the throne, with French advisers and officers to assist him, and a few regiments to serve as a nucleus to his army, Spain could turn out a force which would be a very valuable addition to the strength of any European power. With Spain as our ally we can, in addition to the force that she can put in the field, neglect altogether our southern frontier, and employ our whole army elsewhere. With her as an ally of Austria or of England, we should have to keep an army in the south to guard our borders."

Two days after leaving Paris, the party arrived at Peronne, where a considerable body of troops were collected, of which, although an aide-de-camp, Desmond now learned for the first time the duke was to take the command. No movements of importance had taken place in the field, and as the force at Peronne still wanted several regiments, to bring it up to the intended strength, some weeks passed before it was set in motion.

The four aides-de-camp, however, had a busy time of it. The main army was stationed in the neighbourhood of Lille, and frequent communications passed between Berwick and Vendome.zThe allies were inactive. Eugene had, early in April, met Marlborough at the Hague, and had concerted with him the plan for the campaign. He had then gone to Vienna to bring up reinforcements, and until these arrived Marlborough hardly felt in a position to take the offensive, as the French armies were considerably stronger than his own, and he had not yet been joined by the troops from Hanover. Except to receive orders, the aides-de-camp saw little of their commander. He was absorbed in the difficult problems of the war, and was occasionally absent for two or three days at the camp of Vendome. He always spoke kindly to them when on duty, but at other times dispensed altogether with their attendance, and as a rule took his meals alone.

"You see him at his worst," d'Eyncourt said one day to his new comrades, "He is a different man when he is in the field. Then he is full of life and activity, looking into every detail himself, endeavouring to infuse some of his own energy into others, full of care for the comfort of his troops, though ready to endure any hardship himself. Then you see the real man; a noble character, idolized by the soldiers and loved by us all. You must not judge him, in the slightest degree, by what he now is. He has a great deal on his mind, and has, so it is whispered, no small trouble in keeping the peace between Vendome and Burgundy. The failure, too, of the expedition to Scotland must have greatly disappointed him, and I have no doubt he expected to be put at the head of any French army sent over to place James upon the throne. However, he may congratulate himself now that he was not with it, for no honour and no gain has been earned by any concerned in it."

"That certainly is so," Desmond agreed. "It was a mismanaged affair altogether. To begin with, twenty thousand men should have been sent instead of six thousand; and in the next place, the fleet should have assembled at Brest or Bordeaux, for in that case, although the news of its assembling would assuredly have reached England, it would not have been known whether it was intended that the landing should be made in Ireland, Scotland, or on the English coast, while by gathering at Dunkirk no doubt was left as to the destination. This was proved by the fact that, when the English fleet watching the port was driven off by a gale, and an opportunity was thus given for a start, instead of coming back again, as we had hoped, only to find that we had left, it sailed straight for the north, making absolutely certain that we were bound for Edinburgh."

"Well, we must hope," O'Sullivan said, "that next time the force will, as you say, be fully twenty thousand men, will include the Irish Brigade, will be led by Berwick, and will land in Ireland."

At this moment an orderly entered.

"The duke requires your attendance, Lieutenant Kennedy."

Desmond at once went to the duke's apartments.

"You will start at once for Lille, Mr. Kennedy, and will report yourself to Marshal Vendome. I have arranged with him that one of my aides-de-camp shall accompany the force that is about to advance, and shall keep me informed of what is being done. I have selected you because I know you to be active and shrewd. The marshal is too much occupied to send me such full reports as I should wish, and I look to you not only to give me facts, but to convey to me your impressions of what you see passing around you. Do not fear to speak plainly. Your communications will be strictly private, and your views will be thus of far more use to me than the official expressions of the marshal and his staff.

"You will, of course, take your servant with you, and I have told off three troopers to accompany you, for the purpose of bringing your reports to me. There is no probability of a general engagement at present, and until we obtain some idea of Marlborough's plans, no extensive operations will be undertaken."

From the manner in which he spoke, Desmond had no doubt that Berwick himself was in favour of taking the initiative without delay, but that he had been overruled. It was indeed of importance to the French that, before advancing, they should secure possession of the towns of west Flanders, so that the great roads would all be open to them. Half an hour after leaving the duke, Desmond was in the saddle, and, followed by the four soldiers, rode for Vendome's camp. According to instructions he halted for the night at Arras, and reached Lille at ten the next morning. He at once presented himself to the marshal, and handed to him the letter from Berwick, of which he was the bearer.

The duke glanced through it.

"I have been expecting you, Lieutenant Kennedy, and have arranged that you shall mess and ride with the junior officers of my staff. I will order a tent to be erected for you, at once. Should any portion of my force move without me, I have arranged that you shall accompany it. You will find many of your compatriots in camp, for we have five battalions of the Irish Brigade with us, among them that of O'Brien, to which the Duke of Berwick informed me you belonged before you were appointed to his staff, having distinguished yourself markedly on several occasions."

The marechal-de-camp coming in, Vendome placed Desmond in his charge, requesting him to introduce him to the various officers of his staff, with whom he would have to mess, and to see that he was well cared for. He was well received by the young French officers, all of whom, with scarce an exception, belonged to good families, and Desmond was not long in discovering that they regarded their occupation rather as a pleasant and exciting diversion, than as a matter of duty, and that the greater portion of their time was devoted to pleasure. They rode, practised with the pistol and rapier, made excursions into the country, dined, and spent their evenings as if the army were nonexistent. A few only, and these were men who had served as officers, took their profession seriously, and divided among themselves what work had to be done, the young nobles gladly relinquishing it to them.

Chapter 12: Oudenarde.

Desmond did not remain long at the marshal's camp, but accompanied expeditions that were sent to Bruges, Ghent, and Ypres. The inhabitants of these towns had, for some time, been in communication with the marshal. They were hostile to the English, and had a standing feud, of many years' duration, with the Dutch.

As soon, therefore, as the French columns approached, they opened their gates. The weak garrisons that had been placed there, finding themselves unable to at once control the population and defend the walls, evacuated the town before the French arrived.

Beyond writing confidential reports to Berwick, Desmond had had little to do, and spent most of his time with his own regiment, by whom he was heartily welcomed, and with the other Irish battalions encamped near them. He and the other officers captured in the Salisbury had been given up as lost by their comrades; and the appearance of Desmond, in his staff uniform, was the first intimation they had received of his escape, of which he had more than once to give a detailed account.

In doing this, he made no mention of the seizure of Lord Godolphin. He knew that the minister was anxious that this should not get abroad, and, as he had behaved fairly to them, Desmond considered that he ought to remain silent on the subject; and merely said that, on their arrival at Rye, they had made an arrangement with a man who was in the habit of conveying persons secretly, to or from France, to take them across the channel.

"You amaze me more and more, Kennedy," the colonel said. "Six months ago, when you joined, you seemed to me little more than a boy, and yet you have been through adventures that demanded the brain and courage of a veteran. We missed you all much; but I hope we shall soon get the others back again, for I had news the other day, from Paris, that arrangements for their exchange were going on, and no doubt they will rejoin as soon as they land.

"There is little chance of you, O'Neil and O'Sullivan coming back to the regiment; but, at any rate, as Berwick's force is sure to join ours, as soon as operations begin in earnest, we shall often see you."

It was the end of June before the main army advanced. Desmond had returned to Peronne after the capture of the three Flemish towns, and was warmly praised by Berwick for the manner in which he had carried out the work entrusted to him. On the 6th of July, he received orders to accompany the duke.

"There is bad news," Captain Fromart said, entering the room where the four aides-de-camp were together. "You know the marshal had commenced the siege of Oudenarde. We have news now that the enemy has suddenly advanced towards him, and he has been obliged to raise the siege, and fall back across the Scheldt. The troops are to go forward at once. The duke will ride on, with all speed, in accordance with Vendome's urgent request. All four of you are to go on with him. I shall accompany the force here.

"There is no time to be lost. The duke's horse is to be at the door in a quarter of an hour, and it will not please him to be kept waiting. You had better leave your spare horses, for the present. I have already warned the escort."

It was a short notice, but by the time named the four aides-de-camp were in their saddles, as were their soldier servants, for by this time Desmond's two friends had obtained servants from a dragoon regiment. They were but just in time, for they had scarcely mounted when the duke came out, sprang into his saddle, and went off at a canter.

The distance was some fifty miles. They stopped once for two hours, to refresh themselves and their horses, and rode into Vendome's camp soon after nightfall. A large tent had been already erected for Berwick's use, close to that of the marshal; and another, close by, for the use of the officers who might come with him.

A quarter of an hour later, a soldier entered the aides-de-camp's tent, with a large tray.

"The Duke of Berwick bids me say, gentlemen, that he is supping with the marshal, who has sent these dishes to you from his own table."

"Please to give our thanks to the Duke of Vendome, for his kindness," Desmond said; but when the soldier had left the tent, he went on, "I have no doubt that this is the result of a suggestion on the part of Berwick, and greatly obliged to him we must feel. We had just been saying that we supposed we should get nothing to eat till tomorrow morning, while here is a supper worthy of the marshal, and four flasks of wine, which I doubt not are good."

It was ten o'clock before the duke returned to his tent, when he at once sent for his aides-de-camp.

"There will be nothing more for you to do, tonight, gentlemen. Sleep soundly, for we shall have a hard day's work tomorrow. We are to cross the Scheldt again at daybreak. The enemy are on the other side of the Dender, and the next day a pitched battle will probably be fought. You may be surprised that we do not wait until my forces arrive, but we have heard that Eugene's reinforcements are within two days' march of Marlborough, and, as they are more numerous than those I command, it has been decided to accept battle at once. Good night."

"The general is in a good temper," d'Eyncourt said, as they reentered their tent. "I expect that his views have been adopted, and that there was a warm discussion over them."

This was indeed the case. The Duke of Burgundy, an obstinate man without any knowledge of war, had been in favour of pushing forward, crossing the Lys as well as the Scheldt, and attacking the allies as soon as they met them. Vendome, on the other hand, was of opinion that the army which was now collected near Ghent had better advance against Oudenarde, which might be carried by a coup de main before Marlborough could come to its assistance, which he might be some days in doing, seeing that he was in command of a mixed force, composed of Dutch, Danes, Hanoverians, Prussians, and British. Burgundy then maintained that they should retire, and fight near Ypres, where they would be close to the frontier, and could retire upon Lille in case matters went against them. Berwick, however, at last managed to persuade him to agree to Vendome's plan, as the capture of Oudenarde was a matter of the utmost importance, and it would be as easy to fall back thence to Lille as it would be from Ypres.

This Burgundy had sullenly assented to, and the next morning the army marched to the position fixed upon. This was on steeply rising ground, with the river Norken running at its foot. Beyond this were two other eminences, on each of which stood a windmill. That on the west was called the windmill of Oycke, and that on the adjoining hill the windmill of Royegham, the latter flanking the main position. Oudenarde being found to be strongly garrisoned, it was decided, in spite of the opposition of Burgundy, to cross the Scheldt at Gavre, and then to give battle to the allies between that river and the Dender.

Marlborough had, however, been joined by Prince Eugene, who had, like Berwick, hurried on in advance of his army, and the two great generals decided, instead of attacking the French by the road from Brussels, to sweep round across the Scheldt at Oudenarde, and by other bridges across the river, and so to place themselves between Vendome and France.

A portion of the French army was already in movement, when the news came that the allies were fast coming up. Early the next morning their advance guard, composed of twelve battalions of infantry and the whole of the cavalry, reached the Scheldt; and, having thrown bridges over the river, crossed, and soon came in contact with the French advance guard, under Biron. There was some severe fighting, in which neither party gained any great advantage, the French maintaining possession of the village of Eynes.

While this conflict was going on, Marlborough and Eugene, with the main body, had reached the river, and were engaged in crossing it; and Vendome determined to attack them while carrying out the operation. He was, as usual, opposed by Burgundy, who wished to continue the march to Ghent. Marshal Vendome pointed out that, in a country so broken and interspersed with hedges, an army possessing the greatest strength--for the French numbered eighty-five thousand, while Marlborough had but eighty thousand under him--would lose the advantage of that superiority; and, upon Berwick strongly siding with the marshal, Burgundy was forced to give way.

The discussion lasted some time, enabling the allies to pass bodies of troops across the river, where they were formed up at a village a few hundred yards north of Oudenarde; and immediately Marlborough felt strong enough to risk an attack, orders were sent to Cadogan, who commanded the advance guard, to drive the enemy out of Eynes.

Four English battalions attacked the seven French battalions in the village, while the cavalry crossed higher up, and came down on the back of the village.

Three of the French battalions were surrounded and made prisoners, while the other four were dispersed.

It was now evident, even to Burgundy, that an action could not be avoided, but again an angry dispute took place. Vendome would have stood on the defensive, with the river Norken to be crossed before he could be attacked. He was, however, overruled by Burgundy, who had nominally chief command. Marlborough took advantage of the delay, and posted his troops in front of the castle of Bevere, and sent the twelve battalions at Eynes to reinforce his left, against which he saw the main attack of the French would be directed. He then lined all the hedges with infantry, and stationed twenty British battalions, under Argyle, in reserve.

Crossing the Norken, the French fell upon the Dutch and Hanoverians, who constituted the left wing, and who, though fighting obstinately, were driven back. Marlborough moved from the centre with twenty battalions to reinforce them, and despatched Eugene to command on the right.

A desperate fight now took place. On both flanks, the ground was broken by enclosures with deep wet ditches, bridges, woods, and small villages; and the cavalry were unable to act on such ground. The infantry on both sides fought with extreme resolution; every hedge, ditch, bridge, and house being defended to the last. Seldom, indeed, in modern warfare, has so obstinate and terrible a fight taken place. Frequently the combatants were mingled together, and fought with bayonets and the butt ends of their muskets.

Gradually, however, the Dutch and the Hanoverian battalions won their way forward, and drove the French back to the village of Diepenbeck, where the latter successfully maintained themselves. Marlborough then ordered General Overkirk to move round and seize the hill at Oycke, which, although it flanked the enemy's position, was not held by them.

This he did, with twenty Dutch and Danish battalions, who had only just crossed the river. He then pressed on and seized the mill of Royegham, thus cutting the communication between the French at Diepenbeck and the troops that still remained on the plateau beyond the Norken. Eugene then swung round his right, and, pressing forward, surrounded the French on that side, so completely enveloping them that his men and those of Overkirk each believed the other to be French--for darkness had now fallen--and fought for some time before the mistake was discovered.

As, in such a country, it was impossible to move troops in regular formation in the darkness, Marlborough gave orders for the troops to halt in the positions they held. Had the light lasted two hours longer, the whole of the French army would have been slain or captured; but, under cover of darkness, the greater portion made their way through the intervals of the allied troops. Many fled to Ghent, while thousands made for the French frontier. Vendome lost in killed and wounded six thousand men, and nine thousand prisoners, and his total loss exceeded twenty thousand; while the allies lost five thousand, of whom the great majority were Dutch, Danes, and Germans.

The French troops on the plateau withdrew, under the direction of Vendome, in good order; and before morning a large number of fugitives had rallied. Marlborough sent forty squadrons of horse in pursuit of them, but the French showed so firm an attitude that the cavalry were unable to seriously interfere with their retreat. Berwick had remained, during the day, near the marshal; and had placed his aides-de-camp at his disposal, for the difficulty of the ground, and the distance from the plateau of the various points at which the troops were engaged, rendered communication much slower than it otherwise would have been, and Desmond and his companions were frequently sent off with orders.

It was the first time Desmond had been under fire, and the effect of the roar of musketry, the whizzing of bullets, and the shouts of the combatants, gave him a much stronger feeling of discomfort than he had expected. The roar of cannon was not added to the other sounds, for the guns of the day were clumsy and difficult to move; and, owing to the rapid marches and countermarches of both armies, the greater portion of the artillery had been left behind, and only a few guns were on the field, and these, in so close and confined a country, were of little use.

Desmond felt now that he would far rather be fighting in the thick of it, with O'Brien's regiment, than making his way alone along the lanes, impeded constantly by columns advancing to the front, while he was met by a stream of wounded men making their way to the rear.

At first, all was exultation among the troops, for as the Hanoverians and Dutch were forced to give way before the assault of the main body of the French, shouts of victory rose; and it was confidently believed that they would, this day, avenge the two great victories Marlborough and Eugene had gained over them.

Having delivered his orders to the officer in command, Desmond rode back. Vendome and Berwick had both dismounted, and were standing together, with a few of their staff, at the edge of the plateau, examining the field with their telescopes.

"I have delivered your message, sir," he said, riding up and saluting. "The general bade me tell you all was going well. The enemy were falling back, and will soon be in full flight."

"Very well, Mr. Kennedy. By this time, he will have found out that he was a little too sanguine."

The fire had, indeed, for the past few minutes broken out with augmented fury. Marlborough had arrived at the threatened point, and had placed himself at the head of the Dutch and Hanoverians, and, animated by his presence, these had not only ceased to fall back, but were in turn advancing.

"The battle is not won yet, Kennedy," O'Sullivan, who had returned a few minutes before from the front, said, as he joined him. "On our left we are being driven back, for a large force has reinforced the enemy there, and unless our main column defeats the allied left, and pushes them into Oudenarde, we shall have night coming on before we have finished; and, as our cavalry cannot act in these cramped fields, Marlborough will be able to draw off without any great loss."

For an hour, there was no change. Then Berwick, looking round, beckoned to Desmond.

"Mr. Kennedy," he said, "a strong force of the enemy moved, half an hour ago, towards their left. I have lost sight of them, owing to the high hedges and trees, but it does not seem to me that they can have joined in the battle. Our troops are strongly posted at Diepenbeck, and should be able to maintain themselves there against the whole allied army; but the enemy cannot see our dispositions, and would surely have pushed forward and made a desperate assault on the village, had they been joined by the strong force I saw moving in that direction.

"It may be that this force has been held in reserve, in case our line should be reinforced, and again advance. Marlborough may be content to hold his own on his left, while Prince Eugene, who, we have heard, commands on their right, turns our flank on that side.

"I wish you to ascertain, if possible, what this force is doing, and where it is posted. If you ride across to the mill, on the eminence behind Diepenbeck, you may be able to get sight of them; or, if the smoke renders it impossible to discover matters from that point, ride on to the farther hill, and, descending there on the enemy's left, you will be able to make your way close enough to ascertain what is going on. You are well mounted, and need not greatly fear capture, for they would hardly care to divert a party of cavalry in pursuit of a single officer. Still, it is as well not to push your horse too hard on your way out, for you may possibly need all his strength."

A minute later, Desmond was cantering his horse down the declivity to the Norken. Crossing by the bridge near Mullen, he turned to the right and rode up the hill of Royegham. Here a strong brigade, composed of cavalry and infantry, under General Grimaldi, was stationed. Desmond rode up to him.

"The Duke of Berwick has sent me to ascertain, sir, the position of a strong body of the enemy's troops, whom he observed marching from the river towards our right. May I ask if you have noticed them?"

"We saw them move away, after crossing the river, but have not seen them since. I should fancy they are engaged in front of Diepenbeck; but the ground is so undulating, and the view so obscured by smoke, that we have not caught sight of them since they issued from Oudenarde--indeed, the hill behind Diepenbeck prevents our seeing down into the low land beyond."

"I will ride on there, sir," Desmond said. "Certainly a better view can be obtained than from this side."

A canter of a mile took him to the summit of the hill at whose foot Diepenbeck stood. He could see the masses of French troops, gathered in and in front of the village; but beyond that a veil of smoke covered the country, and entirely obscured the contending parties, whose position could only be guessed by the incessant rattle of their musketry fire.

Turning again, he rode down the dip that separated the hill from that of Oycke. He had just gained the crest, when he saw a large force marching rapidly towards the mill. Seeing at once the serious nature of the movement, he turned and galloped, at full speed, to the point where the generals were still watching the progress of the fight.

"I could learn nothing of the force you spoke of from General Grimaldi at Royegham, nor on the heights above Diepenbeck; but, riding towards Oycke, I saw them advancing at full speed towards the windmill, at which they had already almost arrived."

An exclamation of anger broke from the duke.

"This is what comes," he muttered, "of placing a fool in command of the army."

Turning away, he at once communicated the news to Vendome, who stamped his foot furiously on the ground.

"Just when victory was in our grasp," he said, and turned his glass towards Oycke, which was some four miles distant.

"I can make them out now," he said. "There is a black mass issuing from the village of Oycke, and ascending the hill in the direction of Royegham. It is too late to reinforce Grimaldi there. They will be upon him before we can cross the Norken. But, at any rate, we must send a brigade down to Henhelm, where, with Grimaldi's men, they can try to keep open the road from Diepenbeck."

Ten minutes later they could hear, by a sudden outburst of fire, that Grimaldi was engaged. The sun had already set, but Berwick was able to make out, with his glass, that the left was giving way before the attack of Eugene, and that the twenty battalions under Argyle, which had hitherto remained inactive, were advancing by the main road leading, through Mullen, to the plateau on which they stood.

"The day is lost," Berwick said bitterly. "The troops at Diepenbeck are completely cut off. Darkness alone can save them from annihilation. And to think that, if it had not been for Burgundy, we could have maintained ourselves here against double the force of the allies! So long as the system of giving the command of armies to royal incapables continues, we cannot hope for success."

Vendome lost no time in issuing orders. The troops still on the plateau were brought forward, whence their fire would command its approaches. Aides-de-camp were sent in all directions, to order the generals of divisions to draw off at once, and to make their way up to the plateau; and Berwick's four aides-de-camp were told to make their way, if possible, by different routes to Diepenbeck, and to give orders for the troops there to maintain themselves, at all costs, until darkness had completely fallen; and then to make their way as best they could to the plateau; if that was impossible, to march for either Ghent or Lille.

"The service is a desperate one, gentlemen," Berwick said, as he turned to give the orders to his officers, "but it is necessary, for if the force remain there until morning, they are all irretrievably lost. It is getting dark already, and you may, therefore, hope to pass unnoticed between the intervals of the enemy. If you get there safely, do not try to return at once, but, like the rest, endeavour to make off during the night."

Without waiting for orders, Mike followed his master. Going down, they met the remnants of Biron's division flying in disorder. They separated at the bridge of Mullen, and, with a word of adieu to his comrades, Desmond turned to the right, and rode for Groenvelde.

Suddenly, a volley of musketry was fired from the hill to the right. Desmond staggered for a moment in the saddle, and the bridle fell from his left hand. Mike was by his side in a moment.

"Where are you hurt, master?"

"In the left wrist, I fancy. By the way the hand hangs down, it must have smashed both bones. However, there is no time to wait, now. It is a matter of life and death to get to Diepenbeck."

"One moment, your honour. Let me put your hand into the breast of your coatee; then, if you keep your elbow tight against your body, it will keep it steady."

Although Mike carried out his suggestion as gently as he could, Desmond almost fainted with pain.

"Take a drop of brandy from your flask, master. It won't take half a minute, and then we will be off."

They continued their journey. The rattle of musketry, ahead of them, showed that the combat had already commenced close by; between either the advancing troops of Argyle, or those who had crossed the hill of Royegham; and Grimaldi's brigade, which was probably endeavouring to hold them in check, until the troops at Diepenbeck came back.

It was already too dark to distinguish the uniforms, except at a distance of a few yards. Dashing on, he saw a dark mass ahead--three officers rode out.

"Who are you, sir?" they shouted.

"I am carrying a report from the general," he replied, in English, and without drawing rein dashed on, passing within twenty yards of the column, and reached Diepenbeck without further interruption.

In the centre of the village, the French general was sitting on his horse, surrounded by his staff. The combat beyond raged as furiously as before. Desmond rode up, and saluted.

"I am the bearer of orders from Marshal Vendome, sir," he said. "He bid me tell you that a large force of the enemy has crossed the hills of Oycke and Royegham, and is already in your rear, the enemy's right overlapping your left; while the whole British reserve is pressing forward, and will ere long effect a junction with both these forces. Your retreat, therefore, is entirely cut off. The orders are that you shall maintain yourself here as long as possible, as in the darkness and confusion, it is unlikely that the allies can attack you from the rear before morning.

"The marshal himself holds the plateau, and will continue to do so. You are to make your way tonight, if possible, in battalions and in good order, through the intervals between the various divisions of the enemy; or, if that is not possible, singly. All are to endeavour to join him on the plateau. Those who cannot do this are to make for Ghent or Lille."

"Your order scarcely comes as a surprise, sir," the general said bitterly. "We have heard firing in our rear for some time, and we were afraid that things had gone badly with us, after all."

He at once gave orders that the troops behind the village were to take up a position to resist any attack made in that direction. Desmond dismounted, as did Mike, and the latter took the two horses, fastened them to a tree, and then, with Desmond's scarf, bound his arm firmly against his side.

"We have made a mess of it entirely, your honour," he said, "and have got a terrible bating. Sure we were lucky in getting here. Faith, I thought we were caught when you were hailed."

"It was a narrow escape, Mike; and if they had waited till I had got a little nearer, and had seen my uniform, I must have surrendered."

"It seems to me that we are like rats in a trap, Mr. Kennedy."

"Something like it, Mike; but it is hard if we can't get through them, in the dark."

"That we will do, sure enough," Mike said confidently; "but which way should we go?"

"That I can't tell you. You see, they are in strength in front, Marlborough and Eugene are on the left and partly behind us, and the troops you saw come across the hills are somewhere in the rear. If it were daylight, not a man of us would escape; but as it is, it will be hard if we cannot make our way through.

"What I am thinking about chiefly, at present, is the safety of O'Sullivan, O'Neil, and d'Eyncourt. They ought to have been here as soon as we were. They may either have lost their way in the darkness, or fallen into the hands of the enemy. However, I shall not give them up for another half hour."

The firing was now abating, and presently died away completely; except for a few scattered shots, showing that the allies had been halted where they stood, and were no longer pressing forward. Another hour passed, and Desmond's comrades were still absent.

In the meantime, the general had called together the colonels of the several regiments, had explained the situation to them, and repeated Vendome's orders. The news came like a thunderbolt upon them, for the din of firing round the village had completely deadened all distant sound, and they were wholly unaware of what was passing in other parts of the field.

"I must leave the matter to your individual discretion," the general said. "Those of you who think your men can be relied on, can try to escape and join the marshal in a body. Those who have not that confidence in their regiments--and indeed some of these have been almost annihilated--had best tell them to scatter. Those who remain here will assuredly be made prisoners in the morning.

"It is possible that that may be the better plan, for it is better to surrender than to be cut to pieces. I therefore leave the matter entirely in your hands. I myself shall remain here. We have done all that men can do in the way of fighting, and, as I was told to hold this place till the last, I shall remain at my post."

Desmond was present when this conversation took place.

"We will wait another hour, Mike," he said, as he rejoined his follower. "We may be sure that the greater part of the enemy's troops will be asleep by that time. They must have made a tremendous march, for the news last night was that they were twenty miles away; and they have been fighting twelve hours. After such work as that, the men will drop down to sleep as soon as they have halted."

"Shall we go on horse or on foot, your honour?"

"I think the best plan will be to lead our horses, Mike, across this country. It would seem natural to do so, and once through them, we could then gallop round and join the troops on the plateau."

"I should say, sir, that if I were to steal out to where they have been fighting for the last six hours, I might get a couple of uniforms to put over our own. They will be lying thick enough there, poor chaps. If we had them on, we might pass through any troops we might meet, as we both speak English."

"That is a good idea, Mike, if you can carry it out."

"Sure I can do that, and without difficulty, your honour. I expect the enemy have drawn back a little, so as to be in some sort of order if we were to fall upon them in the night; and I know that all our men have been recalled. I will fasten the horses to this tree, and perhaps your honour will keep an eye on them."

"I will stay with them, Mike."

The soldier at once made off. The village was now crowded with troops. All order was at an end, and the regiments were considerably mixed up. The officers went among them, saying that an attempt was going to be made to pass through the enemy, and join the force on the plateau. They pointed out that there was at least as much hope in being able to do so as in making off singly.

Many of the soldiers, not having themselves suffered defeat, responded to the call; and several bodies, four or five hundred strong, marched out into the darkness. The majority, however, decided to shift for themselves, and stole away in threes and fours. Of those that remained, some broke into the village wine and beer shops and drank to stupefaction; while others, exhausted by the efforts of the day, threw themselves down and slept.

Mike was away half an hour.

"I have got an officer's cloak for you, and a helmet with feathers. I think he must have been a staff officer, who was killed while delivering his orders. I have got a soldier's overcoat and shako for myself."

"Capital, Mike! Now I think that we can venture, and we will go the shortest way. We might very well lose ourselves among these hills, if we were to try to make a circuit."

Having put the Dutch uniforms over their own, they set out, taking the way to the left until they came to the main road by which the British reserve had advanced. Then they mounted their horses.

"It is no use trying to make our way through the broken ground, Mike. There is another road that goes through Huerne. We will strike that, and must so get round on the right of the enemy. Even if we come upon them, we are not likely to excite suspicion, as we shall be on a road leading from Oudenarde.

"I was noticing that road from the height. It runs into this again, near Mullen, and the enemy are not likely to have posted themselves so near to the river."

They rode on through Huerne. The village was full of wounded. No one paid them any attention, and they again went on, until suddenly they were challenged with the usual "Who comes there?"

"A staff officer, with despatches," Desmond replied.

He heard the butt of the soldier's musket drop upon the ground, and rode forward.

"Can you tell me, my man," he said as he reached the sentinel, "where the Duke of Marlborough is to be found?"

"I don't know, sir," the man replied. "Only our regiment is here. I know there are a number of cavalry away there on the left, and I heard someone say that the duke himself was there. There is a crossroad, a hundred yards farther on, which will lead you to them."

Thanking the man, Desmond rode on. A few bivouac fires had been lighted, and these were already beginning to burn low, the troops having dropped asleep almost as soon as they halted.

"I hope we shall meet no more of them, Mike," Desmond said, as they went on at a brisk trot. "I sha'n't feel quite safe till we get to Mullen."

They met, however, with no further interruption. As they crossed the bridge, they halted, took off the borrowed uniforms, threw away the headgear and put on their own hats, which they carried under their cloaks, and then rode on up the hill, after having first satisfied the officer commanding a strong guard placed at the bridge that they were friends.

Another ten minutes, and they were upon the plateau. Desmond had no difficulty in finding out where the headquarters were established at Hayse, and, riding there, he at once went into the house occupied by Berwick, and reported his return.

"I am glad to see you back again, Kennedy," the duke said, heartily. "It is something to have recovered one friend from the wreck. Now, what is your news?"

Desmond related what had happened to him from the time he left, and said that a large proportion of the troops at Diepenbeck had already left, and, as he heard no outburst of firing, he hoped most of them had got safely away.

"I see you are wounded."

"I have had my wrist smashed with a musket ball, fired by a party on a hill to the right, belonging, I suppose, to the force that came up from Oycke."

"You had a narrow escape of your life," Berwick said. "If you had been hit a little farther back, the ball would have gone through your body. Sit down at once. I will send for my surgeon."

And he instantly gave orders for the surgeon of the staff to come to his tent, and then made Desmond, who was suffering terribly from the agony of the wound, drink a tumbler of wine.

"I know you are all busy, doctor," the duke said, as the surgeon entered, "but you must do something for Mr. Kennedy, who is badly wounded in the arm."

The surgeon examined the wound, and shook his head.

"Both bones are fractured," he said, "and I am afraid that there is nothing for it but amputation."

"Then leave it till tomorrow, doctor," Desmond said faintly. "There must be a number of poor fellows who want your attention much more than I do."

"That would do, if I could make you a cradle, but we are badly off for all surgical appliances."

"Could you cut one out of one of my jack boots?"

"A capital idea, Mr. Kennedy. Nothing could be better. And I will put it in operation, at once, with some of my other patients."

"Mr. Kennedy is full of expedients, doctor, and it seems to me that this may be really a valuable one. All the cavalry men have jack boots, and I will give you an order to requisition as many as may be required. The men can get new ones from the stores at Ghent."

The surgeon at once cut off the foot of one of Desmond's boots, and then divided the leg longways. "There," he said, taking up one of the halves; "you could not wish for a better cradle."

He took out some lint that he had brought with him, together with some flat splints, bound the hand in its proper position, and then laid the arm from the elbow to the fingers in the cradle, round which he tightly put a few bandages to keep it in position.

"Now for your scarf," he said, and with this made a sling to support the arm.

The whole operation did not take five minutes.

"Now, Mr. Kennedy, you had best lie down and get what sleep you can. I will take the other half of your boot, and the other boot also. It will be no use without its fellow. It will make three wounded men comparatively comfortable, and I will send for some more from the troopers."

"Yes, lie down at once, Kennedy," Berwick said. "We are going to march off at daybreak, and the marshal and I have arranged everything between ourselves. You had better try and eat something, if it is only a wing of that chicken and a few mouthfuls of meat. Your faintness must be due as much to hunger as to your wound, for you have been at work since early morning, and cannot have had time to eat anything."

This was indeed the case, and Desmond managed to swallow a few mouthfuls, and then lay down upon the sofa, where, in spite of the pain of his wound, he presently dozed off, being utterly worn out with the work and excitement of the day.

Before morning, some five thousand of the troops from Diepenbeck had marched into the camp, in good order and with their arms, and as soon as it was daylight the whole force started for Ghent. With deep regret, Desmond had learned from the marshal, before lying down, that none of his comrades had returned; and as they had not reached Diepenbeck, he felt sure that they were either killed or prisoners.

"D'Eyncourt will, of course, be treated as a prisoner of war; but if the identity of O'Sullivan or O'Neil is proved with the officers of that name who escaped from Newgate, it is likely to go hard with him."

After repulsing the cavalry sent in pursuit, the army marched away unmolested, being joined as they went by large numbers of fugitives, who had made their way through the allied lines in small parties. Marlborough's army remained on the ground they had won, collecting and caring for the wounded of both armies.

Two days later, Berwick's corps joined Vendome, and that of Eugene marched into Marlborough's camp. In spite of the loss that he had suffered at Oudenarde, this reinforcement raised Vendome's army to over one hundred and ten thousand men, which was about the same force as Marlborough had under his command.

After Eugene had joined him, standing as he did between Vendome's army and Paris, Marlborough proposed that the enemy's fortresses should be neglected, and that the army should march directly on Paris. The movement might have been attended with success, but was of so daring a description that even Eugene opposed it, while the commanders of the Dutch, Danes, and Prussians were unanimously against it; and he consequently decided to lay siege to Lille--a tremendous undertaking, for Lille was considered the strongest fortress in France, and Vendome, with over a hundred thousand men, was within a couple of days' march of it.

His dispositions were made with extreme care, and a tremendous convoy of heavy artillery, ammunition, and provisions was brought up from Ostend, without the French being able to interfere with its progress. Marlborough, with his British contingent and the Hanoverians, was to cover the operations of the siege, which was to be undertaken by Prince Eugene with the rest of the allied army.

Vendome marched at once with his army, and, making a circuit, placed himself between Lille and Paris, deserting his recent conquests in Ypres, Ghent, and Bruges, all of which fell into the hands of the allies.

Chapter 13: Convalescent.

Desmond was not present with the French army, for many hours after their arrival at Ghent. He suffered intense pain on the ride thither, and was then taken to a hospital that had been hastily formed for the reception of wounded officers. Here the surgeons had agreed that there was nothing for it, but to amputate the arm halfway between the wrist and the elbow. The limb was already greatly swollen.

"Under ordinary circumstances," the surgeon said, "we should wait until we had reduced the inflammation, but this might be a matter of a week or ten days, and there is no time to spare, as the army will probably march away in a few days, and travel would increase the inflammation to such an extent that your life might be sacrificed."

"I would rather have it taken off at once, doctor," Desmond said. "The operation cannot hurt very much more than the arm is hurting already, and the sooner it is over, the better."

Surgery was in its infancy at that time. Anesthetics were undreamt of; but the surgeons of the French army had large experience, and the operation was very skilfully performed, for the time. The stump was then seared with a hot iron.

"You have stood it well," the surgeon said, for, except when the iron was applied to the wound, no groan had issued from Desmond's lips. "Now, your servant must keep these dressings continually soaked with water, and, in a few days, we may hope that you will be able to travel in a waggon without danger."

When the army marched away a week later, Desmond was placed in a waggon, half filled with hay, with several other wounded officers. At Arras, where there was a large military hospital, he was kept for a few days, and then sent on to Amiens, only the most severe cases being retained at Arras, as another engagement might take place at any moment, and the resources of the town would be taxed to the utmost. He gained strength very slowly, and it was six weeks before the surgeons pronounced him to be sufficiently convalescent to be moved.

"It would," they said, "be probably some months before he would be fit to return to active service."

He was sitting, looking listlessly out of the window of the chamber that he and three other officers occupied, when Mike came in, followed, to Desmond's intense surprise, by Monsieur de la Vallee.

"My dear Desmond," the latter exclaimed, hurrying forward and grasping his hand, "you must have thought that we had all forgotten you."

"Indeed, I never thought anything of the kind, Philip. I did not suppose that you had ever heard of me, since we parted at Moulins."

"News travels but slowly, but we did hear that fifteen subalterns of O'Brien's regiment were captured in the Salisbury. I wrote to a friend in Paris, and he told me that you were among the number, but that, on making enquiries, he found you had, in some manner or other, effected your escape, and that you and two other officers had had an audience with the king, and had then gone to the northern frontier on the staff of the Duke of Berwick. I wrote begging him to get, if possible, a sight of the despatches, and if your name appeared, to let us know. Ten days ago, I received a letter from him, to say that you had been wounded at Oudenarde. The Duke of Berwick had, in his private despatch to the king, mentioned your name with very high praise, saying that it was due to you, alone, that so many of the troops hemmed in at some village or other--I forget its name--managed to make their escape during the night, for, although he sent off four aides-de-camp with orders, you alone managed to get through the enemy, though wounded by a bullet which had caused you the loss of your hand. He said he had written to the chief surgeon on Berwick's staff, who was a personal friend of his, to ascertain, if possible, where you were. Of course, I set out as soon as I received his letter."

"What! Have you ridden all the way from the south of France to come to me, Philip?"

"Of course I have, and should have ridden all across Europe, if it had been necessary. I went round by Pointdexter. The baron is laid up with an attack of gout, or he would have accompanied me. He sent all sorts of messages, and so did Anne, and the latter informed me that I need not show my face at the chateau again, until I came accompanied by you. When I reached Paris my friend had learned from the surgeon that you were at Amiens, and so, here I am.

"I met your faithful Mike at the gate of the hospital. I was glad, indeed, to see that he had come out unharmed from that terrible fight. When I told him I had come to take you away, he almost cried with joy."

"It will be the saving of him," he said. "He has been going down the hill for the last fortnight, and it is change and good nursing he wants."

"He will get good nursing, I warrant," I said, "and the soft air of the south will soon set him up."

"It is wonderfully kind of you, Philip; but I am sure I am not strong enough to ride."

"No one is thinking of your riding, at present, Desmond. I have brought down a horse litter with me, and four of my men, with the quietest horses on the estate, and all you have to do is to lie down in it, and talk with me whenever you are disposed. You have a whole batch of adventures to tell me."

"I feel better already, Philip. I own that I have been downhearted of late, for it seemed to me that I should be an invalid for months, and be living in Paris without a friend except Mike, for all the regiments of the Brigade are either with Vendome or in Spain. The sight of your face, and the thought of your kindness, so cheers me that I feel capable of anything."

"Well, we will start tomorrow morning, Desmond. I shall go at once and see the director of the hospital, and get an order for your discharge."

The next morning they set out. Desmond had to be assisted downstairs. There he was laid on a litter, packed with soft rugs. This was raised and placed between two horses, ridden by two of de la Vallee's men. De la Vallee himself took his place by the side of the litter, Mike rode on ahead leading Desmond's charger, and the other two servants fell to the rear, in readiness to change with those bearing the litter, when half the day's journey was done.

Seeing that the exertion of being moved had exhausted his friend, de la Vallee rode for some time in silence. Then, when Desmond opened his eyes and smiled at him, he said:

"I hope you are feeling comfortable?"

"Perfectly. I hardly feel any motion."

Every care had been taken to prevent jolting. The poles of the litter were unusually long, thus adding to their elasticity. The ends passed through leathern loops suspended from the saddle; and were, at this point, covered with a thick wrapping of flannel bandages, which aided in minimizing the effect of any jar. The first day's journey was performed at a walking pace, and they reached Beauvais, twenty-five miles being accomplished.

The fresh air and the slight easy motion were beneficial, and in the afternoon, Desmond was able to talk cheerfully with his friend. There was, however, no continued conversation, Philip saying he would ask no questions about Desmond's doings until he was stronger. His story had better be told while sitting quietly in a room, where it would not be necessary, as it was on the road, for the voice to be raised.

In the evening, however, after partaking of supper, Desmond, without being asked, related the incidents, so far as he knew them, of the battle of Oudenarde, and of the manner in which he received his wound.

"The whole disaster was due entirely to the Duke of Burgundy, or rather to the king, who placed him in command over two generals of the highest skill and reputation. If he had wanted to accompany the army, Burgundy should have done so just as our King James did, merely as a volunteer.

"I am told that the king showed great courage in the battle. For my part, I think his presence was altogether a mistake. He claims that the English are his subjects, and yet he takes part with a foreign army in battle against them. His being present will certainly not add to his popularity in England."

"I agree with you," de la Vallee said. "It would have been much wiser for him to have abstained, altogether, from interference in the matter. It was, of course, a different thing when he attempted to land in Scotland. Then he would have been leading the loyal portion of his subjects, against those whom he considers rebels against his authority. That was quite a different thing from acting, without cause or reason, as a volunteer in the French army, against those whom he regards as his countrymen and subjects.

"I am afraid, Desmond, that, though it may shock you to think so, these Stuart princes of yours are not wise men. Legitimate monarchs of England though they may be, they do not possess the qualities that endear kings to their people. From what I have heard, James was a heavy pedant, a rank coward, essentially not a man to be popular among a spirited people. Charles had a noble presence and many fine qualities. But, although his ideas of kingly power would have suited us well enough in France, his arbitrary measures alienated a large proportion of his people, and brought ruin upon him.

"Your second Charles, in spite of his numerous indiscretions, was not unpopular, because the people were wearied of the stern repression of Puritan rule, and were therefore disposed to look leniently upon his frailties, while they appreciated his good temper and wit. His fatal mistake was allying himself so closely with us--a grievous mistake, indeed, when we remember that for centuries the two nations had been bitterly opposed to each other. As for his brother, he forfeited his throne by his leanings towards the Catholic Church, in whose communion he died. Decidedly, the Stuart kings were not a success.

"As to James the Third, as you call him, I know nothing beyond the fact that he is a protege of the king of France, and has now fought against his own people--a blunder, as it seems to me, of the worst kind, and one which is certain to alienate many of his supporters on the other side of the water. Were he to mount the throne, it would be partly due to the aid of French troops and French money--men and money, mind you, of a power at war with England! He would therefore, necessarily, like Charles the Second, be regarded as a protege of France. He would be bound in gratitude to Louis, and the position of England would be altogether changed. She would become the ally of Spain and France, her ancient enemies; and opponent of her present allies, Holland, Austria, Protestant Germany, and Denmark."

Desmond was silent. He could not but agree with what his friend said, and had himself considered that it was a most unwise step for James to appear in the field, fighting against his countrymen.

"I don't think I am strong enough to argue, Philip," he said with a smile, after a long pause, "and I don't mean to give you a victory, when I am fighting under disadvantages. The Stuarts certainly never did any special benefit to Ireland, and assuredly brought ruin and misery upon us; and at the present moment, I don't seem able to explain why we should be so devoted to the cause of these Scottish Stuarts, rather than to that of Anne, who is, after all, of the same family and race. However, we will fight it out when my brain is not so dull as it is at present."

They slept the next night at Pontoise, having made a somewhat short journey, though Desmond protested that he felt quite equal to going on to Paris.

"You are a good deal better today, Desmond, but there is no hurry, and we will take matters quietly. If you continue to make improvement we shall be able, in another day or two, to travel faster; and I hope that, before we get to the end of our journey, you will be strong enough to sit your horse for a few miles each day."

They made no stay in Paris, but proceeded on their way, the morning after their arrival. Melun and Montargis were their next halting places. Desmond was gaining strength rapidly. His good spirits were returning, and at their evening halt, he had been able to recite the history of his escape from England. His wound had a less angry appearance, and on the day of their leaving Montargis the horses, at his request, occasionally broke into a trot for a mile or two.

"You are looking paler. I think the motion is too much for you," Philip said after one of these occasions, when they again settled down to a walking pace.

"I feel a bit tired, Philip, but one must make a beginning, and I shall never get strong unless I begin to use my muscles. At present, I acknowledge I feel as if I had been beaten all over with sticks, but I have no doubt that I shall shake this off, after a bit."

This was indeed the case, and on the last three days of their journey to Pointdexter, he sat his horse for two or three hours. Philip had, on the last day, sent on one of his men to inform the baron that he would arrive that evening with Desmond, and as they were seen approaching, the baron and his daughter came out from the chateau, and welcomed them as they alighted.

"Do not upset the young fellow by appearing shocked at his appearance," the former had said to Anne. "It was certainly a blow, this morning, to hear that he had lost his left hand, and that the greater portion of the journey had had to be performed in a litter, so you must expect to find him greatly pulled down. But see, they are breaking into a trot, so he has evidently gained strength on the way."

In spite of the warning, the girl's eyes filled with tears as she saw Desmond's thin face and wasted figure, and his left arm in a sling.

"Welcome to Pointdexter, Monsieur Kennedy! Many have entered here, since the old chateau was built, but none who have rendered such vital service to our race. Do not try to speak. I see that you are shaken with your journey. We will soon put that all right."

"It has been a rather longer journey than we have previously made," Desmond said, after dismounting and shaking hands with the baron and his daughter, "and we rode somewhat faster than usual, as we were both of us anxious to be here. It was good, indeed, of Philip to make such a journey to find and bring me to you."

"If he had not done so, assuredly we should. My foot was so bad, with this villainous gout, that I could not put it in a stirrup, but we should have had out the family coach. I had half a mind to do so as it was, and Anne was most anxious to try her powers of nursing, but Philip overruled us, and said that he would be with you a week earlier than we could reach you in the coach, and that, moreover, he was sure the journey in an open horse litter would be far better for you than being jolted in a close carriage. So, as usual, he had his own way; though I must say that, for once, Anne rebelled strongly against his authority."

"You are all very good, Baron," Desmond said; "but, indeed, I think that Philip was right. I can assure you that the journey has done me an immense deal of good, and he will tell you that I am very different, now, from what I was when he found me at Amiens, for I had begun to think that I should never get away alive."

"Do not let us stay talking here," the baron said. "Anne has had some soup prepared for you, under her own eyes; and that, and a glass or two of good Burgundy, will do wonders for you."

Desmond, indeed, was greatly revived, and was able to join in a cheerful conversation with his hosts.

"We are both dying to hear your adventures," the baron said, "and how you managed to escape from that jail in England, as you did, and also how it was that we met with that dreadful disaster at Oudenarde. It really seems that those terrible fellows, Marlborough and Prince Eugene, are invincible."

"They are good generals, Baron. Beyond troubles with the commanders of the forces of their allies, they are able to carry out their own plans. The Dukes of Vendome and Berwick are also able commanders, but they were hampered by the presence of the Duke of Burgundy, who, on several occasions, overruled their opinions and ruined their plans. It is to him, alone, that the defeat at Oudenarde is due. The French soldiers fought as well as ever, and it was the position in which they were placed, and not the superior fighting powers of the enemy, that caused their defeat."

"But how is it," the baron asked, "that with, as I hear, one hundred and ten thousand men, Vendome does not raise the siege of Lille? It seems incredible that, with so great a force, he should remain inactive while the enemy are carrying out their works for the siege."

"That I cannot tell you, sir. We heard all sorts of rumours at Amiens, but it seems that Marlborough had taken up a strong position, and entrenched himself there with seventy thousand men, while Eugene is conducting the siege operations."

"I don't understand it," the baron said, irritably. "There must be more ways of marching to Lille than one. If one road is barred, why not advance by another? The Duke of Burgundy is not with the army now, so the blame cannot be put on him."

"No, sir; but Berwick's army is still, as I hear, under his independent command, and the duke, excellent soldier as he is, is not one to be easily led. If his opinion differs from that of Vendome, he would assuredly maintain it; and as his manner is not conciliatory, and his opinions are very strongly expressed, it may well be that there are, as was rumoured at Amiens, constant dissensions between him and Vendome."

"Well, it seems to me very strange, Monsieur Kennedy, after having during the last reign defeated the best infantry of Spain, humbled Austria, subdued Bavaria, crushed the enemy in Italy, and shown ourselves to be the best soldiers in Europe; that we should now suffer defeat after defeat, by an army containing men of half a score of nationalities, though led by the greatest general that England has ever produced."

"And, Baron, with English troops under him who have, for hundreds of years, shown themselves invincible!"

"Yes, yes," the baron said, hastily. "We know all about Crecy, Poitiers, and Agincourt; and how well they fought in Holland; but I thought, Kennedy, that you were the enemy of the English, and were here with your brave countrymen to fight against them."

"Not in my case, assuredly, Baron. I came over here because there is no opening for Irish gentlemen at home, and because only by the aid of France could our lawful king be placed on the throne. It is true that a section of the English people, under Oliver Cromwell, not only conquered us, but divided a great portion of our land among themselves; and, although we were again defeated by a usurping Dutch king, with the Dutch troops under his command, that is no reason why I should feel any animosity to the people at large, whose qualities I admire, and the majority of whom are, in their hearts, attached to the cause of the Stuarts, and hate those who are keeping the king from his throne. I own that I would rather that it had fallen to my lot to fight for France against Spaniards, Germans, and Italians, than against the English."

"Did you lose many friends at Oudenarde, Monsieur Kennedy?" Anne asked.

"I lost my two greatest friends," Desmond said. "At least, I fear that both are dead. They were the two who escaped with me from the English prison. They, with Monsieur d'Eyncourt, another of Berwick's aides-de-camp, started with me to carry orders to the troops, who were all but surrounded by the enemy. We went by different roads, to increase the chances of one of us getting there.

"I succeeded with but this comparatively trifling wound," and he pointed to his empty sleeve, "but none of the other three got through, nor did their names appear when the lists were exchanged of the prisoners captured. Therefore, I have no doubt that all fell in the performance of their duty. We had been great friends, ever since I came out, and their loss has greatly affected me."

"You are young, and will find fresh friends," the baron said, briskly. "Do not let us dwell on the past. You have now to apply all your energy to getting strong, and if you show as much vigour in that, as in other matters, I hope that in a month's time you will be well on the road towards complete recovery."

"I mean to try hard, Baron," Desmond said, with a smile. "If I continue to gain strength as quickly as I have done during the journey, I shall certainly insist, before long, on being considered convalescent."

Day by day, indeed, his strength increased. At first he wandered about in the park, accompanied by Philip and Anne, for the baron, although somewhat recovered from his attack of gout, still walked with difficulty. In a week, he again took to horse exercise, and was ere long able to join in hunting and hawking parties.

The house was gay, for the baron, as soon as Desmond was able to take his share in conversation, invited many of the neighbouring gentry to the chateau, and introduced him to them as the man who had done so much for his daughter and himself. Several entertainments were given, at which the chateau was thrown open to all comers, in honour partly of Desmond and partly of the approaching marriage of the baron's daughter to Monsieur de la Vallee.

This had been arranged to take place in September. Before that time arrived, Desmond had completely recovered his strength, and being now fit for service, was anxious to join. But his friends would not hear of his departure until after the marriage; and as news came that Lille had been captured by the allies, and it was certain that both armies would soon go into winter quarters, and would fight no more that year, he allowed himself to be persuaded to stay.

The siege had been one of the most terrible in history. The place was nobly defended, and its conquest cost the allies dearly, twelve thousand being killed and wounded, and over seven thousand succumbing to diseases; while of the garrison, nearly seventeen thousand strong, but four thousand five hundred remained alive at the time it capitulated. Its fall caused general consternation throughout France, for it opened the road to Paris, and during the winter Louis made strenuous efforts to obtain peace; but the terms demanded by the allies were so onerous that the negotiations were broken off.

In spite of the general distress throughout the country, the wedding was a gay one.

Desmond had written to the Duke of Berwick, who was now in Paris, saying that he was fit for duty, and would report himself at the end of the month; and, on the day before he was about to leave Pointdexter, he received a reply from him.

It ran as follows:

Dear Monsieur Kennedy:

I am heartily glad to hear of your restoration to health. I mentioned you to His Majesty today, who was pleased to speak very highly of you.

The campaign is virtually at an end, for the present year. His Majesty has informed me that various changes will be made in the spring. Marshal de Villars is to replace the Duke of Vendome in the command of the northern army. The latter has been unfortunate, and misfortune on the part of a soldier is regarded as next door to a crime. Certainly the defeat at Oudenarde was not his fault, but had he taken my advice, Lille might have been saved. Doubtless he was as much dissatisfied with me as I was with him, and perhaps with reason; for, as you know, I am not accustomed to mince my phrases. However, as His Majesty was pleased to say, it is evident that having two generals acting together, each with an independent command, is a mistake, and one that should not be again committed. Therefore, next spring I am to take the command of an army in Dauphiny, and to check the Austrians and Italians.

He said, "If you can spare him, Duke, I should be glad if you would let me have this young Irishman for a time. I shall promote him to the rank of captain, for the great service he rendered in carrying, as you say, at grievous risk and with the loss of his hand, the order to the troops at Diepenbeck to scatter during the night, thus saving me at least ten thousand of my soldiers. I shall also settle upon him a pension of fifty louis a year, for the loss of his hand. I will send him to Spain, having had several complaints from the Duke of Orleans" (who, as you know, is now in command there) "of the incompetence of many of his staff".

I said that, although I had found you a most zealous and useful officer, and had a warm regard for you, I would of course accede to His Majesty's wishes in the matter. Enclosed in this letter is the order for you to join the Duke of Orleans, and a private letter from myself to the duke, giving a sketch of your services and exploits, which will doubtless give you, at once, a place in his favour.

I do not think that this war will last very much longer. France is well-nigh ruined by the sacrifices she has made, and the drain upon the allies must be almost as great. Therefore, I trust that another campaign will bring it to an end. If not, you may be assured that when the duke no longer requires your services--and it is probable that, after a year's campaigning, he will be heartily tired with the difficulties that he, as I did, will meet with from the procrastination and general stupidity of the Spanish--you will be free to return to me, and I shall be glad to number you again among the members of my staff.

Desmond was sorry to leave the service of the duke, but consoled himself with the hope that it would be only temporary; and the prospect of a year's campaigning, in a new country, was by no means displeasing to him. Therefore, after writing a suitable letter to the duke, he took leave of the Baron Pointdexter, with many thanks for his kindness, and, attended by Mike, started for Spain.

"It's glad I am to be on the move again, Captain Kennedy," the soldier said, as they rode away. "Sure, your honour, idleness is not good for a man, especially when he has lashings of the best of food and drink. When I came to buckle on my sword belt, this morning, I found it would not meet within three inches, and the coatee is so tight that I feel as if I was suffocated."

"You will soon work it down again, Mike. From what I hear of Spain, there is no fear of your getting too much food there. Rough work and small rations are, I hear, the rule."

"I am ready for a good spell then, your honour. I hardly know myself now, for I am flabby and short of wind. Still, I am sorry to leave the chateau, for I have had the best time I ever had, in my life. Everyone was mighty kind, and seemed to think that I had done great things in helping to rescue Miss Anne, whereas I did nothing at all, except to follow you."

Chapter 14: A Mission.

On arriving at Madrid in the first week in December, 1708, Desmond, after putting up at an hotel, and changing the uniform in which he travelled for his dress suit, proceeded to the headquarters of the Duke of Orleans, and sent in his name, together with Berwick's letter of introduction. In a few minutes he was shown into his room. The duke looked at him in some surprise.

"Are you Captain Kennedy?"

"I am, Your Royal Highness."

"The Duke of Berwick has very strongly recommended you to me, saying that you had performed excellent service under him, and that he parted with you, with regret, at the express wish of His Majesty. He speaks of you as a young officer, but I was hardly prepared to see one so youthful. He says that you are devoted to your work, active and intelligent as well as brave; and as such your arrival is very welcome to me, for although excellent in battle, I own that my officers are less devoted to the hard work and detail that are as necessary as bravery on a general's staff.

"By the way, I seem to have heard your name before. Let me see, it was in connection, was it not, with that affair of the Marquis de Tulle and Baron de Pointdexter's daughter?"

"I certainly had the good fortune to take part in that affair, sir."

"The king himself was pleased to tell me the details of that adventure, and to speak very highly of your courage and energy in carrying it out. And so, you are really the hero of that affair? He said that you were a young ensign in O'Brien's Irish regiment. You have risen rapidly, sir, for it is but eighteen months since it took place."

"His Majesty graciously promoted me to the rank of lieutenant when I was appointed by the Duke of Berwick to his staff. I obtained my next step after the battle of Oudenarde, for carrying a despatch to the force cut off in the village of Diepenbeck, in which service I received a wound which resulted in the loss of my left hand. I was several weeks in hospital, and then obtained sick leave and went down for two months to Baron de Pointdexter, which visit resulted in my complete restoration to health. At the end of that time the Duke of Berwick, who had also returned from the army, was good enough to recommend me to His Majesty, and he thereupon promoted me and appointed me to join your staff."

"If Marshal Berwick spoke approvingly of your conduct, Captain Kennedy, it is in itself a sufficient recommendation, for the duke is not easily satisfied. I am sure that I shall find you a valuable acquisition to my staff."

The duke invited Desmond to dine with him that evening, and presented him to several of his staff who were among the company. These were, for the most part, personal friends and associates of the duke; gallant gentlemen, but wholly ignorant of war, and adverse to hard work, and it was not long before Desmond found that his services were called into requisition whenever it was necessary that a despatch should be carried to a distance. He was by no means sorry that this should be the case, for he soon tired of the stiffness and ceremony of the Spanish Court, and of the conversation (chiefly relating to ladies in Paris, whose very names were unknown to him) among the French officers, and it was a relief to him, indeed, when he could get away from attendance at headquarters, and enjoy an evening's talk with the officers of one or other of the four Irish regiments there.

Many of these expeditions were attended by considerable danger, for the wars that had for some years devastated the country had resulted in general disorder. Armed bands, under the pretence of acting in the interest of one claimant or other to the throne, traversed the country, pillaging the villages, driving off flocks and herds to the mountains, and ruthlessly slaying any who ventured to offer the smallest opposition. Catalonia and Valencia had been the scene of the greater portion of the conflicts between the rival claimants. Throughout the rest of the country the population looked on apathetically at the struggle for mastery, caring but little which of the two foreign princes reigned over them; but, in the out-of-the-way districts, the wilder spirits left their homes in numbers, enticed by the prospects of plunder, under the leading of one or other of the partisan chiefs.

Desmond had, from the moment of his arrival, spent the greater portion of his spare time in the study of Spanish, and, aided much by his knowledge of French, had made rapid progress, and in three months was able to converse fairly in it. It was, indeed, essential for his work, as without it he could not have made his way about, and safely delivered the orders of which he was the bearer.

In the beginning of March, the duke sent for him.

"I have been greatly pleased, Captain Kennedy, with the activity that you have displayed, and am going to make a further call upon you. This mission is of greater importance than any on which you have hitherto been engaged, and is one which, ordinarily, would be entrusted to an officer of higher rank; but I feel that I cannot do better than place it in your hands. From what we learn, I believe that it is the intention of the enemy to commence the campaign by crossing the frontier, near Badajos. By so doing, they can either follow the valley of the Guadiana to the sources of the river, and then come down into Valencia; or they could cross the sierras, come down into the valley of the Tagus, and march on Madrid.

"In the first place, I wish a report as to the state of the fortifications of Badajos, and the efficiency of its garrison. I am, of course, acquainted with the official reports, sent by the Spanish commander of the town to his Government, but I have come to place no faith whatever in Spanish reports, which, for the most part, are a tissue of falsehoods. Your first duty, then, will be to give me as complete a report as possible of the state of things there; of your impressions of the capacity of the governor, as shown by his preparations; also of the morale of the troops. In the next place, I shall be glad of any information you can gather of the country beyond the frontier, and the state of the roads in all that neighbourhood. Here, again, the native reports are absolutely untrustworthy. The line of the enemy's advance would be either direct from Lisbon through Vicosa, or up the Tagus, which offers them great facilities for carriage, and down through Portalegre and Alvas.

"During the past four years, there has been a good deal of fighting near the frontier, but the reports of the officers commanding the Spanish forces there are devoid of any practical information as to the roads on our side of the boundary. As it has been resolved to give the enemy battle, as soon as he crosses the frontier, it is most important that I should know the best lines by which troops can move, the state of the bridges, and the positions in which a battle on a large scale can best be fought.

"You see, the mission is an important one, and I selected you for it as a proof of the confidence I feel in your ability. While carrying out this duty you shall have the temporary rank of major, as it will less ruffle the susceptibility of the Spaniards, if an officer of that rank be employed, than if a captain be sent to institute such enquiries.

"You will, of course, be provided with a letter to the Governor of Badajos, couched in such terms that he will not consider your mission has any reference to himself, its object being to discover whether the magazines at Badajos are sufficiently well supplied to admit of their being, if necessary, drawn upon for the subsistence of the army; also, whether the garrison needs strengthening, in case the enemy should lay siege to the town before our army is at hand to give battle. Thus you will ostensibly confine your enquiries to the amount of provisions and ammunition, and consult the governor as to whether he considers the force at his disposal sufficient for the defence of the fortress against a vigorous attack. Fortunately, the Spanish methods are so slow that, before you get these particulars, you will have ample time to ascertain the points as to which I am chiefly concerned.

"You will be furnished with a native guide, well acquainted with the passes of the sierras between the Tagus and the Guadiana. This part of your journey will not be unattended with danger, for the mountains swarm with bands of partisans; that is to say, bandits. I shall, however, give you an order, to the officer in command of the garrison at Toledo, to furnish you with an escort of ten troopers under an officer, to conduct you across the mountains. Four of these will accompany you to Badajos, and remain with you until you return to Toledo. Once in the valley of the Guadiana, you should have little chance of falling in with any bands of guerrillas, but an escort will add to your weight and importance in the eyes of the Spaniards."

"I feel greatly honoured, Your Royal Highness, by your selecting me for the mission, and will carry it out to the best of my ability."

"In an hour the papers will be ready for you, and you can start at daybreak tomorrow."

"We are going on a long trip this time, Mike."

"Back to France, your honour?"

"No; we are going to the western frontier, by Badajos."

"It makes no difference to me, sir, where we are going; but, in truth, I shall be glad to go anywhere, for I am mightily sick of this town, where the people have no great love for the French, and the best part of them seem to look down upon us soldiers, as if we were dirt under their feet. It is unsafe to go through the streets alone at night. A score of men have, since we came here, been found lying dead with a knife between their ribs."

"Yes; the population here is very much divided, Mike, and even those who are favourable to Philip have no love for the foreign soldiers whose bayonets keep him on the throne. The duke has, many times, made formal complaints to the king and the city authorities. Philip has given strict orders for the arrest of bad characters, but the city civil authorities protest that they cannot lay hands upon them, and I believe have never taken the slightest trouble to do so."

"How long shall we be away, your honour?"

"I should say, a month. I am to have temporary rank as major, while engaged on this business. Anyone under that grade would receive but little courtesy from the Spaniards."

"They are a mighty haughty lot," Mike grumbled. "I believe they think that, when the flood came, the Spanish grandees had an ark all to themselves, as they could not be expected to put up with a conveyance full of animals."

Desmond laughed.

"They haven't yet taken in the fact that Spain is no longer the great power she was when she was mistress of half of Europe. They were fine fighters then, Mike. For my part, I own that I cannot understand how it is they have fallen off in that respect; for certainly, without our troops, they would make but a poor stand against the Portuguese, backed up by the English and Dutch."

"I have not seen them fighting yet, sir, but to my mind people so fond of using their knives are not likely to be of much account, when it comes to manly, straightforward fighting.

"Well, your honour, if you are to go as a major, you will need some slight alterations in your uniform--more gold lace, and such like. So I had best see about it, at once."

"I did not think of that, Mike; but you are right. I don't know whether, as I only hold temporary rank, I have a right to wear the uniform of a field officer; but, as the duke wishes me to be able to speak with some authority, there can be no harm in making the change, and the additions can easily be taken off, upon my return."

"The duke ought to have given you the full rank, instead of the temporary one, sir. You have done more work, since you came here, than all the colonels and majors on his staff."

"As far as work goes that may be so, Mike; but as the work consisted in carrying despatches about on horseback, it certainly affords no claim for promotion. And, indeed, I have no wish whatever for it. I am already the youngest captain in the service, except the young nobles who got their commissions as colonels, without even serving a day in inferior rank. I feel uncomfortable now when I go to our regiments, to see men who have been years in the service, and gone through many a desperate action, still lieutenants; while I, after two years' service, and still under nineteen, am a captain."

"Yes, sir; but you know that you saved eight or ten thousand men to France at Oudenarde, and you lost a hand in the service of the country. That would count for a great deal."

"It counts for something, no doubt, Mike, but many of these officers have risked their lives a score of times, and been wounded frequently, though they may not have lost a limb."

"Ah well, sir!" Mike said, philosophically, "Luck is everything. And who would go soldiering, if it was not so? When going into battle, everyone knows that a lot of his comrades will be killed, but he trusts to his luck to get through safely. One man gets promoted and another doesn't, and he hopes that luck will come his way next time. I don't say that your honour's promotion has been luck, but you have had luck in being on the staff of the Duke of Berwick, and everyone knows that it is the staff officers who get the credit and promotion, while the men who do most of the fighting get passed over. There would be nothing to say against that if, as in your honour's case, a man was chosen for the staff because he had done something that showed that he was fit for it. But it isn't so here. If a man belongs to a good family, and has interest, he gets a good appointment; and it is mighty seldom that a man is taken from his regiment, and put on to the staff, because he has done something which showed he was a good soldier."

"That is so, Mike. There is no denying it. And I believe it is one reason why so many disasters have befallen the French army. The generals are, as a rule, good, and the soldiers are excellent, but the staff are generally altogether incompetent, and seem to consider that the fact that they are nobles renders it unnecessary for them to give attention to details, or to be more than ornamental figures in the general's train. And when we see the authority of Vendome overruled by a young prince, who is grandson of the king, and nothing else, one must not be surprised that it is the same all through the army."

That evening, Desmond received a packet containing his appointment as major while on special service, details of instructions as to the points to be attended to, and letters from the duke to the commandant of the garrison at Toledo, and from Philip to the Governor at Badajos.

The next morning he started at daybreak, accompanied by Mike, and arrived that evening at Toledo. Here he presented his letter to the commandant.

"Very well, sir," the officer said, when he had read it. "At what hour do you wish the escort and guide to be ready in the morning?"

"I should like to start as early as possible, Colonel. I myself, being well mounted, might cross the sierra in a day; but the troopers' horses could not do that."

"You would not gain anything if they could, Major Kennedy, for even if your horse could carry you over sixty or seventy miles of mountain roads in a day, you would certainly need a couple of days' rest before proceeding farther. If you get as far as Enmedio, which is in the heart of the sierra, you will have done well. You will then have another long day's ride down to Ciudad Real, from which place the officer with six of the troopers will return. The general says nothing about a non-commissioned officer, but I shall take it upon myself to send one to accompany you, with the four men. It will take a good deal of trouble off your hands."

"I am much obliged to you, Colonel."

"Now that we have finished business," the officer said, "we can talk of other things. You will, of course, put up here. I have two or three spare rooms, and the accommodation at the inns is wretched. I am always very glad when an officer rides through, because we hear little enough about what is passing, and as there is no sort of sociability among the Spaniards, life is very dull here, and one is very glad of the change."

"Thank you, Colonel. I will gladly accept your invitation."

The colonel rang a bell, and ordered a servitor, who answered, to show Major Kennedy's servant where to put up his master's horses and his own, to bring up the officer's valises, and to make the soldier comfortable below.

"We shall sup in half an hour," he said to Desmond, when the man had left. "Two of my majors are going to share the meal."

As soon as the valises were brought up, Desmond changed his uniform, got rid of the dust of the road, and was just ready when a servant knocked at the door and said that the supper was served. The meal was a pleasant one. The three French officers were anxious to hear the last news that had reached Madrid from France. The conversation did not flag for a moment during the meal.

After this was over, and cigars were lighted--for the officers had all adopted the custom of the country--the colonel said courteously, "Would you mind telling us, Major Kennedy, how it is that you, who by your name are Irish, although you speak excellent French, have made your way so rapidly as to be already a major?"

"Not at all, Colonel. I am, myself, as much surprised at it as you may be. But, really, my present rank is only temporary. I am going down to Badajos, on a special mission for the Duke of Orleans, and as he thought that I should be received better were I a field officer, instead of captain, he has given me the temporary rank of major while so employed.

"I will briefly tell you how I obtained the other steps. The first was given me, by the king, on my appointment as aide-de-camp to the Duke of Berwick; His Majesty being good enough to take an interest in me, owing to a little adventure in which I had become involved. It concerned, I may say, the almost accidental rescue of a lady, who had been carried off by a nobleman of the court."

"I remember now," the colonel said. "The lady was Mademoiselle de Pointdexter, and her abductor Vicomte de Tulle. It happened a month or so before our regiment left Paris for Spain, and was the chief topic of talk. I recall your name, now, in connection with the affair, and how warmly everyone spoke of your gallantry. Well, Major, how did you gain your next step?"

"I had the good fortune to be the only one who survived, of four aides-de-camp who were sent off by the Duke of Berwick, at Oudenarde, to make their way through the allied lines with orders, to the division cut off from the rest of the army in the village of Diepenbeck, to disperse and make off across the country, as best they could. My comrades were all killed, but I was lucky enough to succeed in reaching the village uninjured, with the exception of a ball in the wrist, which caused the loss of my hand, and, I may say, almost of my life. It was because of the favourable report, which the duke was pleased to make of this service, that I received my rank as captain."

"It was well earned, too, sir," the colonel said warmly. "I confess, I thought when you arrived that, although Irish by name, you must have had some very powerful influence at your back to have risen so early. Unhappily, promotion often bears no relation whatever to merit; and one sees young nobles, with no other recommendation than that of their birth, placed over the heads of officers of five-and-twenty years service. No one is jealous of a man who owes his rise to brilliant deeds of courage, or signal ability; but it is galling to see these young popinjays thrust forward, simply by family influence."

In passing over the hills the next day, a large party of armed men made their appearance, suddenly, on a height above; but, seeing that an attack was likely to meet with a stout resistance, and as little booty would be obtainable, they did not interfere with their passage. Desmond congratulated himself on having an escort, for it would have gone hard with him, had he been accompanied only by Mike.

On the fifth day after leaving Madrid he arrived at Badajos, with the sergeant, the four troopers, and Mike. After some formalities--for the town, being close to the frontier, was liable at any moment to be suddenly attacked--Desmond was conducted to the governor, a pompous Spanish officer.

"Are you yourself Major Kennedy?" he asked, looking with some surprise at his young visitor.

"My name is Kennedy, sir, and I have the honour of being major, and to serve on the staff of his grace, the Duke of Orleans. I am the bearer of a letter to you from His Majesty, King Philip."

The Spaniard took the letter and read it, and Desmond could see, by the expression of his countenance, that he was by no means pleased.

"I do not understand," he said coldly, "why an officer should have been specially despatched to obtain information which I have already duly furnished."

"I understood from the Duke of Orleans, sir, that as news has been received that the enemy's plans were to cross the frontier near this town, it became a matter of special importance to see that it was sufficiently supplied with provisions, and munitions of war to stand a siege. It has been found more than once that, owing to the culpable neglect of subordinates, fortresses when besieged were by no means so well supplied with provisions, powder and shot, as had been supposed. Naturally, the governor of a fortress like this, with a considerable garrison, is too much occupied to personally superintend all these matters, and must leave them in the hands of his subordinates, who on their part commit them to those of sergeants and storekeepers; so that, while everything is reported to be ready, there are really deficiencies. A waste often takes place in the distribution of stores, and the matter was so important that the king requested the duke to send one of his staff to give you every assistance, and to receive your suggestions, which will be complied with to their full extent. As your last report was sent in some three months back, necessarily considerable changes have taken place, in that time."

"Well, sir, I will obey His Majesty's orders, and give you every facility. My officers shall be instructed to open such magazines as you may select, and you will be then able personally to judge as to the quantity and condition of the stores. It will, of course, be impossible, unless with an immense expenditure of labour, to go through the whole of the magazines and to reckon up their contents; but as many as you wish shall be opened, and a party of soldiers told off to count the bales and cases."

"A very few will suffice, sir. Of course, in the event of a battle being fought and a reverse occurring, the enemy might sit down before your town. You would be exposed to a long siege, for it might be some time before the army was again in a position to advance and fight another battle, or raise the siege. I have little doubt that everything will be found in excellent order, but should there be any deficiencies, the duke assured me that they would be at once made good."

"If you will call tomorrow morning, sir," the governor said, "I will have some of the officials, in whose charge these matters are, placed at your disposal; but I am convinced that you will find that my reports on the stores and ammunition in hand are fully borne out."

"The governor is, as I expected, a good deal put out, Mike," Desmond said as he rejoined his follower, who was waiting outside with the horses. "Now, let us find out the best hotel."

"Didn't he ask you to stay with him, your honour?" Mike asked in surprise.

"No. He is much too grand a man for that, and besides, he may have his wife and children with him; and however much a Spaniard may place his house and all within it at your service, it is very seldom that he invites a stranger to enter it. Moreover, glad as they may be to have French help in fighting their battles, they look with suspicion and dislike upon an individual Frenchman.

"Besides, I fancy I shall find that these stores and magazines by no means tally with the report sent in by the governor. I heard the Duke of Berwick one day speaking about it, and he said there was corruption and dishonesty among their officials, from the highest to the lowest. It is probable that both the king and the Duke of Orleans have the same opinion, and that it was for this reason that they sent me here, in order to assure them that the fortress is as well supplied as has been stated. With the other papers, I have received a copy of the governor's report, although I did not think it necessary to tell him so."

The next morning, on going to the governor's, Desmond found a number of officials assembled there.

"These are the officers in charge of the stores and magazines," the governor said. "Colonel Mendez will accompany you, and will see that everything is done to facilitate your examination."

The governor bowed formally. Desmond returned his salute, and then went down with the Spanish colonel, the other officials following. He saw that there was an expression of malicious pleasure in the colonel's face, and guessed that he was, by no means, sorry at the investigation that was to take place.

"I think, sir," Desmond said, "that it will not be necessary for us to have all these officials going round with us. It will be impossible, in one day, to do more than examine one department. As ammunition is the most important of all stores, I would suggest that we take only those in charge of the war material."

"Very good;" and, turning to those behind, he said: "For today, all those save the officers in charge of the magazines can be relieved from this duty. Their turn will come tomorrow, or next day."

With the exception of five or six, all moved away.

"We have three magazines in the town," the colonel went on, "so as to lessen the chance of our resources being destroyed by a single blow. There is the Central magazine, another that is known as the San Juan magazine, and the Western magazine."

"We may as well visit the Central one first, as, no doubt, that is the most important one."

As they went on, a party of twenty soldiers, who had been drawn up there, fell in behind, while Mike and two troopers of his escort also, at his orders, accompanied them. The magazine was formed in what had formerly been an old castle, but which was now used for another purpose, that of a store, its thick walls affording protection against any but very heavy missiles. On entering what had been the courtyard, Desmond saw that the greater portion of it was occupied by storehouses, massively built, and covered by some five or six feet of earth.

"The first of these on the right contains musketry ammunition," Colonel Mendez said, "the next two contain cannonballs; powder is stored in the three houses at the farther end, and the three on the left side contain hand grenades, fuses for mines, signal rockets, and other miscellanies, such as brimstone."

"We will examine number one first," Desmond said. "Which is the officer in charge?"

One of the officials stepped forward, with a key. Desmond saw that his face was pale, and that he had a sullen look.

"I will ask you, before we enter," he said, "how often do you take stock of your stores? I suppose when the governor sends in his half-yearly report?"

"We do not do it that way at all," the man said. "I have a book. It was given to me by the officer I succeeded. Here it is. You will see that he handed over so many barrels of cartridges. On one side of the page I put down the number of barrels issued, and on the other the number I receive, and thus, at any time, without disturbing the contents of the store, I can state the number of barrels it contains."

"Then how long have you held this position, sir?"

"I have been in charge of this store, and of those used for powder in the cellars underneath the castle, for ten years."

"The man whom you succeeded--how long had he been here?"

"I believe he had been here for twenty years, or more."

"And his system of keeping account was the same as yours?"

"Precisely. He handed his books to me, and I have kept mine in the same way."

"Then it is a fact, if I understand you rightly, that there has been no taking of stock for the past thirty years?"

"It was not necessary," the officer said, in a surly tone. "There can be no mistake possible, considering the way in which we made our entries."

They now entered the store. It was some sixty feet long and forty feet wide, with pillars of masonry along the centre to support the weight of the roof. It was lighted only by small loopholes in the thick walls. Four of the soldiers carried lanterns, and they were about to enter, when Desmond said:

"There is no loose powder lying about, I suppose?"

"None," the officer replied. "The barrels were all carefully examined before being taken into the store. They are, as you can see, strongly made. A leakage is out of the question, unless by any accident one should fall off the pile and burst; but such a thing has never happened, as far as I know."

"I see, by your book, that there should be three thousand four hundred and eighty-two barrels, each containing five hundred cartridges. Certainly an ample supply, even for a prolonged siege."

The barrels were piled in four tiers, one above another, forming a wall on each side of a central path, seven feet wide.

"Give me your hand, Mike," Desmond said to his follower, and, standing upon it, he was able to scramble on to the top.

"Twelve barrels deep," he said, as he descended. "Now, let us count the number in each line."

The wall of barrels extended only some two-thirds of the length of the stores, and there were thirty barrels in each line. He made a rapid calculation.

"That is three thousand two hundred, but I see that, in addition, there is a small pile on each side, beyond the others, which would about make up the correct total. Your record is strictly accurate."

The official took up the lantern, as if the matter was now finished, but Desmond said:

"No, sir. I have but begun; and my instructions were to see how much musket ammunition there was here, at present. I only know how many barrels there are.

"And now, Colonel, I will ask you to call your men in, and set them to work. I wish two passages made through each of these piles of barrels. Three feet wide will be sufficient."

"It would be very dangerous to move them," the official said hastily.

"Not if it is carefully done. You tell me the barrels are strong, and that there is no leakage. Even if this should not be the case, there is little fear of the powder coming in contact with the candles in these lanterns; and besides, as the powder is in cartridges, it would not leak out even if one of the barrels were to burst."

The soldiers had set to work at four points, chosen at hazard by Desmond. The barrels, as they were taken down, were ranged along on each side of the central path. When three lines had been cleared out, one of the soldiers gave an exclamation.

"This is lighter than the one I carried out last!" he said.

"Carry it out into the courtyard," Desmond said. "I should like to look at the contents."

It was taken out to the courtyard, and one end carefully taken out.

"You see, Colonel," Desmond said, as he looked at its contents, "you would have been reduced to great straits, long before you expected it."

The colonel, who belonged to the artillery, looked into the barrel, which was full of earth.

"Empty it out!" Desmond ordered.

They did so. There was not a single cartridge in it.

"This is scandalous!" the colonel exclaimed. "I did not expect that everything would be found right, but I had no idea of such villainy as this!"

He turned to the men.

"Arrest the commissary, at once," he said.

But that official was nowhere to be found. He had slipped away, as soon as the men began to take down the barrels. Some soldiers were at once sent off in search of him.

"We will continue the work," Desmond said, "and see how extensively this fraud has been carried on."

The same result was met with in each of the openings. The first three lines consisted of barrels filled with cartridges; the seven lines behind contained nothing but earth.

"You see, Colonel, instead of having over three thousand two hundred barrels of cartridges, you have less than a thousand. It is almost beyond belief! It is clear that this fellow, and probably the man who was in charge before him, have been in collusion with the contractors for these cartridges, and allowed them to send in seven barrels of earth for every three of cartridges. No doubt, they calculated that there was little chance of the fraud being detected--never, indeed, until there was a prolonged siege--for they would naturally serve out the barrels from the front row, as they were required, filling their places with fresh ones as supplies came in."

The other storehouses were now examined. The number of cannonball alone tallied with the account. There were large deficiencies in the store of powder, and, indeed, among almost all the other munitions.

"It is infinitely worse than I thought," the colonel said, "and I fear that the storekeepers are not the only people concerned in these frauds."

"Now, Colonel, if you do not mind, I should like to go to one of the provision stores at once. Possibly, after what we have discovered, some pretext to stop further examination may be invented, if we wait till tomorrow."

Great as had been the fraud in the magazines, that in the supplies of provisions was even greater. There was a deficiency of many hundreds of sacks of flour and beans. The meat stores were entirely empty, although they should have contained a large number of tierces of salted beef. This was a matter of minor importance, for in case of the approach of an enemy, the people of the country round would drive their cattle into the town, and, indeed, the allowance of meat to a Spanish soldier was so small that he could do well without it, existing entirely upon bread and fried beans. Of wine there was scarce half the amount indicated. A great number of the barrels had been filled only with water.

It was late in the afternoon when the work ceased.

"I should require a fortnight," Desmond said, "to get accurate figures. This, however, is comparatively unimportant. It is quite sufficient to know that in no case is there half the amount, either of ammunition or of provisions, given in the governor's last report, and that fraud on a large scale has been carried on; and I cannot but think that some men, at least, of higher rank than these storekeepers must have been privy to the affair."

"There has certainly been something wrong in the supply of clothes, Major

Kennedy. My men have had no new ones served out to them for the past year and a half, although I have made repeated applications during the past two months."

"Yes; I noticed when I walked about in the town, yesterday, that many of the troops were almost in rags, and I have no doubt there has been fraud in the clothing department, as well as in all the others."

"Well, sir, as a Spaniard I lament this terrible exposure. Blame, however, must not be laid entirely upon the military. The supply of provisions of all kinds, of cloth for clothing, and, indeed, of everything but guns and ammunition, is in the hands of the junta of the province, and of the civil authority here. Many of the members must be concerned in the matter, and I have no doubt that the officials here are heavily bribed to shut their eyes, and to arrange matters so that the frauds may escape attention.

"I know that once, when I proposed to the governor to examine some of the barrels of cartridges as they came in, he answered me very sharply, and told me that my business was to work the guns, and not to meddle with the duties of the storekeeper."

"Then do you think, Colonel?--"

"I think nothing," the officer replied. "The governor is the governor, and it is not for me to discuss his conduct in any way, nor even to admit the possibility of his knowing of this affair."

Only two or three of the storekeepers had been arrested. The rest had slunk away, as soon as they saw how matters were going.

Chapter 15: Treachery.

At this moment an officer came down, and said that the governor wished to see Colonel Mendez and Major Kennedy, at once. As they entered the room, they saw the governor walking up and down in a state of great agitation.

"I hear, Colonel Mendez," he said, stopping before that officer, "that you have, on your own authority, placed several of the commissariat storekeepers under arrest. What does this mean, sir?"

"It means, sir, that Major Kennedy has discovered enormous deficiencies in the stores, and there can be little doubt that a number of persons must have been concerned in the matter, besides those in charge of the storehouses. Wholesale bribery must have been practised, by those who supplied the goods to those whose duty it was to receive them."

"I shall order a commission of enquiry to sit at once, and beg that you, Colonel Mendez, will send me in a detailed report of the matter, which is, I need hardly say, one of extreme gravity."

"I was right," Colonel Mendez said, as they left the governor's house. "I suspected that something was wrong, ever since he refused to allow me access to the magazines. I have no doubt that he has been acting in collusion with the contractors, though he may not have been aware of the extent of their rascality, for his subordinates may not only have accepted bribes from the contractors to carry out the frauds to which the governor may have consented, but may also have taken money from these to allow of still greater ones to be perpetrated."

"What will he do, do you think, Colonel?"

"He will endeavour, by every means in his power, to prevent any word of your discovery from leaking out. And, if I may advise you, I should say it would be well that you should take every precaution for your own safety. His position is a desperate one, for one cannot doubt that your report will be followed by his removal from his post, his dismissal from the army, and the confiscation of everything of which he is possessed. Therefore, it is almost a matter of life and death to him to prevent your report from being sent to headquarters, and to have you removed altogether. This done, the facts might not leak out. It would be supposed, at Madrid, that you had been stabbed by some street ruffian. And, although another officer might be sent down to report, it is by no means likely that he would go so rigorously into matters as you did, but would be contented merely to count barrels and bales, without troubling to investigate their contents."

"But your evidence would be as strong against him as mine."

"Yes; but that evidence is not yet given. He can, in the first place, and I have no doubt will, suppress my report to him. In the second place, he would consider it unlikely that I should venture to make the matter public, for he has powerful friends at court. He is connected with many of the leading families in the province, and might rely upon being able to hush the matter up, so long as it was known only to the heads of our army, who are not unaware that, although the pay of a commander of a fortress is not more than sufficient to maintain his position, they, like most other of our officials, generally retire with considerable fortunes. Therefore, any interference on my part would be more disastrous to my prospects than to his.

"It is humiliating to say so, Major Kennedy, but both our civil and military systems are rotten to the core. There are, of course, honest men in both services, but as a rule corruption is almost universal. Still, although he cannot fear me as he must fear you, it is possible he may endeavour to make himself safe by removing me also from his path; and for a time I shall take good care to remain in my own barracks, as much as possible."

"I will be careful also," Desmond said, "and I thank you much for the warning, which was needed, for it would never have struck me that he would even attempt to suppress the information that I have gained; but I see that it will be necessary to be very careful, especially in the manner of sending off my reports."

"If I were in your place, I should mount my horse at once, and with the troopers of the escort ride straight for Madrid."

"I cannot do that, Colonel, for the examination into the state of the stores here was only a part of my instructions, and I must, if possible, carry these out to the letter before leaving for Madrid. I might, however, send off my despatch by two of the troopers with me."

"I think you may take my word for it, Major, that they would never reach their destination. Even while we are speaking, a messenger may be sent off either to one of these bands in the mountains, or to two or three of the contractors--who are, of course, as deeply involved as the governor, for there is no doubt of their guilt, while no proof can be given to his being a party to it--telling them that it is a matter of life and death to them to prevent you or your messengers from reaching Madrid."

"The lookout is certainly far from comfortable," Desmond admitted, "and I must, tonight, think it over in every way, and decide upon what course I had best pursue."

When he reached the hotel, he told Mike what Colonel Mendez had said.

"By the powers, your honour, it is a nasty scrape that we seem to be in, almost as bad as when you were shut up in that prison in London."

"Worse, Mike; for then we knew that we should be tried, but hoped that Louis would interfere in our favour, and by threatening reprisals obtain our liberty; whereas here we have only ourselves to depend upon, and the blow may come at any moment."

"Well, at any rate, your honour, we will see that none get at you unbeknown. I will lie down in your room against the door, and if the sergeant places a man on guard outside, it is hard if anyone gets at you."

"I hardly think the precaution necessary; but there is no saying what this man might not do in so desperate a situation, so I will tell the sergeant to place a sentry at the door, and to relieve him every two hours. I shall think the matter over, and by tomorrow morning shall decide whether I had best remain here and complete my work, or ride at once to Madrid."

At about two o'clock in the morning Desmond, who had but just dropped off to sleep, was aroused by hearing the sentry outside his door challenge. There was no answer. All remained quiet. Mike leapt to his feet and opened the door.

"What is it?" he asked the sentry.

"I saw two or three men at the end of the corridor. It was too dark to make them out clearly. They were coming this way. I levelled my carbine and cried, 'Who comes there?' and at once they stole away. They could have been after no good, for their steps were noiseless, and they must have come up without boots."

"Keep a sharp lookout, sentry," Desmond said, "and see that they don't steal up to you, for if they do, you may be stabbed before you have time to turn round.

"It is lucky that I carried out your suggestion, Mike, and posted a sentry at the door. Of course, these men the sentry saw may not have been coming here, but at any rate their conduct was suspicious."

In a few minutes Desmond was again asleep. He had had a long day's work, and believing that the affair was over, at least for the night, he did not even try to keep awake.

As soon as Mike heard, by his breathing, that he was asleep, he got up noiselessly and seated himself near the open window, with a loaded pistol. An hour passed, and then he heard a slight stir in the street. He did not look out, but grasped his pistol tightly.

Their room was on the first floor. Presently, he heard a grating sound against the window. It was very dark, and he knelt down so that he would be able to make out any figure that showed above the windowsill. He thought first of rousing his master, but as he had another pistol in his belt, and his sword leaned against the wall, ready to his hand, he thought it better to let matters take their course.

He had heard no further sound, but presently a round object appeared in sight. Stretching out his arm, he fired without a moment's hesitation. There was a sound of a heavy fall below, followed by some muttered exclamations. In a moment, Desmond was on his feet, a pistol which he had laid by his pillow in his grasp.

"What is it, Mike?"

"It is only a gentleman who had a fancy for looking in at the window, your honour, and I have no doubt would have come in, without saying by your leave, if I had not cut the matter short by putting a bullet into his forehead. He had some friends down below. He came up on a ladder."

He looked out of the window.

"They are taking it down now, your honour. Shall I give them another shot?"

"No, Mike; let them go. The lesson has been good enough."

The sentry had also run into the room, on hearing the shot.

"It is all over," Desmond said. "Seeing that you prevented them from getting in at the door, they tried the window. Mike has shot one of them."

There was a sound of feet and loud talking in the passage, and as Desmond went out, the landlord, two of the serving men, and several of those staying at the hotel ran up.

"What is it, senor? We heard a shot."

"Yes; a fellow tried to enter my window, by means of a ladder; but fortunately my man heard him, and shot him before he came in. No doubt it was some prowling marauder, who, seeing my window open, thought that there was a chance of plunder."

"Carrambo!" the landlord exclaimed, "then we shall have enquiries, and all sorts of trouble."

"I don't think you will," Desmond said quietly. "I fancy he had some friends down below, and they will probably carry his body and the ladder away, and, if you hold your tongues, nothing more will be heard of it.

"Mike, do you and the sentry take a lantern and go down and see."

The landlord looked out of the window.

"As far as I can see, everything is quiet there," he said. "Are you sure that your servant was not dreaming?"

"That you will soon ascertain, if you go down with him," Desmond said. "I fancy that you will find some traces of the affair there."

The landlord, followed by his two servants, went down with the soldiers, and then, lighting a lantern and handing it to them, went out, keeping carefully behind them.

"There," Mike said, when he stopped under Desmond's window; "does that look like a dream?" and he pointed to a patch of blood on the pavement.

"It is true enough," the landlord said.

"Pedro and Lopez, fetch pails of water and brooms, and get rid of this blood, otherwise we shall be having enquiries made in the morning."

Mike returned to his master, at whose door the sergeant and the other troopers were standing.

"There is no occasion, sergeant," Desmond had just said, "to keep a sentry at the door any longer. We can be quite sure that we shall not be disturbed again before morning, and indeed, I am not likely to sleep after this."

"Very well, sir; but if you don't mind, I will keep a sentry on watch."

"Just as you like, sergeant, but I feel sure there is no occasion for it. Still, after what has happened, it may perhaps be wise to do so."

"Well, Mike," Desmond said, when they were again alone, "the campaign has opened with spirit. This is something like that journey with the Baron de Pointdexter, when we expected to be attacked every minute."

"Well, we got through that all right, your honour, and it is hard if we don't get through this."

At six o'clock, a volley of musketry was fired.

"They are practising early, sir," Mike said.

"It can't be that, Mike. It is too close. They would go beyond the outer works to practise, and, by the sound, it is certainly much nearer than that, though possibly just outside the walls."

"I will go out and enquire, your honour. When one is at war, it is as well to know exactly what the enemy are doing."

"Take one of the troopers with you, Mike. Pierre speaks Spanish well."

Mike returned in an hour.

"They have shot all the prisoners we took yesterday," he said. "I hear they held a sort of court martial in the evening, at the governor's. It did not sit more than ten minutes. They were all found guilty of fraud and treachery, and were shot this morning."

"Worse and worse, Mike! Evidently, the governor is determined to get rid of all whose evidence might throw any light on this matter. After what has happened here, and these summary executions, I feel very uncomfortable as to Colonel Mendez. Will you go to the artillery barracks with a message from me that, as I have my first report to write out, I shall not continue the investigations today? Take Pierre with you again."

When Mike returned, Desmond saw that his news was bad.

"The colonel had not been seen when I got there, and his servant went up to his room and found him lying dead, stabbed to the heart."

"Another witness gone," Desmond said. "An honourable gentleman, and a pleasant one. Well, Mike, the matter becomes more and more serious. After this there is but one thing open to me, and that is to return to Madrid at once. When I relate the circumstances to the duke, he will see that, had I endeavoured to carry out the rest of his instructions, the chance of my report ever coming to hand would have been slight indeed, and it is all important that he should get it.

"The question is, shall we mount and ride at once, or shall I go and take leave of the governor?"

"Of course, your honour, you can do as you like, but I should say that the sooner we are out of this, the better. The longer we stay here, the more time he will have to take care we don't get back alive.

"There was another thing I did not tell you, sir. As we went to the barracks, we passed some cavalry men talking. They were arguing that the enemy must be marching this way, for at two o'clock last night ten troopers were suddenly called up and sent off, the gates being opened for them by order of the governor."

"Just what I expected, Mike. He has written to warn the various contractors that the frauds have been discovered, and, no doubt, telling them that all messengers from here must be stopped and searched, and all reports and documents taken from them; that if I come myself, I am to be put out of the way; and that if this can be done the matter can be hushed up, as he has taken measures to silence all those who know anything about the affair.

"Well, I think you are right. We need not mind saying goodbye to this scoundrel, as it would only give him time to perfect his arrangements. I have no doubt that he would pretend to be ill, or to be engaged in some business that would detain him, and manage to keep me waiting some hours before he saw me. Order the sergeant to saddle up at once. Let the men eat a meal as quickly as possible, and let each put a bottle of wine and a loaf of bread into his valise, so that we shall be able to ride without stopping anywhere. Say that we shall mount in twenty minutes, and they must not wait to polish up their accoutrements. Tell them to put plenty of forage before the horses, and not to put the bridles in their mouths until the last thing. Let each pour four or five feeds of corn into his forage bag.

"When you have given the orders, have your own breakfast. I will go downstairs and get something there. I packed my valises while you were away."

Exactly twenty minutes later the little troop started. The men had, at Desmond's orders, loaded their pistols and short guns. Avoiding the principal streets, they rode by narrow lanes until they emerged close to the eastern gate. Through this he and his followers rode, without question, at a quiet pace until beyond the exterior fortifications, across the bridge over the Guadiana, and then broke into a canter.

The sergeant and men were not a little surprised at the sudden departure, for they had supposed that they would remain for some time at Badajos. Desmond called the sergeant up to his side.

"I dare say you are surprised at this sudden move, but you know that two attempts were made upon my life last night, and I have no doubt that these would be repeated, and perhaps with greater success, had I stayed there. You were present yesterday, with two of your men, when we discovered that large portions of the stores were mere dummies filled with earth. Whether or not the governor was a party to the fraud I cannot say, but this morning he had all the storekeepers who were arrested shot, and Colonel Mendez, who was present at the investigation, was murdered during the night. It is evident, therefore, that many people are interested in preventing the discovery we made from getting known. Of course, the soldiers who assisted would be aware of it, but they would not venture to speak, and it is only I and your men and my servant who have still to be silenced.

"I tell you this, in order that you may impress upon the men the necessity for the greatest vigilance, such as they would use if travelling through an enemy's country. Messengers were, I hear, sent off yesterday evening in various directions, and I have no doubt that these were to the various contractors concerned in the plot, urging upon them the necessity of preventing the news from reaching Madrid; and perhaps to some of the robber bands in the sierra. Therefore, instead of keeping the main road up the valley, we will ride by country tracks and avoid all large towns. We will not put up anywhere, but will bivouac in the open. In this way I hope that we shall yet avoid any parties of men who may be lying in wait for us.

"The most dangerous part of the journey will, of course, be the passage of the mountains. We must there travel by one or other of the roads through the defiles, and it is possible all these may be watched. If we are attacked, we must endeavour to ride through them. If this is impossible, we will sell our lives as dearly as we can."

"You may trust us for that, Major," the sergeant said. "I have no love for these Spaniards, and we are all discontented at being kept down here to fight the King of Spain's battles, instead of being up in the north, where every man is wanted to prevent the enemy marching to Paris."

They struck off from the road when nearing Merida, and followed a country track until they came upon the road between that town and Torre Mocha. Avoiding the latter place, they took the road to Truxillo, and, late in the afternoon, approached that town and halted in a wood two miles distant from it.

Here Desmond consulted his map. There were two roads from Truxillo. Crossing the sierra, the main and shorter road came down upon the Tagus at Almarez. The other passed through Deleytoza, and came down upon the bridge at Condo. Beyond Deleytoza it appeared to be a mere mule track.

"If there are any parties watching," he said to Mike, "they will expect that my messenger, or I myself, will travel by the main road to Almarez, for not only is it better, but it is shorter. But again, they might think that, if I suspected we might be attacked, I should take the road through Deleytoza, and would, at any rate, make matters safe by watching both roads. It is a difficult question which to choose."

"Well, your honour, if you have got to fight, it would be best to do so on a good road. Our horses would be of no use to us, if we were going single file along a bad road; while on a good road we could charge the spalpeens, and cut our way through."

"You are quite right, Mike, and we will take the main road. They will not be mounted, and I don't think they would stand before a charge of seven men; but they may shoot some of us as we come down upon them.

"See here, Mike, this is my report that I wrote out yesterday evening;" and he took a packet from the inside of his coat. "When we start tomorrow morning I shall put it in my left holster. If I am shot, you will not wait for a moment, but will snatch it out and ride on to Madrid, and deliver it to the duke there. I have, this morning, added a few lines relating the murder of Colonel Mendez, the hurried trial and execution of the storekeepers, and the attempts upon my life, and said I have not the least doubt that the governor is at the bottom of it all."

"If your honour is killed, I will carry out your orders, but if it is only wounded you are, I will try to take you off with me."

"You must do as I order you."

"I obey your honour's orders when they are reasonable," Mike said doggedly;

"but leave you behind, to have your throat cut by those villains! I would not do such a thing, so there is an end of it."

Desmond smiled at the earnestness of his faithful follower.

"Well, Mike, you must be guided by circumstances; but remember, it is of extreme importance that this report should reach the Duke of Orleans. Unless he has it we may lose Badajos, and the cause suffer irreparable injury."

"To the devil wid the cause," Mike said. "The cause doesn't trouble me one way or the other. I don't care a brass farthing whether Philip or Charles reigns over the Spaniards. It is not a nice job they will be taking on, any way, and not worth a drop of Irish blood. Well, if your honour should have the bad fortune to be hit, I shall either carry you off, though there's not a breath in your body, or else go down with you."

As there was no doubt that Mike meant what he said, Desmond did not press the matter further.

The next day they set out at daybreak, and, in two hours, were mounting the slope of the sierra. There were no signs of any men being about, until they reached a point where the road ran between steep hills.

"There they are," Desmond exclaimed, reining in his horse. "There are some thirty or forty of them on the road.

"Now, my men, we will ride forward to those boulders you see, a hundred yards this side of them, and then we will dismount and give them a volley. If you keep that up, it will soon be too hot for them to remain on the road; while we, sheltered behind the rocks, will be safe from their shot. It is certain that your guns will carry farther and shoot straighter than theirs, as the Spanish powder is so much inferior to the French."

Accordingly, they rode forward at a canter to the heap of boulders, then suddenly left the road, dismounted, and took cover among the rocks.

"Take steady aim, men," Desmond said, "then you can hardly miss hitting some of them, standing close together as they do."

The bandits had waited, undecided, at the sudden disappearance of those whom they had regarded as a certain prey; and before they could form any plans, five muskets flashed out, and four of their number fell. A cry of rage burst from them, and there was a general discharge of their guns, the balls pattering thickly against the stones.

The soldiers now fired as quickly as they could load, doing considerable execution. Their foes left the road, and imitated them by taking shelter behind stones. For ten minutes the combat continued, and then a party of men were seen, mounting the hill on either side.

"That is just what I hoped for," Desmond said. "Fire at them, so as to force them to climb a little higher up the hill. As soon as they are pretty well out of gunshot, we will mount and charge down the road. There cannot be many men left there."

His orders were followed. Some of the men on the hillside dropped, and the others continued to mount the slopes. When, as they believed, out of fire, they moved forward so as to take the defenders of the rocks in flank.

"Now, fire a volley among the men in front of us," Desmond said. "We are not likely to hit any of them, but it is sure to draw their fire, and there will not be many unemptied guns as we pass them."

As he expected, the volley was answered by a general fire from their hidden foes. Then the party leapt into their saddles, and, pistol in hand, galloped up the road. Several hurried shots were fired from the front, and then, at a shout from their leader, some twenty men leapt from their hiding places and ran down into the road.

Desmond was supported on one side by Mike, and on the other by the sergeant. He dropped his reins--the horse had learned to obey the motions of his knees--and, drawing his sword, rode straight at the bandits. Only a few muskets were discharged, and these so hurriedly that the balls missed their aim, and, with a shout, the party fell upon the brigands. The pistols of the troopers and Mike cracked out, but they had no need to draw their swords, for the rush of the horses struck such a panic into the Spaniards that they sprang from the road, leaving the path clear, and the party thundered past them without a check.

"Is anyone wounded?" Desmond asked, when they had passed beyond gunshot of their assailants.

"I have a ball in my shoulder, Major," one of the troopers said. The rest were silent.

"Well, we have been fortunate," Desmond said. "I will see to your wound, my man, when we get a little farther. If those fellows had not been so scared with our sudden charge that they fired almost at random, we might have lost half our number."

They stopped half a mile farther, and Desmond examined the trooper's arm.

"The ball has gone through the flesh," he said, "without touching the bone, so you will soon have the use of it again."

He bound the wound tightly up with the soldier's sash; and then made, with his own, a sling.

"You may as well put the other arm in your jacket," he said, "and I will tie it round your neck. The air is cold upon the hills."

"We did that well, sir," the sergeant said, as they rode on again. "If you had not thought of taking shelter, and shaking them up, we should all have been shot down before we reached them.

"Is there any chance of another attack, sir?"

"None at all. I should think a messenger was sent to them, yesterday, telling them our strength; and no doubt they thought that, with sixty men, they would be certain to overpower us. That is probably the whole of the band, and in any case, as they would not imagine that we could pass them, they are not likely to have set another ambush."

They slept that night at Almarez, made a short journey to Oropesa, and a long one on the following day to Toledo, where Desmond dismissed his escort, with a handsome reward for their services, and upon the next afternoon rode with Mike into Madrid. The Duke of Orleans looked astonished when he entered the room.

"What! Back already, Major Kennedy? Surely you cannot have carried out all the work that I entrusted to you?"

"By no means, Your Royal Highness; but what I did carry out was so important that I deemed it my duty to ride back at once, to acquaint you with what I have discovered. There is the report, sir."

The duke took it.

"It is a bulky one," he said. "Tell me its purport in as few words as possible."

"I have discovered, sir, that the report sent by the governor of the supply of provisions and stores in Badajos is altogether inaccurate, that frauds to an enormous extent have been perpetrated, that the supply of powder and cartridges is less by two-thirds than was represented, and that similar deficiencies exist in every department."

"This is indeed serious," the duke said. "The possession of Badajos is essential to us. It blocks the way to an enemy's advance, and indeed, they can scarce move forward until it is captured. Now, tell me more about it; or no, I will read your report, and then question you concerning it."

A heavy frown settled on the duke's brow, as he perused the document.

"Infamous!" he exclaimed, when he had finished. "And you say that two attempts were made to murder you that night, and that the Spanish colonel who gave you so much assistance was assassinated, and the commissaries shot the next morning? It shows how anxious the governor was to remove from his path all those who could inculpate him.

"And how did you manage to get out of the toils? For it was clearly of no use killing the minor witnesses, and allowing you to ride here to report the facts."

"I saw that, sir; and as I learned that eight or ten troopers had been sent off, late the night before, I concluded that the road would be sure to be beset, for doubtless some of the contractors would feel it as essential as the governor did, that my mouth should be silenced and my report suppressed. I therefore started early. Keeping by byroads, we were not molested until we had nearly reached the summit of the sierra, when we found a party of some sixty men barring the road. We had a fight with them, and succeeded in getting through with no further damage than a ball through the arm of one of my escort, and that, fortunately, was only a flesh wound."

"But tell me how it was that so small a party escaped so easily?"

Desmond then recounted the incidents of the fight.

"Admirably contrived, sir!" the duke said warmly. "Excellent generalship! You first attack their centre and drive them off the road, then you compel them to weaken themselves by throwing out flanking parties. You keep these out of musket shot, and then charge on their weakened centre after drawing their fire. I am not surprised that, with such generalship, you got off almost scatheless.

"And now, sir, I must ask you to come with me to the king. The matter is too serious for a moment's delay. I must lay the whole case before His Majesty."

Leaving Desmond in the antechamber, he went in to the king, read the full report to him, and added the details he had heard from Desmond.

"I have met with many bad cases of Spanish corruption and peculation," the king said, when he had finished, "but this is by far the worst. Steps must be taken instantly to secure the governor, arrest the contractors, and fill up the magazines. What do you propose?"

"I think, sir, that if we send forward, at once, a regiment of French soldiers from Toledo, accompanied by Colonel Crofton's regiment of dragoons, there is no likelihood that any resistance will be offered--indeed, I should imagine that the governor will have taken to flight, as soon as he learns that his plans for the assassination of Major Kennedy have failed."

"So I should think," the king said; "and certainly he will have warned his accomplices, the contractors; and probably, by this time, they are all on their way either into Andalusia or to the north. Any that are found shall certainly be hanged.

"This young officer of yours must be a wonderfully shrewd fellow. I should like to question him as to how he discovered these frauds."

Desmond was called in.

"This is Major Kennedy, Your Majesty," the duke said. "That is his temporary rank, which I bestowed upon him in order to add weight to his mission."

"I have noticed him before, cousin," Philip said, "when I had gone to your quarters, and wondered to see so young a man in the uniform of a captain.

"Now, sir, will you give me an account of how you discovered these frauds?"

Desmond then related how he had caused the piles of barrels to be opened out, so that he could examine those next to the wall as well as those in front; and how he had similarly examined the other stores.

"Very good, indeed, sir," the king said. "Most officers would have contented themselves with, at most, counting the number of barrels and sacks; and that you should have so thoroughly investigated the matter shows both zeal and shrewdness."

"He has shown that on various occasions," the duke said, "as you may judge from the promotion that he has received. As you see, by the loss of his hand, he has suffered as well as fought on behalf of France. When Your Majesty is at leisure I will, some evening, relate to you a story which I heard from the king himself, of the manner in which he, twice, rescued a fair damsel from an evil-minded noble who carried her off."

"I shall hear it with pleasure, cousin. You say he holds only temporary rank. I think that, after the signal service he has rendered, it should be made substantial."

"I certainly intend to make it so," the duke said.

"Pardon, sir," Desmond said, "but, while thanking you for your kindness, I would beg to be allowed to remain a captain. Already I have obtained more promotion than others have done, after many years of good service, and I should regret very much passing over the heads of so many of my old companions."

"It is the first time that I have had promotion declined," the duke said, smiling. "However, for the present, at least, I will let the matter remain so."

With an expression of warm thanks, Desmond retired.

"We must lose no time over this matter," the king said. "For aught we know, this scoundrel may be in communication with the enemy, and may be prepared to open the gates of the fortress at the first summons."

"I will act at once," the duke replied. "I will, this evening, send orders to Toledo for a regiment to march at nine o'clock tomorrow morning, and, if you will send a similar order to Colonel Crofton, he will overtake the infantry before they get to Almarez."

"I will do so, and will also send with them three field officers, with full power to arrest, try, and execute all those who have taken part in this treacherous fraud."

On the duke leaving the king, Desmond joined him in the antechamber, and as they walked towards the French headquarters, said:

"I hope, sir, that you will permit me to start tomorrow with any force you may be sending, as I wish to carry out the rest of the mission with which you entrusted me."

"By all means, do so if you wish it," the duke said. "Colonel Crofton's regiment will start at nine o'clock tomorrow morning, and you may accompany it. On the road it will overtake one of our regiments from Toledo."

Chapter 16: Captured.

"I have a job for you, Mike."

"What is it, your honour?"

"I want you to take off all the marks of a field officer from my clothes. I am going to be a captain again."

Mike looked with surprise at his master.

"Well, your honour, it is ungrateful bastes they must be. Sure I thought that the least they could do was to make you a full major, though if they had made you a colonel, it would be no more than you deserve."

"I was offered the majority, Mike, but I declined it. It would be absurd, at my age, to have such a rank, and I should be ashamed to look officers of our brigade, who have done nigh twenty years of good service and are still only captains, in the face. I would much rather remain as I am."

"Well, it may be you are right, sir, but it is disappointed I am, entirely."

"You will get over it, Mike," Desmond laughed.

"That may be," Mike said doubtfully, "but I should have felt mighty proud of being a colonel's servant."

"I don't suppose you will ever be that, Mike. You know that, after the last war was over, several of the Irish regiments were disbanded, and no doubt it will be the same when this war is finished, so you could not count upon seeing me a colonel, at any rate not for another twenty years."

"Ah, your honour, I hope we shall be back in old Ireland years before that!"

"I hope so, too, Mike. I have only been out here for two years, and yet I am beginning to feel that I should like a quieter life. No doubt the loss of my hand has something to do with that, but I would give up, willingly, all chance of ever becoming a colonel, if I could but settle down in the old country, though I fear there is very little chance of that."

"But sure there may be fighting there, too, your honour," Mike said; "and if King James goes across the water, there is sure to be divarsion that way."

"I hope not, Mike. It is not that I do not feel as loyal as ever to the cause of the Stuarts, but if they cannot come to their own without Ireland being again deluged with blood, I would rather they would stay away. Twice Ireland has suffered for the Stuarts: first, when Cromwell came over, carrying fire and sword through the land, and divided half the country among his followers; next, when Dutch William did the same. I am loyal to the Stuarts, as I said, but I am still more loyal to Ireland, and would rather that King James remained all his life at Saint Germain, than that those scenes should ever come again."

"That's true for you, sir; and when I come to think of it, I should be just as easy and comfortable in a snug little cot in Killarney, which is my county, whether King James or Queen Anne was ruling it in England."

"Quite so, Mike; and if I had, as you say, a snug little cot to go to, and an income to live comfortably in it, and no fear of being hauled off to prison and hanged for joining the brigade, I should not be sorry to settle down.

"We start back for Badajos tomorrow morning."

"Faith, your honour, it has been so hard getting away from there, that I should not have thought you wished to put your foot inside the place again. You might not be so lucky in getting off, next time."

"We are going in a different way, Mike. Colonel Crofton's regiment of Irish dragoons is going with us, and a French infantry regiment from Toledo."

"Then I am well content to go back, your honour, and I hope we shall see that murthering governor hung."

"I think you have a good chance of seeing that, Mike, if he has not taken himself off before we arrive there; which I think he is pretty sure to do, directly he hears we have got through safely; for he will know that, as soon as my report is handed in, he is a lost man."

"Bad cess to him! At any rate, I hope I shall light upon him some day, sir, and pay him out for sending those fellows to kill you at night, and to hinder us in the hills. As to his cheating the Spaniards, that is their business, and they can reckon with him for it; but I should like to pay our debt myself."

"I don't suppose there is much chance of your having an opportunity of doing that."

"Then why are we going back, your honour?"

"To carry out my original orders, Mike--survey the roads, and passes, and bridges. The duke cannot rely upon Spanish testimony in these matters, and it is most important that we should ascertain, accurately, how good are the roads by which he would advance with the army into Portugal, or where best to oppose the enemy if they cross the Guadiana."

"I am glad to hear you say so, sir, for I was afraid that we were going to have a long stay here again, and I would rather be on horseback, riding all over the country, than walking up and down these streets till my feet fairly ache."

"That is my opinion, too, Mike. We have had a good many rides with despatches, but between times it is stupid work, hanging about the general's quarters waiting for orders."

The next morning, Desmond joined Colonel Crofton's regiment as it was on the point of starting from the barracks. It was in the service of Spain, and had taken a brilliant part in several engagements. Desmond was acquainted with the colonel and his officers.

"Good morning, Kennedy!" Crofton said, as he rode up and saluted him. "I had a note from the Duke of Orleans, last night, saying you were going on special service, and would travel with us as far as Badajos. King Philip sent for me, later on, and himself gave me instructions, besides handing me the written orders. It seems you have discovered that the governor is mixed up, with a lot of contractors, in swindling the state by supplying earth instead of powder and flour."

"So far as the governor goes, Colonel, there is no absolute proof. I have not the smallest doubt that he was the prime mover in the matter, and that the commissaries only received a small portion of the bribes paid to him. It is hardly possible that every one of them should have betrayed his trust, unless sure of the governor's protection. I cannot prove that he had all these men shot in order to silence them, employed men to assassinate Colonel Mendez, or set men to murder me in my hotel and afterwards to intercept us in crossing the sierra. Still, I have no shadow of doubt in my mind that it was so.

"However, I do not think you will find him at Badajos. No doubt, as soon as he heard I had got safely down into the valley of the Tagus, he made off. There is just a possibility that the contractors, knowing that their lives will be forfeited by the discovery of the frauds, might at once have sent in supplies of powder, flour, and other things, to take the place of the casks and sacks of earth; in which case he would probably deny the truth of my statement altogether, and declare that I had simply invented it in order to do credit to myself. But I hardly think that possible. In the first place, there are the soldiers both of my escort and of Colonel Mendez, who assisted in the work of examination; besides which more than half the commissaries escaped while this was taking place, and, on an offer of pardon, would no doubt gladly come forward and give evidence, especially as the execution of their comrades will have shown them that the governor is determined to throw them over."

"Yes; I don't suppose we shall find the arch-scoundrel there, unless, indeed, he can rely upon the support of his garrison; in which case he may have ridden to Portugal, offering to surrender the place at once to them, and will close his gates against us."

"I don't think there is any chance of that, Colonel. In the short time during which I was there, I was able to see that the troops were deeply discontented. They were almost in rags, and the landlord of the inn told me that they were kept on the scantiest rations, and those of a very inferior kind. So I do not think, for a moment, he could trust them to act against a royal force."

Desmond's anticipation proved to be correct. As they descended into the valley of the Guadiana, they met an officer of the garrison, who was bearing a despatch from the senior military officer, saying that the governor and his family had suddenly left without issuing any orders, and, as he had taken all his portable property with him, it was supposed that he did not intend to return. Under these circumstances he wrote to ask for orders.

Colonel Crofton sent him back with instructions, to the colonel commanding the troops, that he was coming with a regiment of dragoons and one of infantry, and had full authority from the king to take all measures that seemed to him desirable. Accordingly, when they arrived at Badajos they were met, at the gate, by the colonel commanding the troops, and a party of his officers.

"I have the king's authority," Colonel Crofton said to him, "to act as temporary governor until another may be appointed. I do not know whether you are aware of the circumstances that led to the flight of Don Juan de Munos?"

"No, sir, we have heard nothing. Rumours were current, among the men, that some strange discoveries were made when the stores were examined, but beyond that I know nothing. In fact, at the time, the assassination of Colonel Mendez of the artillery created such an excitement that nothing else was spoken of."

"Well, Colonel, if you will accompany me to the governor's house, I will enter into the matter fully with you. You may well believe that it is serious, as I have been despatched here with my regiment, and with one of French infantry, for both of whom quarters must be found at once."

"There is plenty of room, sir. The barracks will contain ten thousand men, and at present we have but four thousand here."

"Then I beg, Colonel, that instead of coming at once to my quarters, you will tell off officers to conduct the troops to the most convenient of the buildings now empty. After that, I shall be glad to see you and the commanding officers of the other regiments.

"You will, of course, take up your quarters at the governor's house, Captain Kennedy," he went on, as he rode forward. "As you are going to be employed in surveying duties, you will naturally be a good deal away. But your presence here will be absolutely necessary, as a witness against any of these rascally contractors we can lay our hands on."

When the four colonels arrived, after seeing that the troops were housed, Colonel Crofton obtained from them the names and addresses of the various contractors; and, half an hour later, parties of the cavalry regiment in garrison were despatched, under officers, with orders to arrest and bring them into Badajos. During the meal, Colonel Crofton explained to the four colonels the discovery of the frauds, which naturally excited the greatest indignation among them. He then requested them and Desmond to accompany him to the stores. This they did, after sending to the barracks for a party of fifty men for fatigue duty.

The gaps made during Desmond's explorations had been carefully filled up again, but upon fresh openings being made, his reports were fully borne out. Some hours were spent at the central magazine, and orders given that the other magazines should be opened and examined on the following day.

Desmond did not join in this search, but started early, with Mike, to carry out his own mission. He had been furnished with reports, sent in by the provincial and local juntas, as to the state of the roads, but, as he had expected, he soon found these to be grossly inaccurate. The roads marked as excellent, and fit for the passage of artillery and trains, were found to be mere bridle roads. Others, marked as highroads, were almost impassable lanes. The bridges across the streams were, for the most part, in such a bad condition as to be unsafe for a country cart and, until repaired, impossible for the passage of artillery.

He carefully noted all the points at which work was required to render them in any degree practicable for the passage of troops, and reported fully to Colonel Crofton. The latter, who was provided with full authority, despatched the greater portion of his troops, with a large number of peasants, with materials to fill up the deep ruts, repair the bridges, and make the roads, as far as possible, fit for the passage of an army.

In ten days, Desmond had surveyed all the roads down both the valley of the Guadiana and that of the Tagus, and had sent off his report to Madrid, together with his observations as to the points at which a defensive position could, in his opinion, be best taken up. Having done this, he prepared to undertake the second part of his mission, and to investigate the roads on the Portuguese side of the frontier.

"Now we shall have to keep our eyes open, Mike," he said. "So far as we have heard, there are no bodies of the enemy's troops anywhere in this neighbourhood, but there is a bitter enmity between the Spanish and Portuguese, and we shall be liable to be attacked by the peasants."

"Are we to ride in our uniforms, your honour?"

"Certainly we are, Mike. If we are captured in uniform, we should be dealt with as prisoners of war and have a right to fair treatment. If we are taken in disguise, we shall be shot as spies."

"Faith, your honour, the alternative is not a pleasant one. If we go as civilians, we may be shot as spies; if we go in uniform, we may be murdered by the peasants."

"That is so, Mike. But, you see, we are not likely to fall into the hands of the peasants. We are both well mounted, and the peasants will be on foot, and a great proportion of them unarmed; so that, beyond the chance of being hit by a ball, the risk is not great."

Accordingly, on the following day they rode out, and for nearly a week examined the lines of route across the frontier. They followed the roads between the foot of the mountains and the frontier, as far as Portalegre, but avoided the towns of Campo Mayor and Arronches; crossed the hills, and struck upwards by the bank of the Zarina to Frontiera, and thence west as far as Lavre. They met with no interference by such peasants as they saw working in the fields, or by those in the small villages through which they passed, these supposing the uniforms to be those of English or Dutch officers.

They found that the roads were fully as bad as those of Spain, and would present great difficulty to any army with artillery and a long train of waggons. In one of the places they heard from a peasant, with whom they conversed, that there was another pass over the mountains from Elvas. Of course, the man spoke in Portuguese, but the language sufficiently resembled Spanish for Desmond to understand its meaning.

"We must investigate that road, Mike, for, if it is practicable, it would be the most direct for an army coming from Lisbon. Of course, we shall have to make a wide circle round Elvas, as there is sure to be a strong garrison there, and any soldiers riding about the country would be certain to know that our uniform was French. When we have done that road, we shall have finished our work."

Accordingly, they passed round the fortress at a distance, and presently came upon the road. It showed signs of having lately been repaired, in some parts, but these were so badly done that they increased rather than diminished the difficulties it presented to the passage of troops. They had ridden some ten miles, and were already among the mountains, when they dismounted to rest their horses and to eat the food they carried with them.

Suddenly, looking down the road behind them, they saw a squadron of cavalry coming along.

"This is awkward, Mike. There is nothing for it, now, but to ride on, and when we have reached the foot of the mountains on the other side, strike across country until we come upon the road running direct to Badajos. They are a good two miles behind us, so we need not blow our horses."

Mounting, they proceeded at a trot up the road. As far as they could see, the cavalry behind them did not quicken their pace, which showed that they were on some ordinary duty and not, as Desmond at first supposed, in pursuit of them, some peasant having, perhaps, taken word that an officer and soldier in strange uniform had been seen riding round the town. They therefore took matters quietly, and indeed, sometimes the road was so steep that it would have been impossible for the horses to go beyond a quick walk.

Suddenly, on reaching the crest of the rise, they saw, at a distance of a hundred yards ahead of them, a party of officers, followed by an escort of dragoons.

"We are caught this time, Mike!" Desmond exclaimed. "Escape is impossible. I will ride straight up and surrender. Fortunately they are English uniforms, so we are certain to get fair treatment, which we could not be sure of, had they been Portuguese."

So saying, he rode forward at a trot. The party had drawn rein at his approach, and he rode up to one who was evidently a general officer.

"Sir, I surrender as a prisoner of war. My name is Kennedy, and I am a captain on the staff of the Duke of Orleans."

"And what are you doing here, sir?"

"I am surveying the road, General, by which the allied army is likely to advance. Our information on that score is very defective, and I believe the duke wishes to ascertain, from my report, the state of the roads by which the advance would most probably be made."

The general's question had been in French, and he replied in the same language.

"You do not bear a French name, sir," the general said.

"No, sir, I am an Irishman," Kennedy replied, in English. "I belonged, before I received a staff appointment, to one of the regiments of the Irish Brigade."

"You are a daring fellow, thus to venture so far across the frontier."

"I simply obeyed my orders, sir; and, had I been ordered to reconnoitre Lisbon, I should have attempted to do so."

"Well, sir, I shall have an opportunity of talking to you, later on. I, as you see, am engaged in precisely the same work as you are; namely, in ascertaining, for myself, the state of the roads across these mountains."

"Then, General," Desmond said, with a smile, "I should say that your investigations are hardly satisfactory."

The general also smiled.

"Not so much so as I could wish," he said. "And now, may I ask why, seeing that you are well mounted, you did not turn and ride for it, when you first perceived us?"

"The reason is simple, General. A squadron of cavalry were coming up behind me, and there was evidently no possibility of escape."

"No doubt they were sent out to meet me. Well, sir, if you will give me your word not to attempt to escape, you can retain your sword, and ride with us."

"I give my parole, sir, with many thanks for your courtesy."

"And now, Captain Kennedy," the other went on, "it is probable that you have, about you, the result of your investigations along these roads, which I must request you to hand to me; as it may be as useful, to me, as it would have been to the Duke of Orleans, and may save me a good deal of trouble."

Desmond took out the notebook in which he had, each day, jotted down the result of his observations, with suggestions as to the points where repairs were most needed. He had each night, on his return to Badajos, written up his reports from these, intending, when he had completed the work, to take it himself to Madrid.

The general glanced through the notebook.

"You have done your work very thoroughly, Captain Kennedy, and have rendered me considerable service. Now, we will move forward again. Please follow with my aides-de-camp."

These were two pleasant young men, who were glad of a talk with an officer from the other side.

"How long have you been riding about here, if it is fair to put the question?" one said.

As the notebook contained all the particulars of his journeys on that side of the frontier, Desmond replied at once:

"Eight days, I think. I have been up the road to Portalegre, and by that to Lavre; and if I had not, unfortunately, accidentally heard of this road over the mountains, I should now be on my way to Madrid; but luck has been against me."

"Promotion must be very rapid in your army," the other aide-de-camp said, "or you would hardly be a captain already."

"I was fortunate enough to attract the notice of the King of France, and the Duke of Berwick, on various occasions, and when one has such a piece of good fortune as that, promotion is rapid."

"It is lucky for you that you fell into the hands of the Earl of Galway, instead of into those of the Portuguese generals, who would probably, in spite of your uniform, have made short work of you."

"I did not know that the general was the Earl of Galway," Desmond said. "Certainly, it was lucky that I fell into his hands. Indeed, if I had not seen the English uniforms, I should have turned and charged the squadron behind us; preferring very much to be killed fighting, than to be hanged or shot like a dog."

In a few minutes they met the squadron of cavalry, who had, as the general supposed, been sent out by the Governor of Elvas to meet him. Half of these now took their place in front, and the remainder, drawing aside to let the party pass, fell in behind. Mike had, without orders, fallen in with the earl's escort; and more than once Desmond heard his laugh, as he chatted with the troopers. On arriving at Elvas, the general directed his aides-de-camp to obtain a room, for Desmond, in the house in which they were quartered; and as no one attended to him, Mike undertook his usual duties as his servant.

The next morning, one of the aides-de-camp came in, and said:

"The general wishes to speak to you, Captain Kennedy."

On entering the general's apartment, the earl asked him to take a seat.

"I could not see you yesterday evening," he began, "as I was learning from the Governor the state of the stores here. I should like to have a talk with you. May I ask you, in the first place, how you have so early attained the rank of captain? My aide-de-camp tells me that you said you had attracted the notice of the King of France. It must have been by some singular action, and as I have an hour to spare, before I ride out, I shall be glad if you can tell me some particulars about yourself; unless, indeed, they are of a private nature."

"Not at all, sir. The story is generally known to members of the court at Versailles, and indeed to all Paris;" and he then related to the earl the story of his release of Anne de Pointdexter from her imprisonment, the journey to the south, the attack on the party by the Vicomte de Tulle, and her second rescue from him.

"Thank you, sir," the general said, when he had concluded. "I am not surprised that, after so romantic an adventure, the King of France took notice of an officer who had shown such courage and intelligence. You see, sir, that you and I are, to a certain extent, in a similar position. From motives of religion, principally, you Irish have left your country, and are fighting for a foreign monarch. I, as you are doubtless aware, belong to a French Huguenot family, and, being forced to leave France by the severe edicts, entered the service of Holland, and followed the fortunes of King William, and am now fighting against the troops of the country of my birth. In other respects, there is a similarity. We have both lost a hand in the service of our adopted countries; I at the siege of Badajos, and you at--?"

"Oudenarde, sir."

"I have been thinking it over," the general went on. "I might, of course, send you to Lisbon as a prisoner, but one extra prisoner would not largely benefit my government. You have not been taken in action. Your papers have saved me an immense deal of trouble, for we are no more able to rely upon the information given by the Portuguese than, I should think, the Duke of Orleans can upon that of the Spaniards.

"Therefore, sir, I think that, in the present case, I can make an exception to the rule. In an hour I shall mount and ride down the road to Badajos, and I shall there restore your liberty to you, and permit you to recross the frontier. It would be a thousand pities that so young and gallant an officer should waste, perhaps, some years of his life in an English prison, for the number of prisoners taken in Flanders is so great that it is impossible for the French to find officers to exchange for them. You will understand that, dealing with allies so jealous and susceptible as the Portuguese, I can hardly take the step of releasing you, as it would be at once rumoured that I had been in communication with a French officer, doubtless from some sinister motive.

"I think, Captain Kennedy, that it would be as well," he said with a smile, "that you should withdraw your parole, and do so before we start, in the presence of the officers of my staff. Of course, you must be placed under a very strict guard, and although so near the frontier, you will find it very difficult to escape. Still, such things are managed."

"I thank you most deeply, sir," Desmond said, understanding the tone in which the earl spoke, "and I shall ever retain a deep feeling of gratitude for your generosity."

When the party assembled, in readiness to mount, Desmond walked up to the earl, and said in a tone that could be heard by the officers round:

"Sir, I have changed my mind, and beg to be allowed to withdraw my parole."

"You are at liberty to do so, Captain Kennedy; but nevertheless I shall take you with us today. I shall not, of course, ask you to give any information as to matters on the other side of the frontier, but there are points on which you could inform me, without detriment to your friends."

"That I shall be happy to do, sir."

The earl called up four troopers.

"You will place this officer and his servant between you," he said, "and keep a vigilant lookout upon their movements."

Desmond had not even told Mike of the conversation with the earl, thinking it better that he should remain in ignorance that this escape was connived at by an English general, and his follower was therefore greatly astonished when he heard that his master had withdrawn his parole, and that they were henceforth to be strictly guarded. The party rode until they reached a rise from which they could obtain a view of Badajos, and of the country extending far up the valley of the Guadiana. The ground in front of them sloped gradually.

The earl took his place with two or three officers of his staff, fifty yards in front of the rest, and, dismounting, examined Badajos with his telescope. Then he asked one of his aides-de-camp to bring Captain Kennedy to him.

"You may as well bring his servant, too," he added. "No doubt he knows the country as well as his master does, and may not be so unwilling to answer questions."

The order was carried out, and Desmond and Mike rode up with the aide-de-camp, followed closely by the four troopers. The earl at once began to question Desmond as to the names of the villages visible up the valley. He had remounted now, but his staff, who had dismounted when he did, remained on their feet, as it was evident that he had no intention of moving forward for some time.

While they were speaking, the earl, accompanied by Desmond, rode forward some twenty yards, as if to obtain a better view. Mike had followed him, but the four troopers remained behind the group of officers, having no orders to follow the general so closely.

"This is good ground for galloping, Captain Kennedy," the earl said quietly. "You are within two miles of Badajos."

"Thank you deeply, sir.

"Now, Mike, ride for it!" and, spurring his horse, he dashed off at a headlong gallop.

There was a shout of surprise, the officers of the staff ran to their horses, which were being held by the orderlies, and the four troopers at once galloped forward, snatching their carbines from the slings.

"Do not fire," the earl shouted as they passed. "Take them alive."

As the officers came up, the general signalled to them to stop.

"Don't go farther, gentlemen," he said. "The troopers will doubtless overtake them; but for aught we know, there may be a Spanish force in the village just on the other side of the frontier, and, instead of capturing two prisoners, you might be taken or shot yourself; and I am not disposed to lose any of my staff, just as we are about to commence operations in earnest."

Desmond looked back. He saw that only the four dragoons were following.

"They will not overtake us, Mike," he said, "our horses are certainly better than theirs."

Indeed, they had increased their lead fast. A few minutes later, they heard a trumpet call in their rear, and their pursuers at once checked their horses, and rode back in answer to the recall.

"Tare an' ages," Mike exclaimed, "but that was nately managed. Who would have thought that they would have let us give them the slip so easily!"

"Well, Mike--but this you must never mention to a soul--the earl gave us this chance of escape, I believe. He had, you know, a long talk with me, and said that they had so many French officers captured in Flanders, that one more or less would make little difference. He had asked about my adventures, and seemed much interested in them, and remarked that our positions were somewhat similar, both being exiles on account of our religion, and so serving in foreign armies against our own countrymen. At any rate, it was on his suggestion that I withdrew my parole not to attempt to escape."

"Then he is a rale gintleman, sir, and mighty obliged I feel to him, for I have had enough of English prisons, though indeed, it was only three or four days that I stopped at Harwich."

The party on the hill had watched the pursuit, until the earl said:

"Well, gentlemen, I fancy he has slipped from our hands. I admit that I am hardly sorry, for he was a very fine young fellow, and it would have been a pity for him to be spending, perhaps some years of the best part of his life, in prison.

"Captain Chetwynde, will you order the trumpeter to sound the recall? They are leaving our men behind fast. It is no use losing four troopers as well as two prisoners."

More than one quiet smile was exchanged between the English officers, for, from the tone in which the earl spoke, they had no doubt that he was by no means sorry at Desmond's escape, and that possibly he had even taken him forward with him to afford him a chance of making it. They had, indeed, been a little surprised that, when Desmond withdrew his parole, the earl had not ordered him into strict confinement, instead of taking him with him on his reconnaissance.

The pursuit over, Desmond rode on at a canter to Badajos, and reported to Colonel Crofton that he had been taken prisoner, but had managed to effect his escape, as he was but carelessly guarded.

"I shall now, sir, return to Madrid. I have completed the work I was told to carry out, and shall finish writing up my report this afternoon, and start tomorrow morning."

"I congratulate you on your escape. The Portuguese are not very particular, and might, as likely as not, have paid small regard to the fact that you were in uniform."

"Fortunately, sir, it was not by them that I was captured, but by a small party of English dragoons, who were, I fancy, like myself, investigating the state of the roads."

Desmond had not been called upon to give evidence before the commission of enquiry, it being found that all the contractors had left their homes, a week before the troops arrived at Badajos, taking all portable property with them. Some had apparently gone to Andalusia, while others had made for Catalonia. All had unquestionably made a considerable sum of money by their frauds, and would take good care not to fall into the hands of the French.

"They will never be able to return here," Desmond remarked to Colonel Crofton.

The latter smiled.

"You do not know these people yet, Captain Kennedy, or you would not say so. Some of these fellows are certainly among the richest men in the province, and we may be quite sure that, in a very short time, when the affair has blown over, they will, partly by influence and more by bribery, obtain from the central junta an order that no proceedings shall be taken against them. Anything can be done with money in Spain. There are many upright and honourable Spaniards, but very few of them take any part in public affairs, and would not associate with such men as those who are in the ascendant in all the provincial juntas, and even in the central body in Madrid. "In France there is distress enough, and no doubt the men who farm the taxes are no more scrupulous than they are in Spain, but there is not the same general corruption, and the French nobility, haughty and despotic to their tenants as they may be, are not corrupt, and would scorn to take a bribe. Now that there is a French king on the throne here, there may be, when matters have settled down, some improvement; but it will be a long time, indeed, before the nation can be regenerated, and even the king will soon find that, if he is to reign peaceably, he must not interfere too violently with methods that are so common that they have come to be accepted as inevitable, even by the people who suffer by them.

"I can assure you that I, myself, have been many times approached by men who supply forage and other things to the regiment, and when I have indignantly refused to entertain any proposals whatever, they have not been at all abashed, but have said boldly that it was the general custom. I do not believe they thought any the better of me for refusing even to listen to their offers, but regarded me as a sort of Don Quixote, with ridiculously exaggerated ideas of honour."

On the morning following his return to Badajos, Desmond started on his way to Madrid. Although this time he had no apprehension whatever of a planned attack, he thought it safer and better to travel north from Badajos, and skirt the foot of the sierras until he reached the banks of the Tagus, where there was a strong garrison in each of the towns, and the country was, in consequence, free from the incursions of bands from the hills. The journey passed without an incident, and on reaching Madrid and presenting his report, he received high commendation from the Duke of Orleans, and spent a long day with the general's staff, explaining his report, and going into details as to the nature of the roads, the repairs necessary, and the positions which were, in his opinion, most suitable for battle.

On the following day, the members of the staff were all summoned to meet him by the Duke of Orleans, who informed them that he had received a sudden summons to return to Paris, and that Marshal de Bay would, in his absence, be in command of the French troops. The announcement came as a great surprise to Desmond, but was not unexpected by the other officers.

During the winter, the King of France had been engaged in efforts to bring about a general peace, and had offered terms that showed he was ready to make any sacrifices to procure it. The allies, on the contrary, were bent upon continuing the war. The victory of Oudenarde, the capture of Lille, Namur, and other fortresses, opened the way to Paris, and knowing the general distress that prevailed in France, they raised their demands higher and higher, as they perceived the anxiety of Louis for peace. One of the obstacles to this was the situation in Spain, and it was reported that Louis was ready to yield on this point also, and not only to consent to the cession of the Spanish dominion in Spain, but to his grandson Philip surrendering the crown to the Archduke Charles; and that, ere long, the French troops would be withdrawn altogether. While, during the month that had elapsed since Desmond first left Madrid, these rumours had increased in strength, it was known that couriers were constantly passing to and fro, between Madrid and Versailles, with private communications between Louis and Philip; and there was great excitement, in Madrid, at the rumour of this desertion of their king by France.

The rumours were indeed correct. The king had informed Philip that, great as was the affection he bore for him, the state of France, which was necessarily his chief care, would compel him, ere long, to recall his troops from Spain. Philip had entreated him not to desert him, and declared that, in any case, he would remain in Spain, confiding in the support of the people who had selected him as their monarch. At present, however, the communications were proceeding, and nothing definite had been arranged.

The whole of the staff were to remain with Marshal de Bay, in the same position as they had held under the duke, and, except for the departure of the prince, matters went on as before.

Chapter 17: An Old Friend.

The command had been effected so suddenly that Desmond had not been able to make up his mind to request the Duke of Orleans, to whom he had been attached personally, rather than to the French army in Spain, to allow him to return with him to France, in order that he might again join the Duke of Berwick. Before, however, he could decide whether to do so or not, the duke had taken his departure.

Desmond spoke to the head of the staff, with whom he had been constantly thrown in contact before he left Madrid, and whilst explaining to him, on his return, the details of his report, asked him for his advice.

"I should think you had better remain here, Captain Kennedy. There is likely to be a great battle fought, in a few weeks; but if the rumours we hear are correct, we may not be here very much longer. Certainly I hope there will be no change until then, for if we win the battle, and so relieve Spain from the risk of invasion for a time, we can leave the country with a better grace, as Philip would then only have to battle with his rebellious subjects in Catalonia."

"I should certainly not wish to leave when a great battle is about to be fought," Desmond said, "and will, therefore, continue to serve under the Marshal de Bay until it is certain what is going to be done."

In a short time a general movement of the troops, both Spanish and French, began. Desmond and the other aides-de-camp were actively employed in keeping up communication between the various columns, which were to assemble near Badajos. Moving forward at the same rate as the troops, the march was a pleasant one. It was April now, the country looked bright, and the heat was not too great for marching.

The marshal had gone on with the greater portion of his staff, Desmond having been detailed to accompany the division from Toledo. When within two days' march of Badajos, an orderly brought a note from the marshal, requesting him to ride forward at once. This he did without loss of time.

Marshal de Bay had taken up his quarters at Badajos, and on arriving in the town, Desmond alighted at the governor's house.

"It was a stupid mistake of mine," the head of the staff said, "in sending you on detached duty. I forgot at the moment, when I nominated you, that your knowledge of the locality would be invaluable to us. I only thought of it yesterday when, on the marshal asking for some information on this matter, I pulled out your report. He examined it and said, 'This is very complete and valuable, Colonel. Whom is it made by?'

"'By an officer of your staff, sir, Captain Kennedy.'

"'Where is he?'

"'He is coming down with the Toledo column, sir.'

"'Please send for him at once,' he said. 'One of the others should have been detached for that service. He is just the man we want here.'

"Accordingly we sent for you, and here you are."

"This is an excellent report of yours, sir," the duke said, when the colonel introduced Desmond to him. "As we came down, I noticed that the roads had, in many cases, been thoroughly repaired at the points mentioned in your report as being particularly bad, and the bridges in many places greatly strengthened. Had it not been for that, I do not know how I should have got my guns along.

"And now, sir, I want to ask you a few questions as to the road on the other side. By your report, I see that you consider the road through Campo Mayor to be the only one by which an army could move, and that a large body of workmen must be employed to make the other road fit for the passage of cannon."

He then asked a number of questions concerning this road.

"I see," he said, "you have marked several places, in your report, where an enemy coming down that road could post themselves strongly, and others which might be defended to advantage by us."

"Yes, sir; but of course, the suitability of those places would depend largely upon the respective strength of the armies."

The marshal nodded approvingly.

"From all I hear from our agents in Lisbon," he said, "the enemy's forces will be superior to our own in numbers, but the main portion are Portuguese, who have shown very little fight, hitherto. Their cavalry are almost entirely Portuguese. The only really fighting portion of their forces are the English and Dutch, who are most formidable foes; but against these we have our French regiments, on whose bravery we can rely. Were it not that I think the Portuguese will probably, as at the battle of Almanza, fly as soon as the engagement begins, I should fall back and take up a strongly defensive position. As it is, in spite of their superior numbers, I think we can meet them on an equal field."

The conversation lasted over an hour, and then Desmond retired, leaving Colonel Villeroy with the marshal. As he left the house, an officer standing at the door seized his hand.

"My dear Kennedy," he said, "who would have thought that we should have met again here!"

Desmond staggered back. He could not, for a moment, believe the evidence of his eyes and ears.

"Why, O'Neil, I thought you were dead."

"I am worth a good many dead men, yet," the other one laughed. "Let us go into this wine shop and crack a bottle. We can then talk over matters quietly."

"And O'Sullivan, is he alive too?" Desmond asked.

"No, poor fellow. He has never been heard of since that tremendous licking we got. There is not a shadow of hope."

Then many questions were asked, on both sides; and when these were answered, Desmond said:

"Now about yourself, O'Neil. I thought I was the only one that got through safe."

"So you were, for the other three of us were all on our backs."

"But we did not hear of you as among the prisoners, of whom a list was furnished by Marlborough."

"No; the name of Patrick O'Neil did not appear. I was shot through the body, and during the night I lay insensible, but in the morning I opened my eyes and began to think. It seemed to me that the name was not one that would be likely to please. In the first place, because it was evident, by my age, that I was not one of the Limerick men; in the next place, because of that little matter of my escape from the jail in London. I had no fear of being shot. I should be a prisoner of war, but I should not be likely to be over kindly treated, and when they exchanged prisoners I should certainly not be one of those sent back. You see, what with Blenheim and Ramillies and Oudenarde, they had taken ten of our officers for every one of their officers captured by us, so I thought it best to pass as a French officer.

"It was easy to do so, as my French was good enough to pass anywhere, and, you see, I had on a French staff uniform. Luckily my horse had been shot at the same time as I was. He was lying dead beside me, and within reach of my arm, so that I was able to lean over and get my flask from one of the holsters. I had a terrible thirst on me, and could have drunk a barrel.

"As I heard no firing, I knew that the fighting was over; and in two or three hours a party came along with a stretcher, having a doctor with them. When he saw that my eyes were open, and that I was alive, he examined my wound and shook his head.

"'He is badly hit,' he said, 'but you may as well carry him in.'

"So they took me into Oudenarde, which had been turned into a big hospital.

"'You are not to speak,' the doctor said to me, before they lifted me up. 'You must keep yourself perfectly quiet.'

"When they got me into the hospital, they found a hole behind as well as in front, which I heard one of the doctors say was a good thing. They dressed the wounds and left me. I could see by their faces, the next time they came, that they were surprised to see me alive. One of them said to the other:

"'The bullet must have passed through him without touching any vital point. He may do yet.'

"He bent down, and asked me in French what my name was, and I said 'Victor Dubosc, lieutenant;' so they stuck a card with my name over my bed, and asked me no more questions. I lay there for six weeks, and then I was well enough to get up and walk about.

"Three weeks later, I went down with some other convalescents to Ostend, and there we were embarked, and taken to Portsmouth. Then we were put in boats and rowed to Porchester, which is a place at the end of a sort of lake behind Portsmouth. There was an old castle there, with a mighty high wall, enclosing a lot of ground, where there were huts--rows of them--all filled with our prisoners. Some of the huts were a little better than others, and these were for the use of officers. A regiment of soldiers was in tents outside the walls, and a hundred men were always on guard with loaded muskets.

"I said to myself, often and often, 'If Kennedy were here, he would soon hit upon some plan for getting away;' but for the life of me, I could not see how it was to be managed. It was a dull time, I can tell you. The food was bad, and the cooking was worse. Only a few officers were there, most of them being sent to some place a long distance inland; but, as we were all wounded, I suppose they thought that the loss of blood would keep us quiet.

"One of the officers, having a little money hidden about him, bought a pack of cards from an English soldier, and we passed most of our time playing; but it was poor work, for we had nothing to play for. At last, I said to myself, 'Patrick O'Neil, there must be an end of this or your brain will go altogether. It is not worth much at the best of times, or it would have thought of some plan for getting out of this place before now.'

"At last, I hit on a plan. It was a dangerous one, there was no doubt of that; but as I was desperate, I did not think much of the danger. The worst they could do was to shoot me, which I suppose is what they would have done. My idea was to pounce suddenly on one of the sentries, who kept guard all night; to gag him, and tie him up, before he could give the alarm; and then to dress up in his clothes, and take his matchlock.

"But the difficulty was, what was I to do next. The soldiers came on duty for twelve hours, coming in at six in the morning and going out at six in the evening.

"It was clear to me that it could only be done in the dark, and I had to wait for nearly two months. It was the beginning of October before it was dark enough, at six in the morning, for me to fall in with the others and march out without being noticed.

"At last, the time came. I stole out of my hut an hour before the change would be made, and crept along quietly, till I heard a sentry marching up and down between our huts and those of the soldiers. I had torn up a blanket into strips, and twisted them together to make ropes; and with these in one hand, and a big piece ready to shove into his mouth in the other, I stole up close to him; and when he turned his back to me, I jumped upon him. Luckily, instead of carrying the musket on his shoulder, he had it under his arm, so that I was able to seize the lock with one hand, and clutch him by the throat with the other. I gripped pretty hard, and the man, in half a minute, slipped down to the ground.

"Before he could recover, I had stripped off his coatee and cloak; then I tied his hands and feet, fastened the gag firmly in his mouth, and dragged him in between two huts, where he would not be found till morning. Then I took off my own coat and threw it over him, for the night was chilly, and put on his cloak and shako, and took his place.

"In half an hour I heard a tramp of men, and knew the relief had entered. Then there was a bugle call, and two or three sentries passed towards the entrance. I ran on, too. When they fell in, I managed to get in the last section. Some sergeants ran down the line counting the men, and reported that all were present. The gates were opened, and we marched out.

"As soon as we got among the tents, we fell out, and I had no difficulty whatever in getting off without being observed. Leaving my musket and shako behind me, I went up a long lane which brought me on to the main road, crossed that, climbed a hill beyond, and came down into a wooded country.

"At the first cottage I came to, I stopped. A man and woman came out on my knocking. They looked kindly and good tempered, and I told them a pitiful story, about how I had been unjustly accused of striking an officer, and had been sentenced to two hundred lashes; and that I had managed, in the night, to cut a slit in the back of the guard tent and escape.

"As I had been walking along, a sudden thought had struck me. At Oudenarde, I was wearing the same boots I had worn when we were captured together. When we took the money out, we each left, if you remember, five pieces of gold in one of our boots, which I had never thought of till that day; and, as I came along, I opened the sole and took them out. It was a perfect godsend, as you may guess.

"The man and his wife expressed such sympathy that I did not hesitate to say: 'I want to get rid of my coatee, and of this cloak. The coatee would be of no use to you, and you had best burn it, but the cloak, if you alter it, might be useful; or, if you cut it up, will make a cover for your bed. I will give you that and a gold piece--it is a French one I got in the wars, but you can change it easily enough, when you go into the town marketing--if you will give me a suit of your clothes.'

"This the man readily consented to do, and the woman set before me a large bowl of milk, and some bread, which I ate as soon as I had put on a pair of breeches, smock, and broad hat. Now I felt perfectly safe. They might send news all over the country of the escape of a French officer, but as I had never spoken a word of English, from the time that I was taken, no one would suspect a countryman speaking English to be the man whom they were in search of.

"After leaving the cottage, I travelled quietly to Rye. I thought it best to go there, for it was likely that it would be difficult, elsewhere, for an unknown man to get a passage to France, and it struck me that the man who took us across before, would carry me over the first time he was going with despatches. I found him easily enough, and though I was not dressed quite in the same way as I was when we called on him before, he recognized me at once.

"'Another job for me?' he asked.

"'Not a special one,' I said. 'I am going across again, but there is no occasion for you to make a special trip, and indeed my employer forgot to give me an order upon you. I should have gone back, if I had remembered it, but I thought you would not mind giving me a passage the next time you sailed across.'

"As the man remembered that we had made ourselves pleasant on board, he agreed at once to take me, next time the boat should be going. I laid out a pound in getting a coat more suitable for travelling in France than the peasant's smock. Then I took a lodging in a small inn.

"Three days later, a messenger came down with an order for the man to take him across at once, and as the captain charged me nothing for my passage, I had enough left to pay for my place in a diligence, and on arriving in Paris duly reported myself, at the barracks, as having returned.

"My first enquiry, of course, was about you and O'Sullivan. I found that he had never been heard of, but that you had lost a hand, and had been promoted to a captaincy; had been very ill, and had gone to the south of France on sick leave.

"After I heard that, I remained for two or three months at the depot, and then learned that the Duke of Berwick had just arrived from Dauphiny. I at once went to see him. He told me he could not put me on his staff again, as his numbers were complete, but would give me a letter to the Duke of Orleans, asking him to employ me in that capacity. When I got down here, I found that the duke had left, and that the Marshal de Bay was in command.

"On reading Berwick's letter, he at once appointed me one of his aides-de-camp. You were away, I found to my great disappointment, and I was sent off into Catalonia, with orders for four battalions to be sent at once to Badajos. I arrived here yesterday, in time for the shindy."

"Fortunately, O'Neil, I do not think there is much fear of another Oudenarde. There is no royal duke here, to interfere with our general; and the Portuguese are not to be compared with the Hanoverians, and Dutch, and the other allies that fought against us there."

"I hear, from the others, that you have been occupied in reconnoitring the country."

"Yes, and I was captured, but was fortunately able to give them the slip."

Desmond did not care to tell even his friend that his escape was due to the kindness of the British general.

The next morning, Desmond was sent off to hurry up a body of troops which was still some seven or eight marches away. The news had come that the allied army was in motion, and would probably concentrate near Portalegre. This seemed to show that they intended to invade Spain by Badajos, and the valley of the Guadiana; for, had their aim been to advance up the valley of the Tagus, to Madrid, they would have marched towards Montalvao, and so on by Alcantara to Almarez.

After two days' hard riding he met the column, which, on receiving the order from the marshal to hasten forward with all speed, performed double marches until they arrived at Badajos. Desmond found that the allies had not wasted their time, and that their advance guard was already at Campo Mayor. The Spanish army were posted on the Caya river, a stream that flowed down from the sierra, and fell into the Guadiana at Badajos.

Their position was a defensive one. The army of the allies was known to be some twenty-two thousand strong, of whom some five thousand were cavalry. The Spanish had about the same strength of cavalry, but were inferior in infantry. The number of guns also was about equal, both sides having about forty cannon.

On the 7th of May, the two armies faced each other on opposite sides of the river Caya. As neither party made any movement of advance, Marshal de Bay determined to force on an engagement, and sent orders to the cavalry to cross the river, and to place themselves on the road between the enemy and Campo Mayor.

The allies suffered, as the French had done at Oudenarde, by conflicting counsels. The Earl of Galway was in command of the British, and of two or three Dutch regiments. The Marquis de Frontiera was in command of the Portuguese, who formed by far the greater portion of the force, and, as soon as the movement was seen on the other side of the river, he determined to cross and attack the Spaniards.

The Earl of Galway was strongly of opinion that it would not be wise to take the offensive, but that the army should remain in its present position, until the intentions of the enemy were clearly ascertained. Their cavalry, he urged, could do little by themselves, and it was evident that the infantry could not be attacked while they remained under the shelter of the guns of the fortress. The Marquis de Frontiera, however, and the other Portuguese generals, were unanimous in insisting that battle should be given at once, and the former gave orders for the Portuguese cavalry, with a body of foot and five field pieces, to march immediately.

Seeing that, if unsupported, this force must meet with disaster, the Earl of Galway reluctantly ordered the troops under his command to advance. The river was fordable, and they met with no opposition, until they crossed it and formed up in order of battle. The Portuguese horse were now divided on each wing, the British were in the centre; a portion of the Portuguese infantry were on either flank, the rest were in the rear.

"Captain Kennedy, you will carry my orders at once, to our cavalry, to charge the Portuguese horse on the right wing."

Desmond saluted, and was about to ride off, when he paused a moment and asked:

"May I charge with Brigadier Crofton's dragoons, sir?"

The marshal nodded, and Desmond galloped off. Crofton was in command of the first line of cavalry. His own regiment, which was composed partly of Irishmen and partly of Spaniards, was in the centre of the line.

After delivering his orders to the general commanding the cavalry, Desmond rode on to Crofton.

"The cavalry are going to charge, sir," he said, "and I have permission to ride with you."

Crofton waited until the order from the general arrived, and then, drawing his sword, shouted, "The first brigade will charge," and, riding forward, led the way against the Portuguese horse, whose cannon had already opened fire. The Portuguese fell into disorder as soon as they saw the long line of horsemen charging down on them like a torrent, and when it neared them broke and fled. They were soon overtaken, great numbers were cut down, and the remainder galloped off, a panic-stricken mob, and did not draw rein until they reached Campo Mayor.

The Spaniards at once turned the five cannon the fugitives had left behind them upon the allied infantry, and then, after a few rounds had been fired, the cavalry charged the British infantry. But they had now foes of a different metal to reckon with, and although, three times, the horsemen reformed their ranks and hurled themselves against the infantry, they were each time repulsed with heavy loss.

Then, swerving round, they fell on the Portuguese infantry in the second line, whom they dispersed as easily as they had defeated the cavalry.

The Earl of Galway now brought up the brigade of Brigadier General Pierce, which consisted of the two British regiments of Barrimore and Stanwix, and a Spanish regiment which had been recently raised and named after himself. These charged the enemy with great bravery, drove back their infantry for some distance, recovered the five guns the cavalry had lost, and, still pressing forward, fought their way deep into the centre of the Spanish ranks.

Had they been supported by the Portuguese infantry, on their flank, the battle might still have been won. But the latter, in spite of the persuasions and orders of their officers, refused to advance, and, turning their backs, made off in confusion, although not yet attacked by the enemy. Orders were then sent to the Portuguese horse on the left to charge to the assistance of Pierce's brigade. But instead of doing this, they also galloped off the field, and after defending themselves with desperate valour for some time, the little brigade, being unsupported, and being surrounded by the whole strength of the Spaniards, was forced to surrender.

In the meantime the Earl of Galway, seeing that the battle was lost, through the cowardice of the Portuguese, was preparing to withdraw his men, and had only despatched Pierce's brigade to check the advance of the enemy while he did so. Seeing that these, by their ardour, were irretrievably cut off, he gave the order to the

Marquis Montandre to draw off the British infantry, who alone remained firm, and against whom the whole of the French and Spanish forces now advanced; while he himself with a small body of cavalry, charged into the midst of the enemy in hopes of reaching Pierce's brigade and drawing it off.

Although weakened by the loss of that brigade, attacked on both flanks as well as in front, and frequently charged by the Spanish horse, among which Crofton's dragoons were conspicuous for their bravery, the retreating British maintained admirable order. Occasionally, when severely pressed, they charged the enemy and beat them back; till they were able to withdraw from the field with comparatively trifling loss, thus saving the flying Portuguese from annihilation. As at Almanza, the whole of the fighting, and almost all the loss, fell upon the English, although a considerable number of the Portuguese were cut down in their flight, before the Spanish cavalry returned to join in the attack on the retiring English. The allies had, altogether, seventeen hundred men killed or wounded, and two thousand three hundred taken prisoners, of whom fifteen hundred were Pierce's brigade; and eight hundred Portuguese, who were cut off by the cavalry.

Among the prisoners were the Earl of Barrimore, all the officers of Pierce's brigade, Lord Pawlet, one of the earl's aides-de-camp, two of his pages, and his master of horse.

After the battle was over, and Desmond had rejoined the marshal, he was sent to ride over the field, and ascertain who had fallen and what prisoners had been taken. Night was already coming on, and, after fulfilling his mission as far as was possible in the confusion, he came upon two Spanish soldiers, with a prisoner.

"Whom have you there?" he asked, in Spanish.

"I don't know, sir. We found him lying under his horse, which, in its fall, had so pinned down his leg that he could not escape. Several others had fallen round him, and it was only when we heard a cry for help that we turned the dead horse over, and found him under it, and then got him out."

Standing close, there was light enough for Desmond to distinguish the prisoner's features. He gave a slight start of surprise, then he said:

"You have done well, my men. Here is a doubloon, to get some drink with your comrades when you get into the town. I will look after the prisoner."

The men saluted and went off, well pleased to have got rid of the trouble of marching their prisoner into the town. Mike, rather surprised, moved up to take charge of the captive.

"My lord," Desmond said, "I will now endeavour to repay the kindness you showed me.

"Do you see that little hut, Mike, just at the edge of those trees? You must hide the earl there. Our cavalry are still all over the country, hunting down fugitives."

The earl, who was scarcely able to walk, his leg having been injured by the weight of the horse upon it, murmured his thanks, but did not speak again until they had entered the shed, when Desmond said:

"Now, General, I will first cut down your riding boot, to ease your leg. Then, if you will lie down in that corner, we will pile this firewood over you. It will not be safe for you to attempt to go forward for two or three hours yet. I have a report to make to Marshal de Bay. When I have handed it in, I will return at once.

"Mike, do you stay near the hut, and if any searching party should come along, which is scarcely likely, for they have all gone farther afield, you can say there is no need to search the hut, as you, with an officer, have already examined it."

In a few minutes, the earl was completely hidden. Desmond then rode into Badajos, and delivered his report to the marshal. He then went to the stables, took out his spare horse, and, leading it, rode out to the hut again.

"Has anyone been here?" he asked Mike.

"Not a soul, sir."

"Take the horses into the wood, then, and stay with them for the present. It will not be safe for the earl to move for a couple of hours.

"Now, General," he went on, as he removed the firewood, "I fear that you have been very uncomfortable."

"I can hardly say that I have been comfortable, sir, but that is of no consequence. The pain in my leg has abated, since you cut the boot open.

"And now, how can I express my gratitude to you, for thus sheltering me?"

"It is but a fair return of services, sir. You gave me my liberty, and I am doing my best to restore yours to you."

"It is all very well to say that, Captain Kennedy. I am the general in command of the British forces in Portugal, and had I chosen to openly release you, none could have questioned me. It was only because some magnified report of the affair might have reached the ears of the Portuguese Government, and given rise to rumours hostile to me, that I thought it best to let it appear to be an accidental escape. You see, I am by no means popular with the Portuguese. In the first place, I am a Protestant; and in the next place, I am constantly bringing pressure to bear upon them, as to the supply of provisions, the making of roads, the proper feeding and arming of their own troops, and other matters of the same kind; and they would be only too glad to have some cause of complaint against me.

"But your case is altogether different, for you are risking even your life in thus aiding me to escape."

"That may be, General, but it was nevertheless my duty, as a matter of conscience, to endeavour to return the kindness that you showed me; and as, at present, your army will hardly be in a state to take the field against us for a long time, I do not feel that I am seriously injuring our cause."

"Well, sir, I shall be your debtor for life.

"Do you intend to remain always an exile, Captain Kennedy?" the Earl of Galway went on. "It seems to me little short of madness that so many gallant gentlemen should cut themselves altogether adrift from their native country, and pass their lives fighting as mercenaries. I do not use the word offensively, but only in its proper meaning, of foreigners serving in the army of a nation not their own. Nor do I mean to insult Irish gentlemen, by even hinting that they serve simply for pay. They fight for France mainly in the hope that France will some day aid in setting James Stuart on the British throne; a forlorn hope, for although Louis may encourage the hopes of the Stuarts and their followers, by patronizing their cause, which it suits him to do because it gives him the means of striking at England, by effecting a landing in Scotland or Ireland; it is yet a matter upon which he must be indifferent, save in his own interest, and in the advantage it gives him of keeping in his service some dozen or so splendid regiments, on whose valour he can always rely."

"That is true, sir," Desmond replied; "and I own I have no great hope that, by the means of French assistance, the Stuarts will regain their throne. But what could I do if I were to return to Ireland? Beyond the fact that my name is Kennedy, I am in absolute ignorance as to what branch of that family I belong to, and have practically not a friend in the country. Were I to land in Ireland, I have no means of earning my living, and should doubtless be denounced as one who had served in the Irish

Brigade. I own that I should be glad to return there, for a time, in order to make enquiries as to my family. I was but sixteen when I left, and was kept, as it seems to me, purposely, in total ignorance on the subject. It may be that I was the son of a brave officer of that name, who certainly came over to France soon after I was born, and fell fighting some years before I came out; but I have no proof that it was so, and would give a great deal to be able to ascertain it.

"In Ireland they think a great deal of genealogy, and I am often questioned, by Irishmen of old descent, as to my family; and find it extremely awkward to be obliged to own that I know nothing of it, with any certainty. I have no desire to pass my life in battles and sieges, and, if I survive the risks and perils, to settle down as a Frenchman with an Irish name."

"That I can well understand," the earl said. "'Tis a life that no man could desire, for it would certainly be a wasted one. I can assure you that I think the chance of James Stuart, or his descendants, gaining the throne of England is remote in the extreme. When William of Orange came over, there was no standing army, and as James the Second had rendered himself extremely unpopular by his Catholic leanings, he became possessed of England without opposition, and of Ireland by means of his Dutch troops. The matter is entirely changed, now. England has a strong army, against which a gathering, however strong, of undisciplined men could have but little chance. I conceive it possible that a Catholic Stuart might regain the throne of Ireland, if backed by a French army, and if the people were supplied with French arms and money. But that he would retain the throne, after the French were withdrawn, I regard as next to impossible."

"I cannot but think the same, sir. However, as I see no chance of my being able to go to Ireland, even to push my enquiries as to my family, there is nothing for it but to remain a soldier of France."

"In that matter, I might assist you, Captain Kennedy. I have no doubt that my influence, and that of my friends in England, would without difficulty suffice to gain permission for you to visit Ireland on private business, on my undertaking that you have no political object whatever in desiring to do so, and that you engage yourself to enter into no plots or schemes for a rising. Furthermore, I think I can promise that, if you succeed in your researches, and find that you have relations and friends there, I could, if you desire it, obtain a revocation of any pains and penalties you may have incurred, and a restoration of all your rights as an Irishman. That is certainly the least I can do, after the vital service that you have rendered me--a service that, in itself, shows you do not share in the bitter enmity so many of your countrymen, unfortunately, feel against England."

"I have no such enmity, assuredly," Desmond said. "The choice of coming out here, to enter the service of France, was not of my own making; but was made, for some reason which I have never been able to understand, by the gentleman who had borne the expenses of my bringing up, but who was himself a strong supporter of the English rule, and therefore would have been expected to place every obstacle in the way of my entering the Irish Brigade."

Chapter 18: War.

After hearing Desmond's story the earl asked several questions, and obtained further details of his life when a boy, and of his interview with John O'Carroll.

"It is certainly strange," he said thoughtfully, "and worth enquiring into, for it would seem that he must have some interest in thus getting you out of the way, and in your entering a service that would render it next to impossible that you should ever return to your native land."

"I don't see any possible interest that he could have had in that, sir; but, certainly, I have never been able to account for his conduct."

"It is clear that there is some mystery about it," the earl said warmly, "and were I you, I should certainly take leave of absence, for a time, and go over and get to the bottom of the matter. At any rate, I will at once write to London and obtain a safe conduct for you. This you can use, or not, as you may decide, and can then, if you so please, return and continue your service here.

"Methinks that the war will not last very much longer. France is impoverished, the disasters which have befallen her arms in Flanders have rendered the war unpopular, and in England, in spite of the success gained by their arms, the heavy taxation is making men ask why a war should be continued which may benefit Holland, and the German allies, but can result in no good to England.

"And now, Captain Kennedy, I will be making my way to join the remains of my army. I thank you again, most heartily, for your generous conduct; and, believe me, you may always command my services in any direction. I only regret that these unhappy political difficulties should drive you, and so many of your brave countrymen, into the service of a power that has always been, and so far as I can see is likely to remain, an enemy of England."

"I may say, sir, that Lord Godolphin has, for a certain reason, promised to befriend me; and that, if you write to him on the subject of a safe conduct, I think I could rely upon his taking a favourable view of the matter."

"I will do so, certainly," the earl said. "His power is great. If he is favourably disposed towards you, you may consider the matter as done."

They chatted for some time longer, and then Desmond said:

"I think now, sir, that it would be safe to move. Everything is perfectly quiet without, and I have no doubt that, by this time, the cavalry have all returned to Badajos. However, I will accompany you for a short distance, for you may be stopped by some of our advance posts. You had best take the cloak and hat of my follower, and, as I am well known, no questions will then be asked."

"By the way," Lord Galway added as, Mike having brought up the horses, he mounted; "where shall I send a letter to you, with your safe conduct? We are in communication with many persons at Madrid, and can pass a letter through the lines at any time."

"When there, I lodge at the house of Don Pedro Sarasta, in the Calle del Retiro. I will request him to forward any letters to me, should I be absent."

The earl made a note of the address in his pocketbook, and then, putting on Mike's cloak and hat, started with Desmond, who passed him without question through the lines of outposts; which were indeed but carelessly kept, as it was certain that, after the signal victory that had been gained, it would be a long time before any enemy would venture to attack them.

Two days after the fight, the Marquis de Bay moved forward with his army, with the intention of fighting another battle; but Galway and Frontiera had, by this time, reorganized their forces, and occupied so strong a position, near Elvas, that he could not venture to attack them. However, he occupied the country for a considerable distance beyond the frontier, subsisting his army upon the provisions and forage collected by his cavalry in the villages and small towns. As it was evident that, after the proof given of the inability of the Portuguese to withstand any attack, there was no probability of offensive operations being renewed by the allies; and, the heat becoming intense, the force was withdrawn across the frontier and went into quarters, the general returning to Madrid, where he received an enthusiastic welcome from the inhabitants.

By this time, however, the knowledge that the king of France was entering into negotiations, which would necessitate his desertion of Spain, greatly excited the population against the French stationed in the capital. They were hissed and hooted when they appeared in the streets, and for a time, the indignation was so great that the troops were ordered to remain in their barracks. The king himself, however, gained rather than lost popularity, as he issued a proclamation to the people, saying that, having accepted their invitation to be their king, he would remain with them until driven from his throne by force; and he confided absolutely in their affection, and aid, to enable him to withstand any foes who might attempt to dethrone him.

In the autumn another change occurred. Although, in order to obtain peace, he had granted all the demands, however exorbitant, of the allies, and had undertaken to withdraw his troops from Spain, Louis stood firm when to these conditions they added another, namely, that he should himself undertake, by force, to dethrone his grandson. This monstrous demand united, at once, both those who wished to continue the war rather than grant such humiliating terms as those which had been insisted upon, and the party who were in favour of peace, even at that cost. The negotiations were abruptly broken off, and the French troops, who were already on the march towards the frontier, received orders to remain in Spain.

Now that he had O'Neil with him, the time in Madrid passed more pleasantly for Desmond than before. He was frequently away for several days, carrying despatches to the commanders of the forces in Valencia and Barcelona. In the capital the French were again regarded as friends, and as several successes had been gained and places captured, in Catalonia, the hope that the civil war that had so long been waged was approaching its end, and the confidence engendered by the victory on the Caya, made the people doubt whether any attempt at invasion from the west would be contemplated, and they gave themselves up to gaiety. Balls and fetes were frequently organized, and at these the French were among the most honoured guests.

Early in the spring preparations were made for active operations. Lieutenant General O'Mahony had just returned from Sicily, where he had rendered distinguished service. In the previous year, Crofton had been made a major general, and two new regiments of Irish infantry had been formed, of deserters from the enemy in Catalonia and Portugal. These were commanded by Colonel Dermond M'Auliffe and Colonel John Comerford. These two regiments, with another under Colonel Macdonald, marched from Madrid in April.

As the Marquis de Bay was not yet moving he offered O'Mahony, who had the command of the force, the services of Desmond and O'Neil as aides-de-camp. The offer was a welcome one, for, as none of the men in the newly raised regiments was acquainted with the language, Desmond, who now spoke Spanish well, would be far more valuable to him than Spanish officers could be.

For two months the little force moved about in Catalonia, the rapidity of its marches baffling the attempts of the archduke's forces to interfere with its operations. These were principally directed against various small fortresses, held by partisans of Charles. Several of these were captured, thus clearing the roads they guarded, and opening the country for the more important operations that Philip himself was about to undertake.

It was not until July that the royal army approached Lerida, where O'Mahony's force joined it. General Stanhope marched, with the troops under his command, and encamped at Balaguer; where he was joined by Baron de Wetzel, with some troops which had been brought from Italy. As Stanhope's force was insufficient to give battle until joined by the main army of Charles, he marched, on the 31st of July, headed by two English and two Dutch regiments of dragoons, to secure the passes near Alfaro, and so check the advance of the Spaniards.

After performing a long and difficult march, they took up a defensive position. Stanhope found, however, that the river in front of him was so low that cavalry and artillery could pass easily, and even infantry could cross without difficulty. Scarcely had he taken up his position when two brigades of infantry and nineteen squadrons of cavalry were seen approaching, having been detached from the Spanish army to occupy the position which had been secured by the rapidity of Stanhope's march. They therefore waited for their main army to come up, but before it did so, the whole of Stanhope's force had arrived, and was prepared for battle.

Although it was past six o'clock in the evening, Charles, on his arrival, decided to fall upon the enemy before they could encamp, which they might do in a position in which it would be difficult to attack them. Fourteen cannon at once opened fire from an eminence, whence they commanded the position taken up by the advance force of the Spaniards. This position was on low ground in front of the ridge upon which the village of Almenara stood, and nothing could be seen of the force that lay behind this ridge.

The advanced force of Spaniards ascended this ridge, as soon as the artillery opened upon them, and General Stanhope obtained leave from Marshal Staremberg, who commanded the archduke's army, to charge them. With ten squadrons of horse he rode up the ascent, and there, when he gained it, saw to his surprise twenty-two squadrons facing him, flanked with infantry, and supported with another line of cavalry equally strong. He sent back at once for fourteen squadrons from his second line, and when six of these came up he advanced against the Spaniards, who at the same time moved forward to meet him.

The cavalry on Philip's left at once gave way. The centre and right, aided by the fire of the infantry, made a stout fight, but were driven back by the English and Dutch cavalry. The fighting was severe, for of the six English squadrons who charged, two hundred men and twenty-one officers were killed or wounded.

Philip's second line of cavalry gave but feeble support, and Stanhope's horse soon had them all in confusion, and, driving them from the field, pursued them hotly. The fugitives dashed into their own infantry, who were just arriving in force, and their panic communicated itself to them, and a total rout took place. The pursuit was kept up until it was so dark that the troopers were unable to see each other's faces, and they then halted, having defeated the Spanish without the aid of their infantry, which had not come up in time to take any part in the fight. Much of the baggage, together with tents, many cannon, and a quantity of ammunition, fell into the hands of the victors. Owing to the darkness, the number of prisoners taken was small.

O'Mahony and his troops had taken no part in the engagement, as, having arrived late on the previous evening after a long march, they were still at Lerida. It had not been deemed necessary to hurry them forward, as no battle was expected to take place for some days--as, indeed, would have been the case had the force sent forward arrived at the river before Stanhope.

The routed troops arrived under the shelter of the guns of Lerida. Charles did not attack them there, but, making a detour, seized several places in Aragon, with the intention of cutting the line by which Philip would probably retire, and forcing him to fight again. Philip, however, on his part, marched from Lerida in order to retire into Castile by way of Saragossa. Charles followed hotly, and a portion of his cavalry came up to the rear of the enemy in the defile of Penalva. Here the Spaniards posted a strong force of grenadiers, and the defile being too narrow for the cavalry to act, these dismounted, and a hot fight took place, in which both parties claimed the victory. However, Philip retired the same day in great haste. Charles, arriving three hours later, ate the dinner that had been prepared for his rival.

The Spaniards, covered by the defence of the pass, crossed the Ebro and posted themselves in a strong position within a mile of Saragossa. On the 21st of August Marshal Staremberg, with his generals, having reconnoitred their position, gave orders for the attack to take place the next morning, and at daybreak the cannon on both sides opened fire. General Stanhope, who commanded on the left wing, found that the enemy had the greater part of their cavalry facing him, and therefore strengthened his force by four battalions of foot and six squadrons of Portuguese horse.

The Spanish line ran obliquely, from the river on their left to a steep hill on their right, occupied by their cavalry and a battery of artillery. These, therefore, were much nearer to the attacking force than were those on the plain.

The battle began at twelve o'clock, Charles's force marching in two lines, with the exception of Stanhope's cavalry and infantry. These, from their situation, were the first to come in contact with the enemy. The four battalions first pushed forward up the hill, and, driving the Spanish cavalry back, allowed Stanhope's horse to ascend the hill and form on its crest. The battle speedily ranged along the whole line. The Spaniards, with superior numbers, gained ground on their left. Here O'Mahony's corps were stationed, and they drove a portion of the allies across the Ebro again; but this success was more than counterbalanced on the other flank, where Stanhope's cavalry and infantry carried all before them. The latter, posted in a hollow, opened so heavy a fire upon the Spanish infantry, as they advanced, that they fell into disorder; and as their cavalry were driven off, hotly pursued by Stanhope, they fell back upon the centre, which they threw into disorder. Seeing that the battle was lost, the Marquis de Bay gave the order to retire.

Two hours after the first shot was fired, the rout of the Spanish centre and right was complete, but a considerable portion of the troops were rallied by de Bay at Alagon, three leagues above Saragossa. The left wing, under Generals Amezaga and

O'Mahony, were checked in their course of victory by the disaster which befell the centre and right; but, maintaining their discipline, they fell back in good order, and rejoined their defeated comrades at Alagon.

All the cannon and most of the colours of the regiments forming the centre and right fell into the hands of the victors. The loss of the allies was about two thousand men, killed or wounded; and that of the Spaniards and French three thousand killed and wounded, and between five and six thousand prisoners. Philip rode at once to Madrid, and on the evening of the battle the archduke entered Saragossa; while de Bay retired, with the broken remains of his troops, towards Navarre.

Desmond and O'Neil, who had ridden behind O'Mahony, saw the Spanish troops of the archduke yield before the impetuous attacks of the Irish regiments, who, as they pressed their foes backwards, burst into loud cheering, believing the victory already won. Presently, O'Mahony stopped the advance.

"We must not push too far forward," he said. "It seems to me that things are not going so well in other directions. Our centre is being pressed back. What is going on on the right I cannot say, but the enemy seems to have gained the top of the hill, for our cannon there are silent. If the centre is driven back, those we have now beaten will rally, and we shall be taken in flank by the fire of their centre. Therefore, let us be content with what we have done, and wait and see how things turn out elsewhere."

Even before the rout of the Spanish right, their centre was yielding, for opposed to them were the British and Dutch regiments, whose attack they were altogether unable to withstand. It soon became clear that, at all other points on the field, the battle was going against the Spaniards, and an aide-de-camp presently rode up, hastily, with orders from Marshal de Bay for his left to fall back and retire to Alagon.

Deep was the rage and disappointment among the troops of O'Mahony and Amezaga, as they faced about and set out on their march. They were unmolested. The troops they had beaten were in no disposition to follow them, while the allied cavalry and the infantry of their centre were in full pursuit of the rest of Philip's army, the remnants of which the little force joined, at Alagon, before nightfall.

It was some days before the archduke's army moved forward again. The troops were exhausted by the long marches they had made, and there was a difference of opinion among the generals as to the course that had best be followed. The king wished to pursue the beaten enemy and, if possible, to intercept their march towards France, but Count Staremberg and Stanhope were of opinion that they should first occupy Madrid, and then march into Navarre, so as to bar the advance of fresh French troops into Spain, and at the same time open communications by sea with England, whence they could be supplied with reinforcements and stores of provisions.

Finally, Charles gave way, and the allies marched towards Madrid. The main portion of the army halted at Alcala, a day's march from the capital, and General Stanhope marched on with his division to Madrid, which opened its gates without resistance, Philip having retired with his army. Charles entered the city on the 28th of September, 1710.

The alarm, in France, at the news of the defeat at Saragossa was great, and Louis at once despatched the Duke of Vendome to command there. The latter, travelling fast, and gathering up the garrisons of the towns through which he passed, crossed the frontier at nearly the same time as Charles entered Madrid, and effected a junction with de Bay's army; which had, by this time, been increased by some fourteen thousand men, drawn from the garrisons of towns in Navarre, Castile, Galicia, and Valencia.

Vendome had no doubt that the intention of the allies, in marching upon Madrid, was to open communication with the Portuguese, and determined to throw himself between the capital and the frontier. Marching with all speed, he encamped near Salamanca on the 6th of October, and thence moved to Plasencia, thereby securing the bridge of Almarez, and preventing the Portuguese from joining Charles.

Had it not been for the usual indecision and want of energy on the part of the Portuguese Government, the junction might have been effected before Vendome arrived at Plasencia, for both Charles and Stanhope had, after the victory of Saragossa, written urgently, begging that the Portuguese army should at once advance and join them at Madrid; and that, at any rate, if the whole army could not move, at least the troops in the pay of England should push forward instantly. Stanhope, indeed had marched with his division to the bridge of Almarez to facilitate the junction, and had defeated a Spanish force guarding the bridge. However, the Portuguese did not arrive; and when a messenger brought the alarming news that a Spanish and French army had occupied Plasencia, Stanhope fell back towards Madrid.

As large French reinforcements were known to be approaching the frontier, and Philip's army was already much superior in numbers to that of the allies, it was decided, in a council of war, to evacuate Madrid. The forces which had occupied Toledo and other towns were recalled, and, early in December, the army left the capital; the archduke riding at once to Barcelona, while the army, of which Stanhope's division formed the rear guard, followed in the same direction.

The movement had been delayed too long. Vendome and Philip were already at hand, and on the 9th fell upon Stanhope's division at Brihuega. This force, consisting of eight English battalions and the same number of Portuguese horse, defended themselves desperately, and although the town was wholly without fortifications, they repulsed every attack until their ammunition was exhausted, and they were then forced to surrender. Staremberg, on hearing that Stanhope was attacked and surrounded, turned back and marched with all speed to relieve him, but on arriving within three hours' march of the town, heard that he had surrendered.

The Duke of Vendome, hearing of his coming, drew his troops out and formed them in line of battle, and the next morning attacked him vigorously. The allied right held their ground, but the left fled, and Vendome swept his right round and took the centre and right of the allies in the rear. Three battalions of the second line, however, fell in turn upon the French rear and repulsed them, and the left wing, rallying again, renewed the battle.

The combat was indecisive, both parties claiming the victory. Staremberg wrote to Charles that he had captured all the enemy's guns, and had killed six thousand of them; while the French claimed that they had totally defeated the allies, and captured all their cannon, killed four thousand, and taken nine thousand prisoners. The balance of probability lies to some extent with the French, for the day after the battle, Staremberg retired and marched to Barcelona; but the fact that he was not at once pursued shows that the French and Spaniards must have suffered very heavily.

Desmond had passed unscathed through the battle of Saragossa. O'Neil had been severely wounded, but had managed to sit his horse until the division effected its junction with the Marquis de Bay's shattered forces. Great was the wrath among the two Irish regiments at the issue of the battle.

"What is the use," an officer said to Desmond, "of our throwing away our lives, fighting for these Spaniards, when they themselves are useless, save when they meet the Portuguese, who are still more contemptible? Here have we, on level ground, fairly beaten the enemy, while the right and centre, although having a great advantage in position, allow themselves to be scattered like a flock of sheep."

"They had stouter foes to meet than we had," Desmond said. "We had only Spaniards opposed to us, while they had English and Dutch to fight; and as the best French troops have found, in Flanders, that these were at least a match for them, we must not blame the Spanish too severely for giving way before they were attacked."

"There is something in that, I admit, Kennedy. It seems to me that, in this war, it would be much better if the Spaniards and Portuguese had both remained at home, and allowed the French and us fight it out with the English and Dutch. The battles would have been small, but at least they would have been desperately fought."

"But it would be absurd, Moore, for us to lay down our lives in a struggle in which those principally concerned took no part whatever, and which was of no great interest either to us or to the English. After the way in which Louis was ready to throw over Spain and Philip at the beginning of the year, the Spanish alliance can be of no great advantage to him, and I do not think that even Philip's orders would induce a Spanish army to march across the frontier to assist France. Therefore, as Louis can gain nothing by the Spanish alliance, why should he weaken himself by sending forces here to maintain Philip on the throne?"

"But with the Archduke Charles here, he would have an enemy on his frontier. Philip might not assist him, but Charles would be actively hostile. The English and Dutch troops would be pouring into the peninsula, and we should have another Flanders in the south of France."

"Well," Desmond said, after a pause; "the best way I can see out of it is for both Philip and Charles to withdraw, and allow the Spanish to elect a Spaniard for their king; or, if they could not agree to that, which I don't suppose they could do, choose some foreign prince belonging to a petty state which stands altogether aloof from European affairs, and seat him on the throne. If, again, they would not accept him,

England and France should mutually agree not to interfere in the affair, and let the Spaniards indulge in civil war as long as it pleases them."

Moore laughed.

"It might be a good solution, Kennedy, but there is no more chance of Philip or Charles renouncing their pretensions, or indeed of the French on one side and the allies on the other permitting them to do so, than there is of the world becoming an utopia, where war shall be unknown, and all peoples live together in peace and amity."

"Well," Desmond said, "for my part, I am sick of fighting in quarrels that do not concern me, and when this campaign comes to an end I shall, if possible, rejoin Berwick. The cause of the Stuarts is not advanced, in the slightest, by what is taking place in Spain, and if I am to fight, I would rather do so where victory would benefit us."

"I don't know that you are not right," the other assented. "It certainly seems a pity that the best blood of Ireland should be spilled, in Flanders and Spain, in the service of a foreign country. To my mind, the terms of the surrender of Limerick were disadvantageous both to Ireland and England. England has gained a number of inveterate foes who, with good and wise treatment, might now be fighting in her own ranks. Ireland has lost her best blood, men who were her natural leaders, and belonged to the old families, whom all respected."

"I am sure it was a mistake," Desmond said. "If the terms had been an absolute equality in all matters of religion, and the free pardon of all, without confiscation of their property or other disability, it would have gone far to reconcile our people to defeat; for they would have seen that they could not hope for more than the right of free exercise of their religion, if the Stuarts came to the throne again."

"Perhaps you are right, Kennedy. I know that I myself, had it not been for the persecutions and the priest hunting, and the closing of our chapels, should never have thought of leaving Ireland and taking foreign service. But now there is no going back."

"No, I suppose not," Desmond said, gloomily. "Nothing short of an amnesty, ensuring freedom of worship, and perfect civil equality to all, would induce the majority of us to return to Ireland; and, indeed, it is not easy to see what we could do if we got there. The estates of our fathers are in the hands of strangers. We should soon be altogether without resources, and we should be almost driven to conspire again, even though success would in no way mend the matter.

"However, there is no chance of such an act being passed, for, even if the English Ministry desired to do so, the Protestant feeling in England and Scotland would be too strong for them; and Parliament, which strongly represents that feeling, would reject the bill by an immense majority."

"Then there is nothing to do but to go on fighting," Moore said.

"I see nothing else for it, Moore, but I own that I do not care for the life. I have had three years of it now, and don't like the prospect of another thirty."

"You have been fortunate, too, Kennedy!"

"Yes, I have been fortunate in the way of getting promotion; fortunate that I was not, long before this, put under the sod; but it is no great gratification to be a captain, and though in another thirty years, if I live, I may be a general, I don't think even that would reconcile me to the life. It is just as hard, and a good deal more responsible; and if thirty years passed over, and the Stuarts were not restored, they assuredly never would be, and I should have wasted my life for nothing."

"Well, I am very glad," Moore laughed, "that all our fellows do not look at it in the same light as you do, but take things as they come. I don't bother myself about the future."

"It is a good thing," Desmond said, "and it is the national character to take things as they come. I dare say I shall get into the same way, some day, but just at present, I suppose partly because we have got a thrashing, I feel rather down in the dumps."

Desmond continued his duties as aide-de-camp to O'Mahony, and took his share in the various operations, that ended with the army going into winter quarters and Philip making a triumphant entry into Madrid. Then he went to the general.

"General, I wish to ask leave to return to France, at any rate for a time. The Duke of Berwick, when he despatched me to join the staff of the Duke of Orleans, said he would reinstate me on his staff as soon as the duke no longer required my services. When the Duke of Orleans left, I was handed over with the rest of the staff to the Marshal de Bay, under whom I served in the battle of the Guadiana, and until, as you know, I was detailed to accompany your brigade. Now that the campaign is over, I should, at any rate, like to pay a visit to the Duke of Berwick, under whom I served at Oudenarde. I have, therefore, come to ask you to dispense with my services, and to permit me to return to France."

"Certainly, Captain Kennedy. Your assistance has been of great value to me, but there is no chance of anything being done during the winter; and, as many of my officers are now beginning to speak Spanish, they will, should they remain here till the spring, be able to get on very fairly. I shall be pleased, before you start, to furnish you with a testimonial stating the services you have rendered me. Indeed, I have, more than once, mentioned them in my reports."

Chapter 19: In Search of a Family.

On the following day, Desmond left the brigade, and, followed by Mike, rode for Madrid, where was still lying a letter which had arrived, some months before, from England. He had not asked for it to be forwarded, for if he had been killed, and it had been found on him, it might do his memory a great disservice, as it would seem that he had been in correspondence with the British. The letter, which contained an enclosure, was, to his surprise, from Lord Godolphin. It ran:

Dear Captain Kennedy:

Partly at the request of the Earl of Galway, and still more from my own remembrance of your conduct, in that affair you know of, and of the silence that you maintained concerning it, I have pleasure in sending you a safe conduct to visit Ireland on private affairs. The earl tells me that you have rendered him the greatest of services, and this alone should cancel the fact that you have been serving against us in Flanders and Spain. For this, and your conduct to myself, I can promise you that should you, at any time while I am in power, decide to remain in Ireland, I will obtain for you a full and complete pardon, and a restoration to all your rights as an Irish subject of the queen. I will also obtain a reversal of any attainders or acts of confiscation that may have been passed against your family, on your giving your promise that you will not take part in any secret plots or conspiracies against the reigning family, though, in the event of a general rising in Ireland, with the assistance perhaps of a French army, you would be at liberty to choose your own course of action, without incurring more pains and penalties than those which might befall any native of Ireland waging war against the queen.

As both Godolphin and Marlborough were known to be by no means unfavourably disposed to the cause of the Stuarts, Desmond was hardly surprised at the latter part of this intimation. Though he had but small hopes of being enabled to remain permanently at home, it was yet very welcome to him. Certainly, if he remained in Ireland he would consider himself bound to hold himself aloof from all Jacobite plots, although, if the country rose and a French army landed, he would, unless he considered the cause a hopeless one, draw his sword on behalf of him whom he considered as his lawful sovereign.

"It is not sorry I am, your honour, to be turning my back on this country," Mike said, as they rode out from the gate. "The wine is good, which is more than I can say for anything else in it, except that the people are good Catholics."

"I am starting a longer journey than you think, Mike. I am only going to the duke, now, to ask for a year's leave; though I do not think that I shall be absent more than a few months."

"And where are you going, your honour, if I may make so bold as to ask?"

"I am going to Ireland, Mike."

Mike looked at him with astonishment.

"To Ireland, your honour? Sure they will hang you, before you set your foot a week in the country."

"I have obtained a safe conduct, Mike, from Lord Godolphin. You remember him, the nobleman we kidnapped?"

"Sure I remember him, your honour; and he has given you a safe conduct? It is in luck you are, to be going back to Ireland again."

"It is not a visit of pleasure, Mike. I am going over to try to ascertain to which branch of my family I belong."

"And what can it matter, your honour? It's a good name you have made for yourself out here."

"I have done well enough, Mike, but I am tired of being asked, by almost every officer I meet, about my family, when in fact I know nothing myself."

"Well, Captain, it does not seem to me worth troubling about, for if you don't know who they are, it is little they can have done for you."

"It would seem so, Mike. There is a mystery about the whole affair, and I want to get to the bottom of it."

He rode silently for some distance. He knew that Mike would go through fire and water for him, and that, simple as he seemed, he had no ordinary amount of shrewdness; and he determined to tell him all he knew, especially as he intended to take him to Ireland with him.

"Mike," he said at last, "I suppose you would like to pay a visit to Ireland, also?"

"I should that," Mike said, emphatically. "I was but eighteen when I came out here to enlist in the brigade--that is twelve years ago now, and it is few people would be likely to know me again."

"Well, I am thinking of taking you with me, Mike; and, as possibly you may be of use in my search, I will tell you my story."

And he related the history of his youth.

"He must be an unfeeling baste, to treat you like that," Mike exclaimed indignantly. "Sure I know the name, and have heard him spoken of as a traitor who had gone over to the enemy, and turned Protestant to save his estate."

"That is how you would hear him spoken of, Mike, for it is true; but as to his treatment of me, it all depends whether I was forced upon him by threats, or was taken by him out of friendship to my father. If it were the first of these reasons, he cannot be blamed for keeping me at a distance. If the second, he certainly ought to have behaved differently. But neither explains why he, a supporter of the usurper, should have sent me out to France to fight against the English. It is a hard nut to crack."

Mike agreed. "Mighty hard; but your honour will get to the bottom of it, never fear. And why are we going to the duke, master?"

"To get leave of absence. I cannot disappear suddenly, without asking for leave. I shall, of course, tell the Duke of Berwick exactly why I am going, and I feel sure he will grant my request, without hesitation. There is no fighting to be done, just at present, and even if there were, one officer more or less would make no difference.

"Have you any relations in Ireland, Mike?"

"None that I know of, sir, barring a sister, who was twelve years older than myself; and it is little I saw of her, for she married when I was a bit of a gossoon. Her husband was killed in the siege of Limerick, and I heard that after it was over, she went to settle with some cousins in Cork. Whether she is there now, is married again, or is dead years ago, is more than I can say, seeing that I have never heard of her since."

"Was she with her husband in the siege of Limerick?"

"She was that. I heard about her from some men who knew her husband. They said, after he was killed, she went as a servant in the family of an officer and his wife for a bit, but the officer was killed, and the lady died of grief and trouble; and it was hard work she had to live till the place surrendered. That is all I know about it, your honour. It might have been true, and it might not. I was but a boy, and maybe I bothered the man with questions, and he just told me what came into his head to keep me quiet."

"Well, at any rate, Mike, as we shall most likely land at Cork, you might try to find your sister out. If she went through the siege, she will know the names of many of the officers. She may have heard of a Kennedy."

"Maybe of half a dozen, your honour. As loyal gentlemen, they would be sure to be there."

"What was her name, Mike?"

"Sure it was the same as my own before she married, just Norah Callaghan."

"So I suppose, Mike," Desmond said with a laugh; "but what was the name of the husband?"

"Rooney. I have not thought of it this many a year, but it is sure I am that it was Rooney; and now I think of it, a message came to me from her, just before I left the country, saying that should I ever be in the neighbourhood, it is glad she would be to see me; and I was to ask for Mrs. Rooney, who lived with her cousin, Larry Callaghan, a ship's carpenter, in Middle Lane, which I should find by the river bank."

"Well, that is something to go by, Mike. Of course, she may have moved away long since; but if her cousin is a ship's carpenter, it is not likely that he would have left the neighbourhood."

"I wonder your honour never asked about the Kennedys from some of the officers who were at the siege?"

"I did not like to do so. The colonel came to the conclusion that I must be the son of Murroch Kennedy, who came out soon after Limerick surrendered, and was killed at Breda two or three months after he joined the brigade. The officers agreed with the colonel that this gentleman was probably my father, and of course I was contented that it should be supposed so, and therefore I asked no questions about other Kennedys. Of late, however, I have been worried over the matter. In the Irish regiments in Spain, as elsewhere, were a number of officers belonging to good old Irish families, and though I have got on well enough with them--in the first place as Berwick's aide-de-camp, and afterwards as on the staff of the generals here--I could see that when, in answer to their question, it was evident I knew little or nothing of my family, there was a sort of coolness in their manner which I could quite understand, counting back their ancestors, as they did, pretty nearly to the flood. At present, it does not make any difference to me personally, one way or the other, but I am convinced that if, by chance, when I get older, I should fall in love with the daughter of an officer of one of these old families, he would not for a moment listen to me, until I could give him some proofs that I had a right to the name I bear, or at any rate came of a good family. Certainly, at present, I could not assure him on either point. I only know that I have always been called Kennedy, and that it was under that name that I was committed to the care of Father O'Leary. That proves nothing more than that it is the name by which John O'Carroll wished me to be called; and it is as likely as not--indeed a good deal more likely--that it was not the true one."

"Well, at any rate, your honour, you have made the name of Desmond Kennedy well known and liked, both among the Irish and French officers, for it is no slight thing that an officer in an infantry regiment should be taken on the staff of the Duke of Berwick."

"All that is very well, Mike; but it will not satisfy me more than it satisfies others. So I am resolved to try to get to the bottom of the affair, even if I have to go direct to John O'Carroll, though I know that the chance of his telling me anything is but slight. The only way, indeed, that seems likely to lead to anything is to call upon as many of the Kennedys as I can discover, and ask whether Murroch Kennedy, who left Ireland after the siege of Limerick, married and left a child of two years old behind him. If so, and that child suddenly disappeared when his father left for France, there would be every reason for assuming that I was the child in question; though why he should have committed me to the charge of John O'Carroll, instead of to one of his own family, is not easily seen; unless the whole of the Kennedys were in such ill favour, with the English Government, that he thought it better to trust me to one who was in good odour with the supporters of Dutch William, and was therefore safe from disturbance in his estates."

"Sure, your honour, you are arguing it out like a counsellor, and there is no gainsaying what you have spoken. I have no doubt you will ferret it out. With such a head as you have on your shoulders, it is hard if you cannot circumvent that ould rascal at Kilkargan."

"At any rate we will try, you and I. While I am visiting the Kennedys, you can be finding out people who were at Limerick during the siege, and gather all they can remember about the Kennedys there."

As Desmond had expected, the duke, as soon as he heard his story, at once granted him leave of absence.

"I hope you may succeed, Kennedy," he said. "It is a poor lookout to be risking death continually in the service of a foreign king. I grant that we have the knack of making ourselves at home, wherever we may be, and there are Irish officers in every army in Europe; but, however successful Irishmen may be, they cannot but long to be among their own people in their own land. And if, as you tell me, Lord Godolphin will befriend you, I for one shall think no worse of you if you settle down at home when you have found your family. I know that if the sword should be again drawn, with a fair prospect of success, you will declare for the rightful king."

"That I should certainly do, sir; and will assuredly give no promise, or undertaking, to abstain from joining any royal army that may be raised in Ireland. But it is not with any intention of settling at home that I am going there, but simply, as I have told you, to discover to what family I belong, so that I can have a right to the name I bear."

"At what port will you embark?"

"I intend to pay a visit, for a few days, to the Baron de Pointdexter and Monsieur de la Vallee, after which I shall cross into Italy. I have no doubt that I shall be able to find some fishermen, at Toulon, who will undertake to land me somewhere near Genoa, where I shall be able to take a passage in a ship bound for England."

"And I suppose you take your servant with you?"

"With your permission, Duke. He has been my companion for three years. He is shrewd as well as brave, and will give me valuable help in my enquiries."

After remaining a couple of days with Berwick's army, Desmond started with Mike, and received the warmest welcome from the Baron de Pointdexter, and afterwards from Philip and his wife. Then they travelled on to Toulon, where Desmond sold the horses and equipments. He left his uniform and Mike's there, and procured two civilian suits. As he anticipated, he experienced no difficulty in arranging to be landed near Genoa. There he found several ships bound for England or Ireland, and took a passage in one that would touch at Cork, on its way to Dublin. The voyage was uneventful, and the ship, which had no great draught of water, proceeded up the river to the city.

"The first thing to do, Mike," Desmond said, as they stepped ashore, "is to get rid of these clothes, whose French cut will at once attract attention. I shall get a suit such as is worn by an Irish gentleman. You had better equip yourself as my servant. No livery is worn here, but any quiet dress will be suitable."

They put up at a small inn, and remained there until a suit such as Desmond desired was made for him, and Mike found no difficulty in purchasing ready-made clothes suitable to his new position. Desmond had taken rooms as Mr. Kennedy, and had asked carelessly if there were any families of that name living in the neighbourhood.

"There is one who lives a short distance out of the town. It is a small house, and shame it is that one of the old family should come down so; but most of their estates were stolen from them after the war. Still, the old man holds his head as if he was still lord of broad acres, and he is mightily respected among the gentry."

The next day, Desmond hired a horse and rode out to the house of Mr. Kennedy, which was some three miles from the town. He sent in his name, and was shown into a room, where a tall man, with a somewhat haughty air, received him not unkindly.

"Your name is the same as my own," he said, "though I do not recognize the name of Desmond Kennedy among such members of the family as I am acquainted with."

"I have but just landed from France, and my object in coming here is to obtain some information as to my father's family. Hearing that a gentleman of the name lived here, I came first to you. May I ask if you were acquainted with a Murroch Kennedy?"

"Surely I was. He was my first cousin. We fought side by side at Limerick. I was not one of those who cared to enter foreign service. My estates were confiscated, and I have ever since lived here on the wreck of my fortune, taking no part in politics.

"My cousin was of a different mind. He did not, indeed, go out at once with the greater part of the army of Limerick, but still, hoping that the cause was not altogether lost, he lived for some months among the mountains, and took part in a rising which was promptly suppressed, and then joined the Irish Brigade; and I received a notification, from one of his brother officers, that he had fallen at the battle of Breda. And now may I ask, in turn, what Murroch Kennedy's relationship was to you?"

"I will tell you, sir. But first, will you kindly inform me whether your cousin left a child about a year old behind him?"

"Certainly not, sir. My cousin was an unmarried man, at any rate up to the time when he left Ireland."

"Then, sir, my questions are at an end. I may tell you that, about the time your cousin left Ireland, I was sent as an infant to the care of John O'Carroll, the traitor, of Kilkargan, and was brought up under the name of Desmond Kennedy. He showed me but little kindness, and, nearly three years ago, I went abroad and obtained a commission in one of the regiments in the Irish Brigade, and now hold the rank of captain. For many reasons, I am anxious to find out what family I belong to. It was assumed, by my colonel and fellow officers, that I was the son of Murroch Kennedy, and I wished to ascertain whether this was true, and with that object obtained leave of absence, and made my way back."

"I am sorry that I can give you no assistance, sir. Assuredly you are not the son of my cousin, Murroch Kennedy; and had you been, John O'Carroll, the traitor, would have been the last man to whom he would have entrusted you. I know well the history of all the members of my branch of the family, and can answer, with certainty, that no child was lost, or missing, or unaccounted for at the time he went out; and as all were loyal gentlemen, none would have had any dealings with John O'Carroll, who betrayed the cause for which his brother died fighting at Limerick. I will, however, jot down, for your information, the other branches of the family of Kennedy and their places of residence, though I fear that there is but little probability of your search being successful, as, during the years that have elapsed since the late war, many must have died. Others, like my cousin, have taken service in one or other of the continental armies. Moreover, there is also a possibility that the name by which you are known is not your own."

"I feel that myself, sir, and fear that my enquiries will not meet with success. Still, I shall pursue them until I have at least proved that I cannot belong to any well-known branch of the family. I am much obliged to you, for having so courteously answered my questions, and for your offer to give me a list of the various branches of the family."

For the next few minutes, Mr. Kennedy was engaged in making out the list, which he then handed to Desmond.

"And now, sir," the former went on, "that we have finished what we may consider business, will you tell me a little more about yourself? Your story naturally interests me, and I own that I am surprised that a young gentleman who, from what you have told me, cannot be much more than twenty years old, has risen to the rank of captain, in a brigade where so many officers have signally distinguished themselves. Your story, too, is an interesting one, and seems to me in many respects remarkable; and possibly, when I hear more of how you came to be brought up by John O'Carroll, it may throw some light upon the subject."

Desmond gave a detailed account of his life as a boy, and a short sketch of his subsequent adventures.

"A romantic story, young sir," Mr. Kennedy said, when he had finished, "and to whatever family you belong, they should be proud of possessing so gallant a member. You tell me that you have a safe conduct, but you did not mention how you obtained it."

Desmond had abstained from making any allusion, either to the affair with Lord Godolphin, or to that with the Earl of Galway, and he replied:

"Sir, this is a secret that concerns other people, as well as myself, consequently I am not at liberty to explain it. I may say, however, that it was given to me on my engagement that my visit to Ireland was one of a private nature only, and that I would in no way meddle with politics. When I tell you that the Duke of Berwick, himself, granted me the necessary leave of absence, it will prove to you that he, on his part, was well satisfied that the safe conduct had been issued to me without any unworthy offers, on my part, to the Princess Anne's ministers."

After chatting for some time longer, Desmond took his leave and returned to

Cork.

Mike was standing at the door of the inn.

"I have had no success, Mike. Have you fared better?"

"I have not found her yet, your honour, but I have great hopes of doing so. Larry Callaghan died four years ago, and the woman of the house she occupied said that Mrs. Rooney moved, with his widow and children, to some other part of the town. She knew little about them, seeing that she only went into the house after they had left; but her husband worked in the same yard as Larry did, and she thought that he would be able to find out, from some of the old hands, where the widow Callaghan had moved to. She said she would ask her husband when he came home to his dinner, and maybe he would be able to give her some news.

"And so, your honour has learned nothing about yourself?"

"Nothing, Mike, except that I am certainly not the son of Murroch Kennedy, who was a cousin of the gentleman I called on. I was assured that he was a single man, when he went to France. However, he gave me a list of the principal branches of the Kennedy family, but there is no hurry about starting to see them, and I will certainly wait here till you find your sister, which should not be many days, for some of Callaghan's fellow workmen are almost sure to know where his widow lives."

Mike went out, at seven o'clock that evening, and returned half an hour later.

"I have got the address, your honour. She and the widow Callaghan have got a little place outside the town, and take in washing there, and are going on nicely."

"I am pleased to hear it, I am sure, Mike. I have but small hope that she will be able to give any useful information, but for your sake, I am glad that you have found a sister whom you have not seen for so many years. I suppose you will go up there, at once."

"I will that. They will have done their work, and we shall have a comfortable talk, whereas she would not thank me if I were to drop in when she was busy at the washtub."

"Well, you might ask her to come down, tomorrow morning, to see me. Of course, she shall not be a loser by giving up her morning's work."

"Whisht, your honour! When she knows how much you have done for me, and how you have treated me, she would willingly lose a week's work to give you pleasure. Well, I will be off at once."

It was eleven o'clock before Mike returned.

"We have had a great talk, your honour, me and Norah. She would not believe at first that I was her brother, and in truth, I found it hard to credit that she was Norah, who was a purty colleen when I saw her last; but when we had convinced each other that we were both who we said we were, matters went on pleasantly. I told her some of my adventures with you, and that, by the same token, I had a hundred gold pieces that the Baron of Pointdexter had given me, sewn up in a belt round my waist, where it has been ever since I got it, except when we went into battle, or on that expedition to Scotland, when, as your honour knows, I always put it in with the agent in your name, seeing that I would rather, if I was killed, know that your honour would have it, instead of its being taken by some villain searching the dead. I told her that, if she and Mrs. Callaghan wanted to take a bigger place, I would share it with her, and that quite settled the matter, in her mind, that I was her brother. She said, as I knew she would, that she would come and talk to you for a week, if you wanted it; and she will be here tomorrow, at nine o'clock."

"That is very satisfactory. I am afraid nothing will come of our talk; but still, one may get a clue to other Kennedys who were present at the siege of Limerick."

Punctually at nine o'clock, Mike ushered his sister into Desmond's sitting room.

"I am glad to see you, Mrs. Rooney. Your brother has been with me for three years, and has rendered me very many services, and I regard him as a friend, rather than as a servant. I am glad that he has found his sister, from whom he had been so long parted."

"Mike has been telling me how good you have been to him, and that he would go through fire and water for you, and that you have had some wonderful adventures together. He said you wanted to speak to me about the siege of Limerick. If there is anything that I can tell you, your honour, I will do so gladly."

"What I want to know is, what Kennedys were at the siege?"

"There was Murroch Kennedy, and Phelim, who was always called 'Red Kennedy', on account of his colour; and James and Fergus. I knew all those, because they were friends of my master's. It may be that there were many others, but they were unbeknown to me."

"Am I like any of them?"

The woman looked at him searchingly.

"You are not, sir; but you are mighty like my master, barring, of course, that he was a man ten years older than yourself. But the more I look at you, the more I see the likeness."

"I did not know that you had a master, Mrs. Rooney. I thought that you were there with your husband."

"So I was, your honour; but when he was kilt I was left alone, saving for a child that had been born a fortnight before; and what with the bad smells of the place, and the sound of the cannon, and the fact of my grief, he pined away all at once, and died a week after me husband. It is well-nigh starving we all were. Even the fighting men had scarce enough food to keep their strength up, and a lone woman would have died from hunger. So I was mighty glad, when a friend of mine told me that there was an officer's lady who had had a baby, and, being but weak and ailing, wanted a foster mother for it; so I went at once and got the place, and was with her for a month.

"Her husband was killed three weeks after I went there, and the blow was too much for her, and she died a week later. A fortnight after that came the peace, and as everything was in confusion, what wid our soldiers all going away to France, and the persecutions and slaughterings, I took the child with me and went down to my cousin Larry's here. Av course, I could not part with it, and I could not make my way alone across the country, so I came down here with the troops. I was not strong myself, and it was a year later before I was able to take it to its friends."

"What was the name of your master?" Desmond asked eagerly, for her last words had excited a sudden train of ideas in his mind.

"He was Mr. James O'Carroll, a great gentleman, and the head of his family."

Desmond sprang to his feet.

"That explains it all!" he exclaimed. "Mrs. Rooney, I have no doubt that I am your foster child."

"Why, how can that be, your honour, seeing as your name is Kennedy? Though, except for that, you might well be so, seeing that you are so like my master."

"At any rate, Mrs. Rooney, I was reared at Kilkargan, at the expense of John O'Carroll, and was, as I heard, brought there by a woman when I was a year old.

O'Carroll said that my name was Desmond Kennedy, but I had only his word for it."

"Then how is it that you are not master of Kilkargan, for if you are Mr. James O'Carroll's son, it is you that ought to be? I have always thought of you as there. I have not been in the way of getting news. I left my address with Mr. John, but I never heard from him, or you. I thought, perhaps, that he might have lost the address, but I never dreamt that you had been kept out of your own."

"I don't know that I can say that, altogether," Desmond said; "for, if it had been known that James O'Carroll had left an heir, his estates would certainly have been confiscated; whereas, owing to his brother's turning Protestant, and joining the Williamites, he was allowed to keep possession of them. I can understand now what seemed so strange, namely, that he feared I might somehow learn that I was his nephew, and heir to the estates. Therefore, he behaved as if I was the son of a stranger, and when I was old enough, sent me off to join the Irish Brigade, in hopes that he had seen the last of me; for, even if not killed, I should never be able to set foot in Ireland again after fighting for France. 'Tis strange that none of my father's brother officers ever made any enquiries about it."

"They all went with the army to France, sir. They knew, of course, that the child was born, though they may never have seen you, for the mistress never left her bed after you were born. Naturally, after her death they lost sight of me, and might well have believed that the child had died."

"You must give me the names of all the officers who came to the house, Mrs. Rooney. Many of them may be alive still, and their testimony that a child was born would be most important, for at present there is only your word against John O'Carroll's."

"There is more than that, sir. You were baptized on the day she died. My mistress gave me the paper the priest had given to her, saying that it was of the greatest importance to you, and that I was to give it to Mr. John O'Carroll when, as I promised, I took the child to him."

"And did you give it him?" Desmond asked eagerly.

"No, your honour. I took it with me to the castle, but from the reception I got, I thought it best to say nothing about it, but to give it to yourself when you were old enough. I have got it at home now. There it is, certifying that Gerald O'Carroll, the son of James O'Carroll and his wife Elizabeth, was baptized by him on the 6th of September, 1692."

"That is fortunate, indeed," Desmond exclaimed. "And now, tell me how this uncle of mine received you."

"Faith, your honour, he was mightily put out, at first. He said that I was an impostor, and that he would have me given in charge. I told him that I had proofs that what I said was true, and that there were many gentlemen, brother officers of Mr. James, who would speak for me, and say in court that a son was born to his brother before he died. He wanted to get out of me what proofs I had, and who were the officers; but I told him that was my business. Then he cooled down, and after a time he said that, if he were to let it be known that Mr. James had left a son, the estate would surely be confiscated, seeing that his father died as a rebel fighting against the king; but that, as soon as the persecutions had ceased, and it would be safe to do so, he would say who the child was, and give him his rightful place. That seemed reasonable enough, and so I left you with him, and have always supposed that he kept his word; and that, as soon as it was safe, he acknowledged you to be master of your father's estate."

"And now, Mrs. Rooney, I must think matters over, and see how I had best proceed. I feel how much I owe to you, and, if I recover my estates, you shall see that I am not ungrateful. Will you come again tomorrow morning, and bring with you the certificate of my baptism, and all the names that you can recollect of the officers who were intimate with my father?"

Chapter 20: Gerald O'Carroll.

Mike, who had remained silent during the conversation between his sister and Desmond, returned to the room after seeing her out.

"Well, Mike, you have rendered me many services, but this is the greatest of all. Little did I think, when you said you had found your sister, and that she was coming to me this morning, that she would be able to clear up the mystery of my birth, and to place me in a position to prove myself a son of James O'Carroll. I do not say that I shall regain the estates. My having been in the Brigade will certainly render it difficult for me to do so, though possibly, with the patronage of Lord Godolphin, I may succeed. For that, however, I care comparatively little. My object, in coming here, was to obtain proof that I belong to a good Irish family, and that I have no doubt I shall be able to establish."

"And what am I to call you, your honour, now that I know you are Captain Gerald O'Carroll, and not Desmond Kennedy, at all?"

"At any rate, I must remain Desmond Kennedy at present, Mike. It is under that name that my safe conduct was made out, and if I were arrested as Gerald O'Carroll, it would be no protection to me. However, I shall not want to use it long, for it seems to me that my first step must be to return to France, and to see some of the officers who knew my father, and were aware of my birth. Their testimony would be of great value, and without it there would be little chance of your sister's evidence being believed."

"But there is the paper, your honour."

"Yes; that will show that a child was born, but the proof that I am that child rests entirely with your sister. It might have died when its mother did, and they would say that your sister was trying to palm off her own child, or someone else's, as his. Of course, Mrs. Callaghan would be able to prove that your sister arrived immediately after the surrender of Limerick, bringing a child with her, and that she said it was the son of James O'Carroll; and that she went a year later to Kilkargan, and left it there with John O'Carroll. Moreover, I could get plenty of evidence, from those on the estate, that I was the child so left."

"The likeness that Norah saw between you and your father might be taken as a proof, sir."

"I did not think of that, Mike. Yes, if some of these officers will also testify to the likeness, it will greatly strengthen my case. The chain of evidence seems pretty strong. First, there is the certificate of my baptism, your sister's declaration that I was entrusted to her by my mother on her deathbed, supported by Mrs. Callaghan's declaration that three weeks later she arrived in Cork with the child, which she told her was that of James O'Carroll; your sister's declaration that she took me to Kilkargan and handed me over to my uncle, which would be supported by the evidence of the woman he first placed me with; while the servants of the castle could prove that I was brought by a woman who, an hour later, left the castle without speaking to anyone but my uncle.

"John O'Carroll will find it difficult to explain why he took me in, and who is the Kennedy of whom I was the son, and what service he had rendered for him, a Protestant and a Williamite, to have undertaken the charge of the child of a rebel. There is no doubt that the weight of evidence is all on my side, but whether the judges would decide in favour of the son of a rebel, as against a friend of the English party, is doubtful. Possibly Lord Godolphin's influence might be exerted in my favour. He promised in his letter to me to do me any service in his power. Still, even if I lose the estate, which I may well do on the ground of my father having fought and died for the cause of James the Second, I should still have the satisfaction of establishing my name, which I consider of more importance than the estates."

"Sure, your honour, it's a grand thing to belong to a good old Irish stock; but for myself, I would rather be Mike Callaghan and have a fine estate, than Mike O'Neil without an acre of land."

Desmond smiled.

"There is common sense in what you say, Mike, but there is nothing more unpleasant than, when you are with a number of Irish gentlemen or Spanish grandees, who are equally proud of their ancestors, to be unable to give any account of your family, or even to be sure that you have a right to the name that you bear."

"Well, your honour, it is a matter of taste. As for myself, if the whisky is good, it makes no differ to me whether they call it Cork or Dublin, or whether it is made up in the mountains and has sorra a name at all."

The next morning, Mrs. Rooney returned with the certificate of baptism, and a list containing some twenty names of officers who had been frequent visitors at James O'Carroll's. Among these Desmond, to his satisfaction, found Arthur Dillon, Walter Burke, Nicholas Fitzgerald, and Dominic Sheldon, all of whom now held the rank of general in the French service, and to all of whom he was personally known, having met them either when with Berwick or in Spain.

"Those names are good enough," he said. "And if they can testify to my likeness to my father, it will go a long way towards furnishing proof, when required. All of them entered the service under the provisions of the treaty of Limerick, and therefore their testimony cannot be treated as that of traitors; and their names must be as well known in England as in France.

"Now, Mike, our business here is, for the present, concluded. I shall at once return to France, see all these officers who are still alive, and obtain, if possible, their recognition. As I have a year's leave, I can travel about as I choose. Then I shall decide whether I shall commence an action in the courts, or whether I shall first go over to England, see Lord Godolphin, explain the circumstances to him, and ask for his protection and patronage.

"I suppose the case would be tried at Dublin, where the judges are all creatures of England, and there can be no doubt that a notification, from Godolphin, that he considered my claim to be a good one, and was favourable to it, would have no slight influence with them; and would counteract, to some extent, the fact of my uncle's being a Protestant, and what they would consider a loyal man. Before beginning an action, I should certainly communicate with my uncle, and call upon him to resign in my favour; for I would avoid the scandal of proving an O'Carroll to be a scoundrel, as well as a traitor. As it has turned out, the step which he thought would disembarrass him of me has had the other effect, for, if I had not gone out to France, I should never have been troubled by questions about my family; and should not have met you, Mike, or known of the existence of your sister, the only person who could clear up the matter.

"I shall begin to think what O'Neil and O'Sullivan used to say, that my luck would carry me through anything; and certainly, at present, it has been marvellous."

"Which way will we go back, your honour?"

"Not the way we came, if we can help it. We were nearly a month coming from Genoa, and might have been twice as long, if the wind had not been fairly favourable. I think our best plan will be to take passage by sea to London. There we shall have no difficulty in finding a vessel bound for Rotterdam, or the Hague. Then we will buy horses, and ride along by the Rhine. If we can get through Luxembourg into France we will do so, but I think it will perhaps be best to go on through Switzerland, and pass the frontier somewhere near Lyons, where we shall be but a short distance from Berwick's headquarters in Dauphiny."

A month later, they rode into the duke's camp. They had, on leaving Toulon, packed up their uniforms and sent them to the care of a friend on the general's staff. To his quarters they first went, and having changed his civilian costume for a military one, Desmond waited on the duke.

"Why, Captain Kennedy," the duke said, in surprise; "I did not look to see you again, so soon. Have you been over to Ireland?"

"I have, sir, and though there only a few days, gained information that necessitated my return here. I have found out that the name I go by is not mine, and that my proper name is Gerald O'Carroll."

"The son of Major James O'Carroll, who fought by my side at the Boyne, and was through the first siege of Limerick with me! That explains it. Your face has often puzzled me. It seemed to me that I recognized it, and yet I could not recall whose face it was that it resembled so strongly. Now you tell me, I know at once. Your father, when I first knew him, was a few years older than you are; but he had the same figure, face, and expression.

"And so, you are his son! By what miracle have you discovered your relationship to him?"

Desmond, or as he should now be called, Gerald, related as briefly as possible the manner in which he had discovered his parentage.

"Your uncle must be a thorough villain," the duke said, hotly. "That he was a traitor we all knew, but that he should thus rob his brother's son of his inheritance is monstrous and unnatural."

"I am glad, indeed, sir, that you have thus recognized me. Your testimony will go for much, even in an English court, and I hope to receive a similar recognition from the officers who were intimate with my father in the second siege, and whose names I have here."

The duke glanced down the list.

"Well-nigh half of them are still alive," he said, "and all of them are men of rank and repute, whose word would be taken even by an enemy. How do you mean to proceed? Because I am afraid that, even if we could spare them, there would be some difficulty about their making their appearance in a court, in either England or Ireland."

"I quite see that that is out of the question. All I can hope for is, that such of them as recognize my likeness to my father will draw up a paper saying so, and will attest it before a notary, having as witnesses men of weight and honour equal to their own. The production of such certificates could not but have a strong influence in my favour."

"I will most willingly sign such a document," the duke said, "and four of my best-known generals can sign as witnesses to my signature."

"I thank you most heartily, sir. Such a document should, in itself, be considered as ample proof of my strong resemblance to my father."

"That may or may not be," the duke said, "but do not be content with that. Get as many of the others as possible to make similar declarations. One man may see a likeness where another does not, but if a dozen men agree in recognizing it, their declarations must have a great weight. Certainly no Irish judge would doubt the testimony of so many men, whose families and whose deeds are so well known to them."

From Dauphiny, Gerald travelled first into Spain, and the three Irish officers there whose names were on his list all recognized the likeness, even before he told them his name. He put the question to them in a general way.

"I have learned, sir, that the name I bear is not my own, that I am the son of an officer who was killed in the siege of Limerick. May I ask you if you can recognize any likeness between myself and any officer with whom you were well acquainted there?"

In each case, after a little consideration, they declared that he must be the son of James O'Carroll. All remembered that their comrade's wife had borne a son, shortly before the end of the siege. They remembered her death, but none had heard what became of the child, for in the excitement of the closing scenes, and of the preparation for the march immediately afterwards, they had had little time on their hands, and it was hitherto supposed that it had, like so many other infants, perished miserably. They willingly signed documents, similar to that which he had received from Berwick.

He met with almost equal success on the northern frontier, only two out of eight officers failing to identify him by his likeness; until he mentioned his name, when they, too, acknowledged that, now they recalled James O'Carroll's face, they saw that the likeness was a striking one.

Having obtained these documents, he resumed civilian attire, and, riding by crossroads, passed through Flanders to Sluys, without coming in contact with any body of the allied troops. There he had no difficulty in obtaining a passage to London, and on his arrival called upon Lord Godolphin, who received him cordially.

"So you have utilized your safe conduct, Captain Kennedy. I am glad to see my former captor, and I am as grateful as ever to you for the silence you maintained as to that affair. If it had been known to my enemies, I should never have heard the last of it. They would have made me such a laughingstock that I could scarcely have retained office.

"Now, what can I do for you?"

"It is a long story, my lord."

"Then I cannot listen to it now; but if you will sup with me here, at nine o'clock this evening, I shall be glad to hear it. I am so harassed by the backstair intrigues of my enemies, that it would be a relief to me to have something else to think of."

Gerald returned at the appointed time. Nothing was said as to his affairs while supper was served, but after the table had been cleared, decanters of port placed on the table, and the servants had retired, Godolphin said:

"Now, Captain Kennedy, let us hear all about it."

Gerald related the history of his younger days, and of the manner in which he had discovered his real parentage, producing the certificate of his baptism, a statement which had been drawn up at Cork and signed by Norah Rooney, and the testimony of the Duke of Berwick and the other Irish officers.

"There can be no doubt whatever, in the mind of any fair man," Lord Godolphin said, after listening attentively to the whole story, and examining the documents, "that your uncle, John O'Carroll, is a villain, and that you have been most unjustly deprived of your rights. I know him by name, and from the reports of our agents in Ireland, as one of the men who turned his coat and changed his religion to save his estates. Those men I heartily despise; while those who gave up all, and went into exile in order, as they believed, there to serve the cause of their rightful sovereign, are men to be admired and respected. Be assured that justice shall be done you. Of course, you will take action in the courts?"

"I shall first summon him to give up the estate, shall let him know that I have indisputable evidence to prove that I am the son of his elder brother, and shall say that, if he will give up possession peaceably, I will take no further steps in the matter, for the sake of the family name. If he refuses, as I fear is probable, I must then employ a lawyer."

"Yes, and a good one. I will furnish you with letters to the lord lieutenant, and to Lord Chief Justice Cox, strongly recommending you to them, and requesting the latter to appoint one of the law officers of the crown to take up your case. I should say that, when this John O'Carroll sees that you have such powerful friends, he will perceive that it is hopeless for him to struggle in so bad a cause, and will very speedily accept your terms, though methinks it is hard that so great a villain should go unpunished.

"Now, it will be as well that you should have something stronger than the safe conduct that I sent you. I will therefore draw out a document for Her Majesty to sign, granting you a full and free pardon for any offences that you may have committed against her and the realm, and also settling upon you the estates to which you are the rightful heir, in and about the barony of Kilkargan; being influenced in so doing by the great services rendered by you, both to Her Majesty's well-beloved and faithful minister and counsellor, myself, and to her trusty general, the Earl of Galway.

"The queen is not very likely to ask the nature of the service. Unless it be something that concerns herself, she asks but few questions, and signs readily enough the documents laid before her. If she asks what are the offences for which she grants her pardon, I shall say, when but a boy you were maliciously sent abroad to join the Irish Brigade by your uncle, who wished thus to rid himself of you altogether, and who had foully wronged you by withholding your name, from you and all others. I shall also add that you have distinguished yourself much, and have gained the friendship of her half brother, the Duke of Berwick; and you know that the queen, in her heart of hearts, would rather that her brother, whom you Jacobites call James the Third, should succeed her than the Elector of Hanover, for whom she has no love."

"I thank you greatly, indeed, my lord. Never was a man so amply rewarded for merely holding his tongue."

"It was not only that, sir. It was your conduct in general to me. You might have left me tied up in that house, to be found in the morning, and to be made the jest of the town; instead of which, you yourself conducted and guarded me hither, and so contrived it that no whisper spread abroad that I had been carried off between Saint James's and my own house. You trusted to my honour, in not causing a pursuit of you to be set on foot, and behaved in all ways as a gallant young gentleman, and certainly gained my high esteem, both for the daring and ingenuity with which you carried out your plans for obtaining a passage to France, and for your personal conduct towards myself.

"Where are you lodging?"

"At the Eagle, hard by the Abbey."

"Remain there, until you hear from me. Do not be impatient. I must choose my time, when either the queen is in a good temper, or is in such a hurry to get rid of me, in order to plot and gossip with Mistress Harley, who is now her prime favourite, that she is ready to sign any document I may lay before her."

Feeling that his cause was as good as won, Gerald returned in high spirits to his inn, where he delighted Mike by relating how the great minister had promised to forward his suit.

"Ah, your honour, it will be a grand day when you take possession of Kilkargan--bonfires and rejoicing of all sorts, and lashings of drink. Won't all the boys in the barony be glad to be free from the traitor, and to have the true heir come to be their master. None the less glad will be my sister."

"You must fetch her from Cork, Mike. It is owing to her that I am alive, and it will be owing to her if I recover the estate. She shall have the place of honour on the occasion, though all the gentry in the neighbourhood are there. When I tell them what she has done for me, they will say that she well deserves the honour!"

"And you will go no more to the wars, Captain O'Carroll?"

"No, Mike. I have been but three years in the French army, but I have seen enough of fighting, and, worse still, of fighting against men of our own nation. Besides, if the queen grants me the estates of my father, I shall consider myself bound in honour not to draw my sword against her, or to mix myself up in any plot or conspiracy, but to remain strictly neutral whatever may be going on. Indeed, the more I think of it, the more I doubt whether it would be for the good of Ireland did the Stuarts return to the throne. It could only be done at a further cost of blood and misery. The old religious quarrels would break out more fiercely than ever, there would be risings and civil wars, confiscations and massacres, whichever side happened to get the upper hand. That James the Third is the lawful sovereign of the three kingdoms, I shall always uphold, but there are cases when it is to the benefit of the country, at large, that there should be a change in the succession."

"Sure that may be so, your honour; and yet, it is hard that a man should be kept out of his own."

"No doubt it is hard; but it is far harder that thousands of people should be killed, and tens of thousands ruined, for the sake of one man."

"So it is, sir. So it is, sure enough, when one comes to think of it. Ireland has suffered mightily in the cause of the Stuarts, and I don't suppose that, if King James succeeded to the throne, his English ministers would let him turn out all the men who have taken the places and lands of the old families."

"That they certainly would not, Mike. When Charles the Second returned from exile, all those who had fought and suffered for him thought that they would recover their estates, and turn out Cromwell's men, to whom they had been granted. But they were disappointed. The king found that he could not make so great a change, without upsetting the whole country, and that an attempt to do so would cost him his crown; and you may be sure that James would find an equal difficulty, were he to come to the throne."

"Well, well, your honour, you know more of such matters than I do; but I have no doubt that you are right. I am sure we don't want the bad times to come over again, in Ireland."

Three days later, Gerald received a message from Lord Godolphin, saying that he wished to see him; and, on going to his house, the minister handed to him the paper with the full pardon, and the confirmation of his ownership in his father's estates; together with a letter to the lord lieutenant, and the Lord Chief Justice Cox.

The next day, he took ship for Dublin, and on arriving there presented his letters, and was well received by those to whom they were directed.

The lord lieutenant said:

"It is enough for me, Mr. O'Carroll, that Lord Godolphin speaks of you in such high terms, and I question not that he has thoroughly satisfied himself as to your right to these estates. At the same time, I should be glad if you will give me a brief outline of how it is that you never claimed them before, though perhaps it is as well that you did not do so, for, until the passions excited by the war had somewhat subsided, a friend of the Government would hardly have interposed for the benefit of the son of one who had died fighting for James."

Gerald had drawn up three copies of a statement containing a precis of the case, and he handed one of these to the lord lieutenant, saying:

"As the story is a somewhat long one, my lord, I have written it down, in order that you might read it at your leisure."

"I will certainly do so, Mr. O'Carroll. I should like to be personally acquainted with the details of the matter. It will doubtless excite a considerable stir. It is, I believe, the first time that a supporter of the Government has had to defend his title against one of the family that fought on the other side."

"It is hardly a case of royalist and rebel, sir, but the deliberate action of a man suppressing all knowledge of the existence of his own nephew, in order that he might himself obtain the property of his dead brother.

"I have no doubt that, had it been known that I was in existence, I should still have been thrust aside in order to reward his adhesion to the cause of William, but that would have made his position intolerable. As one who has changed his religion and his politics, he is regarded as a traitor by the people of the barony, and avoided by all the gentry round; but the feeling would have been infinitely stronger, if it had been known that he was keeping his own nephew out of his inheritance. My father was, as I understand, immensely popular, and I doubt whether his brother would have dared to show his face within fifty miles of Kilkargan, had it been known that not only was he a traitor, but a usurper."

The lord lieutenant smiled.

"I am not surprised at your warmth, Mr. O'Carroll; but, unfortunately, your case is not a solitary one. There are thousands of men in Ireland who have suffered for the deeds of their fathers. However, I shall understand the case better when I have read your statement."

It was evident to Gerald that the lord chief justice, who had taken a leading part in the prosecution and punishment of persons known to be favourable to the Jacobite cause, was not altogether pleased with Lord Godolphin's letter.

"A strange affair," he said. "A strange and, as it appears to me, an unfortunate business.

"However, sir," he went on, with a changed tone; "I shall certainly do my best to see justice done, in accordance with his lordship's request. I will read carefully through this statement of your claim, and, after considering it, place it in the hands of the crown lawyers.

"But it seems to me that your own position here is a strange one, and that you yourself are liable to arrest, as a member of a family whose head was one of the late king's strongest adherents."

"My own position, sir, is regulated by this document, bearing the signature of the queen and her chief minister;" and he laid the official paper before Cox.

"That certainly settles that question," the latter said, after perusing it. "Of course I shall, for my own satisfaction, read your statement; but I do not wish to see any documents or proofs you may possess in the matter. These you must, of course, lay before your counsel. I think I can't do better than give you a letter to Mr. Counsellor Fergusson, with whom you can go into all particulars, and who will advise you as to the course that you had best take."

Mr. Fergusson, although one of the crown lawyers, enjoyed a wide reputation, even among the Jacobite party, for the moderation and the fairness with which he conducted the crown cases placed in his hands. He had less employment than his colleagues, for only cases in which the evidence of acts of hostility to the crown were indisputable were committed to him, it having been found that he was unwilling to be a party to calling doubtful witnesses, or to using the means that were, in the majority of cases, employed to obtain convictions.

The lord chief justice's letter to him was as follows:

Dear Mr. Counsellor Fergusson:

I have been requested, by Lord Godolphin, to place the case of the bearer of this letter in good hands, and cannot better carry out his request than by asking you to act in the matter. Lord Godolphin has expressed himself most strongly as to the justness of his claim. The bearer's father was, he states, James O'Carroll, a noted rebel who was killed at the siege of Limerick. This alone would, it might have been thought, have proved a bar to any action on his part against the present possessor of the property; but he is the bearer of a document, signed by the queen herself, reinstating him in all rights he may possess, notwithstanding the actions of his father or of himself. It is not for me to make any comment upon the royal document, though I may say that I fear it may give rise to other suits, and alarm many loyal subjects who have become possessed of confiscated estates. However, we must hope that this will not be so, as it is expressly stated that, in this instance, the pardon and restoration of rights are given in consideration of services rendered by this young gentleman to Lord Godolphin himself, and to the Earl of Galway. What the nature of these services may have been does not concern me.

Gerald carried this letter to the address indicated, and on saying that he was the bearer of a letter from the lord chief justice, he was at once shown into the counsellor's room. The latter, a man of some fifty-five years old, with features that told of his Scottish extraction, with keen eyes and a kindly face, took the letter which Gerald presented to him, and begged him to be seated while he read it. As he glanced through it, a look of surprise came across his face, and he read the letter carefully, and then looked at Gerald keenly.

"You are fortunate in having such good friends, Mr. O'Carroll," he said. "Before I go into the case, will you let me know something about yourself? You are, I take it, some twenty years of age?"

"I am but a few months past nineteen."

"By your figure, I should have put you as three years older; by your face, two years. You must have been fortunate, indeed, to have gained the protection both of Lord Godolphin and the Earl of Galway. No less than this would have sufficed to gain for you this rescript of Her Majesty.

"And now, sir, please to give me an outline of your case, as to the nature of which I am, at present, entirely ignorant."

"I have put it down in writing, sir," Gerald said, handing him the third copy of his statement.

"It will take me some time to read this, Mr. O'Carroll, and I would rather do so alone, and ask you any question that may occur to me afterwards. Will you therefore call upon me again, in an hour's time?"

Upon Gerald's return, the counsellor said:

"It is a strange story, Mr. O'Carroll, and a very disgraceful one. You allude, I see, to testimonies of Irish officers in the French service as to your likeness to the late Mr. James O'Carroll. Will you please let me see them?"

"Here they are, sir, together with a sworn statement by my nurse."

The lawyer read the documents through carefully.

"The testimony of the Duke of Berwick, and of the other honourable and well-known Irish gentlemen, as to the striking likeness between yourself and Mr. James O'Carroll, cannot but carry immense weight in the minds of all unprejudiced persons. They prove too, conclusively, that James O'Carroll left an infant boy behind him, and the statement of the nurse goes a long way to prove you are that son; and I think that this is substantiated by the conduct of John O'Carroll; first in receiving you and undertaking your care; secondly, in the neglect, and I should almost say the dislike, he manifested towards the child he had sheltered; and thirdly, in the extraordinary step that he, a professedly loyal subject of Her Majesty, took in sending you off to enlist in the brigade composed of the devoted adherents of the son of James the Second.

"No doubt, at any rate, can arise that you are the child brought by this Mrs. Rooney to Kilkargan. That can be proved beyond all question; and the fact that your nurse was sent off without having any conversation save with John O'Carroll himself, would show how anxious he was that no one but himself should know her errand.

"I must say that you have shown great acumen in mustering evidence, of all kinds, that would bear upon the question. I say frankly that, without this royal rescript, and the influence of these two noblemen, your chance, as James O'Carroll's son, of wresting your patrimony from the hands of your uncle would be small indeed. Politics have, much more than facts, to do with decisions here; but with such powerful credentials, and with the chief minister of England interfering on your behalf, I think that there is no great doubt that you will secure a judgment in your favour. When the facts are known, the feeling of the greater portion of the population will run strongly with you, and against this unnatural uncle of yours."

"I should be desirous, if possible, sir, of avoiding a public trial that would bring discredit upon the name of my family, and would, in the eyes of the supporters of the present Government, act prejudicially to myself."

"You are quite right. How do you propose to proceed?"

"I was thinking, sir, of sending a statement to my uncle, similar to that which I laid before you, going somewhat further into details, and promising that, if he would surrender the property to me and publicly acknowledge me as his nephew, giving what reason he chose for having so long concealed his knowledge of the fact, I would take no proceedings against him, and would do my best to prevent any discredit falling upon him."

"That would do very well," the lawyer said, "but I should abstain from making any allusion to the protectors you have gained. He will learn that soon enough, and it will be well to see what his first impulse is. Do not mention the names of the Duke of Berwick and the others, who have testified to your likeness to your late father. Simply say that many of his comrades have recognized your likeness to him. It is of no use showing him all the cards we have to play. I should not send the letter by post, but by hand. If you like, I will despatch one of my own messengers down with it, with instructions to bring back an answer, but not to say anything, if questioned, as to his being in my employment."

The next morning, the messenger started by coach for Kilkargan. He returned four days later, bearing John O'Carroll's answer. It read as follows:

Sir:

I have received your audacious letter, and proclaim you to be an impostor, worthy of the severest punishment for attempting to personate a son of my late brother. However, for the sake of my friendship for Mr. Kennedy, your father, I give you twenty-four hours to leave the country, before laying any information against you, both as an impostor and as a rebel who has served against the armies of Her Majesty. I shall, however, at once apply for a writ ordering your arrest, which will be served upon you within twenty-four hours of your receipt of this communication. I shall also have this woman, your pretended nurse, arrested for perjury and conspiracy.

Gerald took this letter to the counsellor.

"That is exactly what I expected," he said, after reading it. "It shows the man in his true colours. We shall see what he says when he learns who are employed against him, and what protection you have obtained. My opinion is that, before many hours have passed, you will receive a letter in a different strain. I consider it by no means improbable that the lord chief justice will have written to him privately, warning him that you have received a full pardon, and are restored to all your rights, and that you are strongly supported by Lord Godolphin, who has written to him and the lord lieutenant in your favour; that you have also the protection of the Earl of Galway, an officer who possesses the confidence of Her Majesty; and that the Duke of Berwick, and many of the best-known Irish officers in the service of France, have all given their testimony, in the most positive manner, of your likeness to James O'Carroll, whom they knew intimately; and will say that, at the request of Lord Godolphin that the matter should be placed in the hands of one of the crown lawyers, it has been submitted to me; and that in my opinion, which I wrote him after our interview, a decision in your favour is inevitable; and strongly advising him to make the best compromise with you in his power."

The same evening, indeed, a mounted messenger, who had ridden posthaste from Kilkargan, arrived with another letter from John O'Carroll. It began:

My Dear Nephew:

I wrote yesterday in haste, on the receipt of your communication. It seemed to me that you were rushing on destruction, by avowing yourself to be the son of my brother James; and that you would be liable to be arrested as a Jacobite agent in the service of France. Therefore, I wrote the letter that I did in hopes that you would leave the country, for the time had not yet arrived when you could safely be recognized by me as the rightful owner of Kilkargan. I have heard, however, that you have received a full pardon for past offences, and a restitution of your rights, and I am only too glad to be able to retire from the false position in which I was placed, and by which I incurred the hostility and dislike of my neighbours and tenants. As you know, I have lived an almost solitary life here, and have spent far less than the income of the estate. I am well aware that, acting as I have done as your trustee, you have a right to demand from me an account of the rents I have received; but I trust that you will not press this matter, as you'll at once come in for the receipt of the rents; and I shall be enabled to live in comfort, in Dublin, upon the savings I have effected, and a small property I received as a younger brother's portion.

You will, of course, understand why, during your stay here, I refrained from any outward demonstrations of affection for you. I felt that suspicions might have arisen, had I not done so, that you were my brother's son, in which case the estate would surely have been confiscated. Seeing that the bent of your inclinations was for an active and stirring life, and as the English army was barred to you, I thought it best that you should go abroad, and so be out of the way until the time should come when matters would so quieten down, in Ireland, that my influence might avail to secure an indemnity for you for serving in France, and enable me to hand over your estate to you.

Your affectionate uncle, John O'Carroll.

Gerald laughed aloud as he read the letter.

"Is it good news, your honour?" Mike, who happened to be busy in the room, asked.

"Nothing could be better. My dear uncle has heard that Lord Godolphin and the Earl of Galway have become my patrons, that the queen has restored to me my rights, and Mr. Counsellor Fergusson has taken up my case. He therefore declares that, as it was always his intention to restore the estate to me, as soon as I could safely return, he is now ready to do so, and only hopes that I will not insist upon his handing over the back rents; which, indeed, I question whether I could do, as the estate was granted to him, personally, by the Government.

"However, of course I shall not press that. I shall be only too glad to obtain possession without the scandal of having to show, in the public courts, that my father's brother was a villain."

"The ould fox!" Mike exclaimed indignantly. "I felt sure, when you told me what the counsellor had said, that he would wriggle out of it somehow. I would give all the gold pieces I have in my belt for half an hour's talk with him, with a good shillelah!"

"Well, we can afford to let bygones be bygones, Mike. And after all, he did me a service, unwittingly, in sending me over to France. In the first place, I had three years of stirring life; in the next, I have made many good friends, and have gained the patronage of two powerful noblemen, without which I should have assuredly never come in for Kilkargan at all."

"That is true for you, your honour. And without it, I might be still a private in O'Brien's regiment, instead of being your honour's body servant."

"And friend, Mike."

"Yes, sir, as you are good enough to say so."

Mr. Fergusson put John O'Carroll's letter down, with a gesture of disgust, after he had read it.

"It is what might have been expected from such a man," he said. "A traitor to the cause he once adhered to, false to his religion, and a usurper of his nephew's rights.

"At any rate, Mr. O'Carroll, I congratulate you. It has prevented a grievous scandal from being made public, and the large expenditure entailed by such a case. You have now only to go down and take possession."

"I shall write to my uncle, and give him a week to clear out, and to make what explanation he chooses of the change."

Gerald wrote at once to his uncle. It was coldly worded, and showed unmistakably that he was, in no way, deceived by the professions in his letter. He told him that he considered it fair that he should retain the savings he had made, as he had personally been confirmed in the ownership of Kilkargan, the Government being ignorant that his brother had left a son. He said that he thought it would be more pleasant, for both of them, that they should not meet, and wished, therefore, that he would leave, before his arrival to take possession.

John O'Carroll at once summoned the tenants, and astonished them by informing them that, he was glad to say, he was free at last to lay down the position he had held as owner of Kilkargan. That his brother James had left a son, whom they all knew as Desmond Kennedy, but whom he had been obliged to treat with coldness, lest suspicions should be excited as to his identity. Had this been known, he would assuredly have been proscribed as the son of a rebel, and debarred by law from any inheritance. He was delighted to say that the time had come when he could publicly acknowledge him, and place him in possession of the estate, as Her Majesty had granted him a special indemnity against the pains and penalties incurred by his father's act of rebellion and treason, and had restored to him his full rights.

A burst of cheering, such as had not been heard in Kilkargan since James O'Carroll rode out, at the head of a troop raised among his tenantry, to fight for King James, greeted the announcement; and, for the first time since that event, John O'Carroll was, for the moment, popular. Subsequent reflection, and their knowledge of his character, soon dissipated that feeling; but in their joy at the announced approaching arrival of their new master, John O'Carroll rode away, with his followers, without the manifestation of hostility that would otherwise have attended his departure.

Bonfires blazed all over the barony when Gerald rode in, accompanied by Mike. The tenants, and a number of the gentry who had known him when a boy, assembled at the castle to meet him; and even his father could not have met with a more enthusiastic welcome than that which was given him.

The next day, Gerald wrote to the Duke of Berwick, telling him what had taken place, and resigning his commission in the Irish Brigade.

"I intend," he said, "to abstain from all part in politics. Although no condition was made, in my pardon for serving abroad and in the restoration of my estate, I feel that, having accepted these favours, I must hold myself aloof from all plots against Queen Anne, though my heart will still be with him whom I hold to be my lawful sovereign. Unless a large army from France was landed here, I believe that any attempt at his restoration would only bring down fresh misery upon Ireland. But, should a force land that would render success almost a certainty, I should then, with the great bulk of my countrymen, join it."

In due time he received an answer, approving the course he had taken.

"I myself," the Duke said, "am under no delusions. With the ten regiments of the Irish Brigade, twenty thousand French troops, and arms sufficient to distribute to the whole country, I believe that Ireland and Scotland might again come under the rule of the Stuarts; but nothing short of such a force would be of any avail. So convinced was I of this that, in 1691, after the successful defence of Limerick, I saw that the cause was for the time lost, and that further resistance would only prove disastrous to Ireland. I therefore resigned my command, and went over to France to serve as a volunteer, and took no part in the war at home. Therefore, I think that you are fully justified in the course you have taken. When the present war, which I think is approaching its end, terminates, and you can again visit France, I trust that I shall see you; and I am sure that you will receive the heartiest of welcomes from your comrades in the Brigade."

Gerald followed out strictly the line he had laid down for himself, and kept aloof from the plots and conspiracies that, for years, agitated the country, entailing disaster upon all concerned in them. Mike was installed as his body servant, and majordomo of his household; and Norah Rooney as housekeeper at the castle.

Three years later, in 1713, the treaty of Utrecht brought the war to an end. Communications being restored between the two countries, Gerald wrote to the Baron de Pointdexter, and told him of the changes which had taken place in his position. He received a warm letter in reply, urging him to go over and pay him and his son-in-law a visit.

But Gerald had had enough of travelling, and wrote to say that he could not leave his estate, as there was much to look after. Letters were, however, frequently exchanged between them, and when, three years later, Gerald married the daughter of the Mr. Kennedy he had visited near Cork, a present of a superb set of jewels, the joint gift of the baron and Monsieur de la Vallee, arrived for the bride.

After the conclusion of the peace, some of the Irish regiments were disbanded, and as the British Government, wiser than before, offered a free pardon to all men and officers who would return, many availed themselves of it; and among these was O'Neil, who delighted Gerald by riding up, one day, to the castle.

"You did not expect to see me again, Kennedy; or, as I hear we ought to call you, O'Carroll. Not knowing where I should find you, I took the liberty of writing to Baron de Pointdexter, and he informed me of your good luck, and your change of name."

"And you have left the French service altogether, O'Neill?"

"Yes, and glad enough I am that I shall be able to end my days at home."

"And what are you thinking of doing?"

"Anything I can get."

"Well, O'Neil, I have some interest with the lord lieutenant. As I am no longer regarded as one likely to join in plots, I think that, were I to ride with you to Dublin after you have been here for a time; and speak to him for you, as one who had seen the errors of his ways, and was anxious to live peacefully, he would procure you some appointment."

O'Neil stayed there for three weeks, and they then rode to Dublin. The lord lieutenant granted Gerald's request, and gave O'Neil an appointment which would enable him to live in comfort; knowing that there is nothing, for keeping a man peaceable, like giving him something to do; and that an idle man is a dangerous man, while one who has a comfortable position can be trusted to hold himself aloof from any business that might imperil his place.

O'Neil thoroughly justified Gerald's recommendation of him, and, a couple of years after his return, married a young and well-endowed widow; and, to the end of his life, abstained carefully from mixing himself up, in any way, in politics.

Gerald saw the failure of Prince Charlie's expedition to Scotland; and the terrible disasters, that befell all who had taken part in the movement, showed him the wisdom of the course he had adopted--of standing aloof from all intrigues in favour of the descendants of James the Second.

www.bookjungle.com *email: sales@bookjungle.com fax: 630-214-0564 mail: Book Jungle PO Box 2226 Champaign, IL 61825*

The Codes Of Hammurabi And Moses
W. W. Davies

QTY

The discovery of the Hammurabi Code is one of the greatest achievements of archaeology, and is of paramount interest, not only to the student of the Bible, but also to all those interested in ancient history...

Religion   **ISBN:** *1-59462-338-4*   **Pages:**132   *MSRP $12.95*

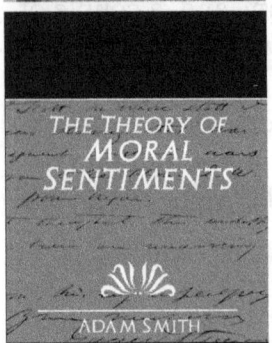

The Theory of Moral Sentiments
Adam Smith

QTY

This work from 1749. contains original theories of conscience amd moral judgment and it is the foundation for systemof morals.

Philosophy   **ISBN:** *1-59462-777-0*   **Pages:**536   *MSRP $19.95*

Jessica's First Prayer
Hesba Stretton

QTY

In a screened and secluded corner of one of the many railway-bridges which span the streets of London there could be seen a few years ago, from five o'clock every morning until half past eight, a tidily set-out coffee-stall, consisting of a trestle and board, upon which stood two large tin cans, with a small fire of charcoal burning under each so as to keep the coffee boiling during the early hours of the morning when the work-people were thronging into the city on their way to their daily toil...

Childrens   **ISBN:** *1-59462-373-2*   **Pages:**84   *MSRP $9.95*

My Life and Work
Henry Ford

QTY

Henry Ford revolutionized the world with his implementation of mass production for the Model T automobile. Gain valuable business insight into his life and work with his own auto-biography... "We have only started on our development of our country we have not as yet, with all our talk of wonderful progress, done more than scratch the surface. The progress has been wonderful enough but..."

Biographies/   **ISBN:** *1-59462-198-5*   **Pages:**300   *MSRP $21.95*

The Art of Cross-Examination
Francis Wellman

I presume it is the experience of every author, after his first book is published upon an important subject, to be almost overwhelmed with a wealth of ideas and illustrations which could readily have been included in his book, and which to his own mind, at least, seem to make a second edition inevitable. Such certainly was the case with me; and when the first edition had reached its sixth impression in five months, I rejoiced to learn that it seemed to my publishers that the book had met with a sufficiently favorable reception to justify a second and considerably enlarged edition. ..

QTY

Reference   ISBN: *1-59462-647-2*   Pages:412   MSRP *$19.95*

On the Duty of Civil Disobedience
Henry David Thoreau

Thoreau wrote his famous essay, On the Duty of Civil Disobedience, as a protest against an unjust but popular war and the immoral but popular institution of slave-owning. He did more than write—he declined to pay his taxes, and was hauled off to gaol in consequence. Who can say how much this refusal of his hastened the end of the war and of slavery ?

QTY

Law   ISBN: *1-59462-747-9*   Pages:48   MSRP *$7.45*

Dream Psychology Psychoanalysis for Beginners
Sigmund Freud

Sigmund Freud, born Sigismund Schlomo Freud (May 6, 1856 - September 23, 1939), was a Jewish-Austrian neurologist and psychiatrist who co-founded the psychoanalytic school of psychology. Freud is best known for his theories of the unconscious mind, especially involving the mechanism of repression; his redefinition of sexual desire as mobile and directed towards a wide variety of objects; and his therapeutic techniques, especially his understanding of transference in the therapeutic relationship and the presumed value of dreams as sources of insight into unconscious desires.

QTY

Psychology   ISBN: *1-59462-905-6*   Pages:196   MSRP *$15.45*

The Miracle of Right Thought
Orison Swett Marden

Believe with all of your heart that you will do what you were made to do. When the mind has once formed the habit of holding cheerful, happy, prosperous pictures, it will not be easy to form the opposite habit. It does not matter how improbable or how far away this realization may see, or how dark the prospects may be, if we visualize them as best we can, as vividly as possible, hold tenaciously to them and vigorously struggle to attain them, they will gradually become actualized, realized in the life. But a desire, a longing without endeavor, a yearning abandoned or held indifferently will vanish without realization.

QTY

Self Help   ISBN: *1-59462-644-8*   Pages:360   MSRP *$25.45*

www.bookjungle.com email: sales@bookjungle.com fax: 630-214-0564 mail: Book Jungle PO Box 2226 Champaign, IL 61825

QTY

☐ **The Rosicrucian Cosmo-Conception Mystic Christianity** by *Max Heindel* ISBN: *1-59462-188-8* **$38.95**
The Rosicrucian Cosmo-conception is not dogmatic, neither does it appeal to any other authority than the reason of the student. It is: not controversial, but is: sent forth in the, hope that it may help to clear... New Age/Religion Pages 646

☐ **Abandonment To Divine Providence** by *Jean-Pierre de Caussade* ISBN: *1-59462-228-0* **$25.95**
"The Rev. Jean Pierre de Caussade was one of the most remarkable spiritual writers of the Society of Jesus in France in the 18th Century. His death took place at Toulouse in 1751. His works have gone through many editions and have been republished... Inspirational/Religion Pages 400

☐ **Mental Chemistry** by *Charles Haanel* ISBN: *1-59462-192-6* **$23.95**
Mental Chemistry allows the change of material conditions by combining and appropriately utilizing the power of the mind. Much like applied chemistry creates something new and unique out of careful combinations of chemicals the mastery of mental chemistry... New Age Pages 354

☐ **The Letters of Robert Browning and Elizabeth Barret Barrett 1845-1846 vol II** ISBN: *1-59462-193-4* **$35.95**
by *Robert Browning* and *Elizabeth Barrett* Biographies Pages 596

☐ **Gleanings In Genesis (volume I)** by *Arthur W. Pink* ISBN: *1-59462-130-6* **$27.45**
Appropriately has Genesis been termed "the seed plot of the Bible" for in it we have, in germ form, almost all of the great doctrines which are afterwards fully developed in the books of Scripture which follow... Religion/Inspirational Pages 420

☐ **The Master Key** by *L. W. de Laurence* ISBN: *1-59462-001-6* **$30.95**
In no branch of human knowledge has there been a more lively increase of the spirit of research during the past few years than in the study of Psychology, Concentration and Mental Discipline. The requests for authentic lessons in Thought Control, Mental Discipline and... New Age/Business Pages 422

☐ **The Lesser Key Of Solomon Goetia** by *L. W. de Laurence* ISBN: *1-59462-092-X* **$9.95**
This translation of the first book of the "Lernegton" which is now for the first time made accessible to students of Talismanic Magic was done, after careful collation and edition, from numerous Ancient Manuscripts in Hebrew, Latin, and French... New Age/Occult Pages 92

☐ **Rubaiyat Of Omar Khayyam** by *Edward Fitzgerald* ISBN:*1-59462-332-5* **$13.95**
Edward Fitzgerald, whom the world has already learned, in spite of his own efforts to remain within the shadow of anonymity, to look upon as one of the rarest poets of the century, was born at Bredfield, in Suffolk, on the 31st of March, 1809. He was the third son of John Purcell... Music Pages 172

☐ **Ancient Law** by *Henry Maine* ISBN: *1-59462-128-4* **$29.95**
The chief object of the following pages is to indicate some of the earliest ideas of mankind, as they are reflected in Ancient Law, and to point out the relation of those ideas to modern thought. Religiom/History Pages 452

☐ **Far-Away Stories** by *William J. Locke* ISBN: *1-59462-129-2* **$19.45**
"Good wine needs no bush, but a collection of mixed vintages does. And this book is just such a collection. Some of the stories I do not want to remain buried for ever in the museum files of dead magazine-numbers an author's not unpardonable vanity..." Fiction Pages 272

☐ **Life of David Crockett** by *David Crockett* ISBN: *1-59462-250-7* **$27.45**
"Colonel David Crockett was one of the most remarkable men of the times in which he lived. Born in humble life, but gifted with a strong will, an indomitable courage, and unremitting perseverance... Biographies/New Age Pages 424

☐ **Lip-Reading** by *Edward Nitchie* ISBN: *1-59462-206-X* **$25.95**
Edward B. Nitchie, founder of the New York School for the Hard of Hearing, now the Nitchie School of Lip-Reading, Inc, wrote "LIP-READING Principles and Practice". The development and perfecting of this meritorious work on lip-reading was an undertaking... How-to Pages 400

☐ **A Handbook of Suggestive Therapeutics, Applied Hypnotism, Psychic Science** ISBN: *1-59462-214-0* **$24.95**
by *Henry Munro* Health/New Age/Health/Self-help Pages 376

☐ **A Doll's House: and Two Other Plays** by *Henrik Ibsen* ISBN: *1-59462-112-8* **$19.95**
Henrik Ibsen created this classic when in revolutionary 1848 Rome. Introducing some striking concepts in playwriting for the realist genre, this play has been studied the world over. Fiction/Classics/Plays 308

☐ **The Light of Asia** by *sir Edwin Arnold* ISBN: *1-59462-204-3* **$13.95**
In this poetic masterpiece, Edwin Arnold describes the life and teachings of Buddha. The man who was to become known as Buddha to the world was born as Prince Gautama of India but he rejected the worldly riches and abandoned the reigns of power when... Religion/History/Biographies Pages 170

☐ **The Complete Works of Guy de Maupassant** by *Guy de Maupassant* ISBN: *1-59462-157-8* **$16.95**
"For days and days, nights and nights, I had dreamed of that first kiss which was to consecrate our engagement, and I knew not on what spot I should put my lips..." Fiction/Classics Pages 240

☐ **The Art of Cross-Examination** by *Francis L. Wellman* ISBN: *1-59462-309-0* **$26.95**
Written by a renowned trial lawyer, Wellman imparts his experience and uses case studies to explain how to use psychology to extract desired information through questioning. How-to/Science/Reference Pages 408

☐ **Answered or Unanswered?** by *Louisa Vaughan* ISBN: *1-59462-248-5* **$10.95**
Miracles of Faith in China Religion Pages 112

☐ **The Edinburgh Lectures on Mental Science (1909)** by *Thomas* ISBN: *1-59462-008-3* **$11.95**
This book contains the substance of a course of lectures recently given by the writer in the Queen Street Hall, Edinburgh. Its purpose is to indicate the Natural Principles governing the relation between Mental Action and Material Conditions... New Age/Psychology Pages 148

☐ **Ayesha** by *H. Rider Haggard* ISBN: *1-59462-301-5* **$24.95**
Verily and indeed it is the unexpected that happens! Probably if there was one person upon the earth from whom the Editor of this, and of a certain previous history, did not expect to hear again... Classics Pages 380

☐ **Ayala's Angel** by *Anthony Trollope* ISBN: *1-59462-352-X* **$29.95**
The two girls were both pretty, but Lucy who was twenty-one who supposed to be simple and comparatively unattractive, whereas Ayala was credited, as her Bombwhat romantic name might show, with poetic charm and a taste for romance. Ayala when her father died was nineteen... Fiction Pages 484

☐ **The American Commonwealth** by *James Bryce* ISBN: *1-59462-286-8* **$34.45**
An interpretation of American democratic political theory. It examines political mechanics and society from the perspective of Scotsman James Bryce Politics Pages 572

☐ **Stories of the Pilgrims** by *Margaret P. Pumphrey* ISBN: *1-59462-116-0* **$17.95**
This book explores pilgrims religious oppression in England as well as their escape to Holland and eventual crossing to America on the Mayflower, and their early days in New England... History Pages 268

www.bookjungle.com email: sales@bookjungle.com fax: 630-214-0564 mail: Book Jungle PO Box 2226 Champaign, IL 61825

QTY

The Fasting Cure by *Sinclair Upton* ISBN: *1-59462-222-1* **$13.95**
In the Cosmopolitan Magazine for May, 1910, and in the Contemporary Review (London) for April, 1910, I published an article dealing with my experiences in fasting. I have written a great many magazine articles, but never one which attracted so much attention... *New Age/Self Help/Health Pages 164*

Hebrew Astrology by *Sepharial* ISBN: *1-59462-308-2* **$13.45**
In these days of advanced thinking it is a matter of common observation that we have left many of the old landmarks behind and that we are now pressing forward to greater heights and to a wider horizon than that which represented the mind-content of our progenitors... *Astrology Pages 144*

Thought Vibration or The Law of Attraction in the Thought World ISBN: *1-59462-127-6* **$12.95**
by *William Walker Atkinson* *Psychology/Religion Pages 144*

Optimism by *Helen Keller* ISBN: *1-59462-108-X* **$15.95**
Helen Keller was blind, deaf, and mute since 19 months old, yet famously learned how to overcome these handicaps, communicate with the world, and spread her lectures promoting optimism. An inspiring read for everyone... *Biographies/Inspirational Pages 84*

Sara Crewe by *Frances Burnett* ISBN: *1-59462-360-0* **$9.45**
In the first place, Miss Minchin lived in London. Her home was a large, dull, tall one, in a large, dull square, where all the houses were alike, and all the sparrows were alike, and where all the door-knockers made the same heavy sound... *Childrens/Classic Pages 88*

The Autobiography of Benjamin Franklin by *Benjamin Franklin* ISBN: *1-59462-135-7* **$24.95**
The Autobiography of Benjamin Franklin has probably been more extensively read than any other American historical work, and no other book of its kind has had such ups and downs of fortune. Franklin lived for many years in England, where he was agent... *Biographies/History Pages 332*

| Name |
| Email |
| Telephone |
| Address |
| |
| City, State ZIP |

☐ Credit Card   ☐ Check / Money Order

| Credit Card Number |
| Expiration Date |
| Signature |

Please Mail to: Book Jungle
PO Box 2226
Champaign, IL 61825
or Fax to: 630-214-0564

ORDERING INFORMATION

web: *www.bookjungle.com*
email: *sales@bookjungle.com*
fax: *630-214-0564*
mail: *Book Jungle PO Box 2226 Champaign, IL 61825*
or PayPal *to sales@bookjungle.com*

Please contact us for bulk discounts

DIRECT-ORDER TERMS

**20% Discount if You Order
Two or More Books**
Free Domestic Shipping!
Accepted: Master Card, Visa,
Discover, American Express

www.ingramcontent.com/pod-product-compliance
Lightning Source LLC
Chambersburg PA
CBHW081830170426
43199CB00017B/2692